The English Garden and National Identity:

The Competing Styles of Garden Design, 1870–1914

This book examines the fierce debate on the styles and forms of garden design that took place in England c. 1870–1914. Focusing on the wild garden, the cottage garden, the formal garden, and the synthesis of the formal and natural styles, Anne Helmreich argues that design principles and debates among designers including William Robinson, Reginald Blomfield, Gertrude Jekyll, and Edwin Lutyens were indelibly shaped by the quest for a powerful English national identity. She demonstrates how "Englishness" was purportedly expressed through the leading styles of garden design and why the garden was promoted as a symbol of national identity. A wide range of cultural practices and institutions, from garden treatises, popular journals, historic preservation organizations, art exhibitions, and two world's fairs, are investigated to reveal how the garden, as a physical artifact and as an idea, circulated widely to produce a unifying national image.

Anne Helmreich is assistant professor of art history at Texas Christian University. A scholar of English landscape design, she has contributed to a number of publications, including the *Journal of Pre-Raphaelite Studies, Journal of the Society of Architectural Historians,* and *Journal of Garden History.*

MODERN ARCHITECTURE AND CULTURAL IDENTITY

SERIES EDITOR
Richard A. Etlin, *University of Maryland, College Park*

ADVISORY BOARD
Steven Mansbach, *University of Maryland, College Park*
Narciso Menocal, *University of Wisconsin, Madison*
Andrew Saint, *Cambridge University*
David Van Zanten, *Northwestern University*
Gwendolyn Wright, *Columbia University*

Modern Architecture and Cultural Identity will comprise monographic studies of important movements and buildings by European and American architects created roughly between 1850 and 1950. Unlike the first histories of modernism, which stressed the international aspects of modern architecture, recent scholarship has attempted to clarify the delicate balance achieved by architects working in a modernist idiom who maintained, nonetheless, a strong allegiance to their cultural roots. This series has been developed in response to this trend and will explore the complex interplay among modern identity and local, regional, national, and related cultural traditions.

The English Garden and National Identity

The Competing Styles of Garden Design, 1870–1914

ANNE HELMREICH

CAMBRIDGE
UNIVERSITY PRESS

PUBLISHED BY THE PRESS SYNDICATE OF THE UNIVERSITY OF CAMBRIDGE
The Pitt Building, Trumpington Street, Cambridge, United Kingdom

CAMBRIDGE UNIVERSITY PRESS
The Edinburgh Building, Cambridge CB2 2RU, UK
40 West 20th Street, New York, NY 10011-4211, USA
477 Williamstown Road, Port Melbourne, VIC 3207, Australia
Ruiz de Alarcón 13, 28014 Madrid, Spain
Dock House, The Waterfront, Cape Town 8001, South Africa

http://www.cambridge.org

First published 2002

Printed in the United Kingdom at the University Press, Cambridge

Typefaces Bulmer 11.25/14 pt. and Lo-Type   *System* QuarkXPress® [GH]

A catalogue record for this book is available from the British Library.

Library of Congress Cataloging-in-Publication Data

Helmreich, Anne
The English garden and national identity : the competing styles of garden design,
1870–1914 / Anne Helmreich.
p. cm. – (Modern architecture and cultural identity)
Includes bibliographical references (p.).
ISBN 0-521-59293-3
1. Gardens – England – Design – History – 19th century. 2. Gardens –
England – Design – History – 20th century. 3. Gardens, English – History – 19th century.
4. Gardens, English – History – 20th century. 5. Nationalism – England – History –
19th century. 6. Nationalism – England – History – 20th century. I. Title. II. Series.

SB466.G7 H45 2002
712'.6'0942 – dc21   2001043777

ISBN 0 521 59293 3 hardback

To my family of gardeners

Contents

❧❀❧   ❧ ix

Contents

List of Illustrations

PLATES

Color plates follow page 124

FIGURES

Acknowledgments

This book derives from my doctoral dissertation in art history at Northwestern University, *Contested Grounds: Garden Painting and the Invention of National Identity in England, 1880–1914* (1994). That project began as an inquiry into the state of British landscape painting during the second half of the nineteenth century, following upon recent studies of early-nineteenth-century landscape representations by such scholars as John Barrell and Ann Bermingham, and resulted in an investigation of late-nineteenth-century painters of gardens (Helen Allingham, George Elgood, Alfred Parsons, Beatrice Parsons, and E. A. Rowe). As I pursued this topic after the dissertation, I became increasingly interested in gardens themselves and debates about garden styles that coursed through garden writing at the end of the nineteenth century. I discovered that by focusing on gardens and garden design I reached even closer to the heart of discourses I had analyzed earlier.

My dissertation research was made possible, in part, by funds from the Art History Department of Northwestern University and the Graduate School of Northwestern University. Appointments as the Mayers Foundation Fellow of the Huntington Library, Art Collections, and Botanical Gardens and junior fellow in Studies in Landscape Architecture at Dumbarton Oaks were crucial for both the research and crystallization of my dissertation topic. Resources of the National Gallery of Art, made accessible through a graduate lecturing fellowship and a position as research assistant in the Center for Advanced Study in the Visual Arts, were instrumental for completion of the dissertation and early stages of research for this book. A research grant from the American Philosophical Society and a Texas Christian University research and creative activities grant enabled me to conduct site visits and archival research in the United Kingdom. Appointments as a visiting fellow, Yale Center for British Art; summer fellow in Studies in Landscape Architecture at Dumbarton Oaks; and the Dr. and Mrs. James C. Caillouette Fellow at the Huntington Library enabled me to complete the research and writing of this book. Publication of an expanded color and halftone illustrated book was made possible by a grant from the Graham Foundation. Monies from Texas Christian University – received from the associate provost for Academic Affairs, the dean of the College of Fine Arts, and the Department of Art and Art History – also offset the cost of illustrations and permissions to publish. Chrystal Hall, through an appointment as research assistant, contributed greatly to acquiring and organizing illustrations for this book.

My research directly benefited from the gracious assistance and invaluable scholarly conversations with the staff at the Center for Advanced Study in the Visual Arts; Dumbarton Oaks; the Huntington Library, Art Collections, and Botanical Gardens; Northwestern University; Texas Christian University; and the Yale Center for British Art. I also appreciate the many kindnesses extended to me by staff of the Garden Library of Dumbarton Oaks, including former librarian Annie Thatcher, as well as Linda Lott, with particular thanks for her assistance in obtaining illustrations. Amy Meyers of the Huntington Library was unflagging in her support and her advice, and staff at the library and art collections afforded me the unquantifiable pleasure of having all the research sources I needed at my fingertips. I also wish to thank the art history faculty at the University of Pittsburgh, where I earned my M.A., and Northwestern University, where I earned my Ph.D. I owe my deepest thanks to the members of my dissertation committee, David Van Zanten and Harold Perkin, and my adviser, Hollis Clayson. My colleagues in the Art and Art History Department, as well as participants in the British Studies Reading Group and the Women's Studies Reading Group at Texas Christian University, have helped me clarify my project through their scholarly dialogue.

This book also profited from insights, comments, and suggestions proffered at scholarly venues where I presented aspects of this research: "The History of Landscape Architecture and the History of Photography," chaired by Therese O'Malley and Nancy Micklewright, College Art Association annual conference, 1994; "Nature and Ideology: Natural Garden Design in the Twentieth Century," organized by Joachim Wolschke-Bulmahn, Dumbarton Oaks, 1994; "British Art and National Identity," chaired by John Wilson and Laurel Bradley, College Art Association annual conference, 1995; "Representation and Landscape," chaired by Diana Balmori, Society of Architectural Historians annual conference, 1995; "Nature, Landscape, and Ideas of the Environment in Victorian Britain," organized by Tim Barringer, Royal College of Art, Victoria and Albert and University of Birmingham Seminar in Victorian Studies, 1997; "Formalism in the Garden,"

xvi

organized by Eric Haskell and Amy Meyers, Huntington Library, Art Collections, and Botanical Gardens and The Scripps College Humanities Institute, 1997; "Landscape, Gardens, Nature, and Identity," chaired by Jan Birksted, Association of Art Historians annual conference, 1998; "Social Uses of Nature and Identity Construction," organized by Michel Conan, Dumbarton Oaks Studies in Landscape Architecture Roundtable, 1999. An earlier version of Chapter 2 was published as a chapter in *Nature and Ideology, Natural Garden Design in the Twentieth Century*, ed. Joachim Wolschke-Bulmahn (Washington, D.C.: Dumbarton Oaks, 1997).

I also wish to thank those garden and architecture scholars who shared results of their own researches with me and patiently answered my myriad inquiries, including Michel Conan, Carla Corbin, Tricia Cusack, Lucy Dynevor, Brent Elliott, Dianne Harris, Ned Harwood, Mark Laird, Kim D. Legate, Nicole Milette, Mandy Morris, Andrew Saint, Joachim Wolschke-Bulmahn, and Jan Woudstra. Therese O'Malley and Elizabeth Kryder-Reid deserve my special thanks for many long conversations about such seemingly arcane topics as flower borders and shrubberies. Mark Laird also participated in these exciting conversations and lent his advice generously, particularly to sections of this manuscript dealing with planting arrangements (any errors are of my own making). Robert Williams deserves my special thanks for his astute insights into Edwardian garden design, from which I have benefited greatly.

A number of institutions in the United Kingdom facilitated my research, and my thanks are owed to their staff, including Alan Powers of the Art Workers Guild, the British Library, the Fine Arts Society, the Lindley Library of the Royal Horticulture Society, and the National Art Library at the Victoria and Albert Museum. In the United States, in addition to the institutions already named, I benefited from the resources of the Documents Collection of the College of Environmental Design, University of California, Berkeley; the Library of Congress; and the interlibrary loan office at the Mary Couts Burnet Library, Texas Christian University.

Perhaps most importantly, this study would not have been possible without the gracious assistance of those garden owners who permitted me access to their homes and shared with me their knowledge and enthusiasm. In particular, I am grateful, at Abbotswood, to Mr. M. Fox, head gardener; at Ammerdown, to Lord and Lady Hylton and Don Cox, head gardener, and his assistant; at Athelhampton, to R. G. Cooke; at Caythorpe Court, to Mike Housely, head of estates, De Montfort University, Lincoln; at Goddards, to the Landmark Trust; at Gravetye Manor, to Peter Wood, Lindsay Shurvell, Pauline Wood, and Mark Yates; at Great Chalfield, to Katie Fretwell, historic park and garden surveyor; at Great Maytham, to Lesley and Frank O'Neill, administrators; at High Beeches, to the

Boscawen family; at Little Thakeham (now a hotel and restaurant), to Mr. and Mrs. Ratcliffe; at Moundsmere, to Mark Andreae; at Munstead Wood, to Lady Clark; at Thorton Hough, to Paul Evans and George Kenyon; at Tirley Garth, to Jim Wigan; at Tylney Hall, to Paul Tattersdill, head gardener; at the Manor House, Upton Grey, to Rosamund Wallinger for sharing both her garden and home, and her excellent knowledge of Gertrude Jekyll; at Vann, to Mary Caroe for both her hospitality and her generosity with her knowledge of Jekyll; at Wayford Manor, to Mrs. R. L. Goffe.

At Cambridge University Press, I benefited greatly from the guidance and encouragement of Beatrice Rehl, my anonymous readers, and, most appreciably, series editor Richard Etlin, who aided generously by curbing my excesses and helping me refine and sharpen my arguments.

I am conscious of the feminist critique of putting friends and family last in one's acknowledgments despite their primary role, but I have kept these thanks for last because they are the most heartfelt. I owe a great debt to my friends and family who have unstintingly offered their suggestions and support on every aspect of this project, ranging from polemics of ideology to the identity of a flower or the construction of a sentence. To my circle of family and friends, thank you, and I look forward to continuing our sustaining conversations.

In this study, I make use of the writings of Henry James, whose position as an outsider trying to write from inside is one with which I have come to identify. As someone who has come to know the English landscape as a frequent visitor, I am aware that I may miss nuances available to the native, but, like James, I am also aware that my vantage point allows me glimpses of things that might otherwise be overlooked by those whose surroundings have become naturalized to them.

The English Garden and National Identity

Introduction

D uring the last quarter of the nineteenth century and opening decades of the twentieth century, fiery debates about styles and forms of English gardens intersected with notions of national identity. The leading styles of garden design sought validity through recourse to the label *English,* and the garden was adopted as a symbol of national identity.

This study is grounded in the premise that gardenscapes do not communicate universal values irrespective of time or place, but that each culture endows garden forms with particular sets of meanings and, within that culture, those meanings, and therefore vehicles that express them, are contested and not fixed. The notion of "reading" the garden – treating garden features like semantic devices that can communicate to those familiar with their language – is both a historical practice and a productive mode of historical inquiry. The latter requires understanding, on the one hand, the vocabulary of the discipline and, on the other hand, the broader social, economic, and political context in which that syntax was deployed.[1] The researcher must work both diachronically and synchronically, investigating how the forms or syntax of the garden changed over time and how these changes were embedded in historical events. This study adopts such an approach, looking at changing garden styles during the period 1870–1914 as reflective of both internal debates within the discipline of garden design and broader debates within the culture at large. Briefly stated, varying garden styles can be understood, or "read," concomitantly as expressions of the competing professional agendas of different kinds of designers (such as gardeners or architects) and articulations, through the vehicle of nature, of competing visions of the nation.

Gardens addressed here are those typically associated with what is called the small country house. Difficult to define, this house stands between the mansion and the cottage and is closest in sensibility to the villa, which J. C. Loudon defined as "nothing more than a park with a house of smaller size than that of the *mansion* and *demesne,* surrounded by a pleasure-ground, and with the usual gardens."[2] Architect Ernest Newton, reflecting in 1912 on the previous fifty years of house building, explained that interest in the "smallish house" rather than "country seats" or "noblemen's mansions" defined modern domestic architecture as did a revival of the art of garden design (referring to ornamental or pleasure grounds, distinguished from parkland or utilitarian spaces).[3]

2 &

The revival to which Newton referred encompassed a range of styles linked with nationalities – such as English, Italian, Japanese – that have been richly discussed by Brent Elliott in *Victorian Gardens* (1986) and David Ottewill in *The Edwardian Garden* (1989). The intent of this volume is not to replace these period overviews but rather to address the broader issue of the cultural context in which these styles emerged. What drove stylistic choices? How are artistic form and social, political, and economic change related? Concentrating on these questions gives rise to the issue of Englishness and garden styles that emerged to express desired perceptions of the nation.

For purposes of this study, the garden is considered not just in its physical manifestation, as a locus, but also in its represented form. This allows analysis, as W. J. T. Mitchell has advised, of how "landscape *circulates* as a medium of exchange, a site of visual appropriation, [and] a focus for the formation of identity."[4] During the period 1870–1914, publishing and the print media grew exponentially with the application of new industrial techniques to the business and craft of printing as well as reduced costs of raw materials. Writings about gardens, whether in horticulture or design journals, treatises, novels, literary journals, newspapers, or pamphlets, proliferated in this environment. Authors and publishers took advantage of new technologies of mass reproducing wood engravings and later, photographs, to issue relatively inexpensive, well-illustrated texts so that word and image, sometimes in concert and sometimes in opposition, constituted the meanings of gardens. Gardens thus became the concern of not just a small elite, who previously had most ready access to treatises and other print material related to gardens, but also a broad literary audience that extended into the respectable working classes.

A discourse, the garden also behaves as a myth, holding forth promises of harmony with nature. Myth is innocent, Roland Barthes claims, "not because its intentions are hidden . . . but because they are naturalized." The garden is a perfect example: seemingly without politics, its meanings are always described by its firsthand observers as obvious and commonplace. Of course, as Rudyard Kipling stated, "our England is a garden." But we should take heed of Barthes's warning that "the most natural object contains a political trace."[5] Thus it is useful to conceive of the garden as embodying a collection of ideologies, sometimes contradictory, bundled together and put to numerous uses. At the turn of the century, the latter included counterbalancing fears of change, accentuating desires for an alternative way of life, harmonizing and smoothing over differences, or accentuating them. Through these processes, the garden became constitutive of national identity.

The question of what constitutes a nation is not answered easily, yet scholars make frequent recourse to the notion of a collective form of identity. Ernest Renan, in his essay "What Is a Nation" (1882), argued that "to have common glories in the past, a common will in the present; to have accomplished great things together, to wish to do so again, that is the essential condition of being a nation."[6] Max Weber rested the definition of the nation on the concept of shared values, sentiments, and "memories of a common political destiny."[7] Walker Connor has pointed out that "the nation is a self-defined rather than an other-defined grouping," to which one could add that in self-defining, the nation often sets itself apart from what are identified as Others.[8] John Hutchinson and Anthony D. Smith insist that nationalism is best understood as an ideological movement with both "political and cultural dimensions" that emerges out of a collective, unified drive for independence and depends on identification of a shared, distinctive culture and territory.[9]

The revolutions of the late eighteenth century, stemming out of philosophies of the Enlightenment, are therefore often argued to be the founding moments of nationalism. Nationalism burgeoned in nineteenth-century Europe, with its reaction against the forced internationalism of the Napoleonic Empire, revolutions for greater political equality, wars of territory, and colonial expansion. Nationalism is, in short, a specifically modern movement. Ernest Gellner situates the rise of nationalism at the point of transition from an agrarian to an industrial age, pointing out that industrialization – with its implicit demand for and reward of stabilization and standardization, and its ability to shrink distances metaphorically – concomitantly required and produced a cultural homogeneity bound up in nationalism.[10]

These definitions of national identity that point inexorably to the role of culture have been cited here intentionally. Although national identity has long been conceived as the result of political acts and pronouncements, Gellner and other scholars, such as Benedict Anderson and Eric Hobsbawm, have demonstrated that cultural practices are crucial in defining and shaping national identity. Gellner, for example, argued that "nationalism is a political principle which maintains that similarity of culture is the basic social bond" so that national communities, generally speaking, are defined "in terms of shared culture."[11] According to Anderson, nationalism or nation-ness are "cultural artefacts of a particular kind" emanating from the condition of the nation as "an imagined political community."[12] He points to how cultural expressions, in particular print language, which possesses an inherent capacity for "generating imagined communities, building in effect *particular solidarities*," create ties that bind communities. He has also called attention to how institutions – such as the map, the census, and the museum, which "profoundly shaped the way in which the colonial state imagined its domain" – also produce national identity.[13] To this list can be added images, specifically landscape images that imagine the topography and scope of the nation and represent it back to itself.[14] As a category of landscape imagery, the garden had particular resonance as a means of imagining nation-ness. An enclosed space devoted to cultivation and display of plants, the garden mirrored the notion of nationhood as a bounded territory designated for a particular set of peoples.

The garden, in the period considered by this account, also functioned as an invented tradition: "a set of practices, normally governed by overtly or tacitly accepted rules and of a ritual or symbolic nature, which seek to inculcate certain values and norms of behaviour by repetition, which automatically implies continuity with the past" and include such symbols as the national flag or anthem that signified membership in the exclusive club of nationhood. Invented traditions thus create a sense of community, as well as to "establish or legitimize institutions, status or relations of authority" and to instill "beliefs, value systems and conventions of behaviour."[15] The garden implied continuity with the past as well as membership within the exclusive club of Englishness, and it set in place value systems with significant ideological importance. Like many invented traditions, the garden and the act of gardening also served as means by which to manage the transitions and stresses inherent in modernity as well as establishing a community based on shared interests.

The role of invented traditions is like that of cultural nationalism as defined by John Hutchinson. Cultural nationalism denotes how society defines the nation through "its distinctive civilization, which is the product of its unique history, culture and geographical profile"; the activities of cultural nationalists include "naming rituals, the celebration of cultural uniqueness and the rejection of foreign practices," which create a sense of unity. Hutchinson concludes,

> cultural nationalists should be seen . . . as moral innovators who see, by "reviving" an ethnic historicist vision of the nation, to redirect traditionalists and modernists away from conflict and instead to unite them in the task of constructing an integrated distinctive and autonomous community, capable of competing in the modern world.[16]

Gerald Newman asserts that the eighteenth century proved the ideal breeding ground for English nationalism, given the existing bonds of people to the land and to an increasingly unified culture and Protestant religion, the growth of the middle classes, the existence of a threatening enemy, the desire for order in a period of extreme change, and fear of imminent decline.[17] Yet some of these same factors, in particular the long-standing antagonism between France and Britain (the latter formed by the union of England and Scotland in 1707), created a sense of Britishness, according to Linda Colley, who argues that Great Britain "was an invention forged above all by war. Time and time again, war with France brought Britons, whether they hailed from Wales or Scotland or England, into confrontation with an obviously hostile Other and encouraged them to define themselves collectively against it." Patriotism was fueled by the rhetoric required to assemble, bind together, and activate a fighting force. Colley goes on to observe that Britishness existed as a sort of veneer, "superimposed over an array of internal differences"; and its presence waxed and waned as forces binding the different nations of England, Wales, and Scotland together appeared and disappeared.[18] Throughout the history of the United Kingdom, created in 1801 by the forced joining of Ireland to Britain, what Hugh Kearney has described as "ethnic politics" has been at work.[19] The tearing at the bonds linking the four nations of Britain continued apace into the nineteenth century, fueling the discourse that linked gardens and Englishness.

In the following discussion, Chapter 1 sets forth the historical context and considers the conflicting tropes – workshop of the world or green and pleasant land – by which England was characterized over the second half of the nineteenth century. Succeeding chapters address key episodes in the history of garden design from 1870 to the Great War, which put an end to a certain kind of garden making with the rising costs of labor and other economic reconfigurations. The period 1870–1914 was characterized by intense debates about garden design, which, at their most polarized, pitched informal against formal, peasant styles against aristocratic styles, and nature against architect. This book argues that these debates, and the design principles at stake, were indelibly shaped by the quest for a powerful English national identity.

The beginning of the controversy can be located in 1870, when William Robinson first published his treatise on the wild garden. Chapter 2 investigates Robinson's approach to garden design and how it was embedded in contemporary scientific and aesthetic practices as well as social concerns. To legitimize his aesthetic, Robinson turned to cottage gardens, considered in Chapter 3. The studied informality of cottage gardens, with their connotations of the amateur, are in marked contrast to formal gardens, yet both were promoted as essentially English and became ingredients in turn-of-the-century designs. Chapter 4 addresses the formal garden, a mode of design largely advocated by architects who cast aspersions on Robinson and his fellow landscape gardeners.

The tension between formalists and naturalists erupted into a battle of the styles, analyzed in Chapter 5 not just as a function of conflicting design principles but also as a product of history and its writing. This fiery debate signifies the high stakes faced by garden designers at the end of the nineteenth century. Yet certain critics at the time questioned the validity of the stylistic debate, because they believed a paradigmatic style had emerged, one that fused the formal and natural and thus acknowledged both existing modes of garden designs while rising above the brawl. To support their assertion, these critics pointed to the work of Gertrude Jekyll and Edwin Lutyens. Chapter 6 examines Jekyll's relationship to English rural culture as evidenced in her writings and garden design and analyzes how her work offered readers a national aesthetic based on local practices. Chapter 7 examines a selection of sites designed by Jekyll and Lutyens and establishes how the team drew on motifs already in circulation while also providing innovative solutions to design problems. This book demonstrates that in a period when artists, writers, musicians, politicians, and numerous others embarked on a search for English identity, the garden was an essential vessel for this voyage of discovery.

Chapter 1

Janus-Faced England

 7

Our England is a garden that is full of stately views,
Of borders, beds and shrubberies and lawns and avenues,
With statues on the terraces and peacocks strutting by;
But the Glory of the Garden lies in more than meets the eye.
Rudyard Kipling, *The Glory of the Garden*, 1911

In 1911 Rudyard Kipling penned this homage to England and the hard work that lay behind the ordered facade of English civilization. In choosing a garden as the referent for England, Kipling was making use of a widespread and highly charged metaphor that can be traced at least to the time of Shakespeare's sceptred isle. But in the late nineteenth century, this trope acquired particular significance and power as it permeated every level of visual culture. Disseminated by key cultural institutions, such as world's fairs and commercial art exhibitions; articulated in nearly every form of media, from lavishly illustrated books to daily papers; and associated with a wide range of cultural practices, from tourism and historic preservation to garden design itself, the notion that the garden embodied Englishness reverberated at the turn of the century. Representations of gardens, in text and image, circulated widely and produced a unifying national image that was specifically and deliberately English.

Yet, as Rudyard Kipling reminded readers, "the Glory of the Garden lies in more than meets the eye." Fears of a disintegrating domestic order and a declining international profile drove the desire to equate gardens with Englishness. In visualizing England as a garden and promoting the garden as a symbol of the nation, artists, architects, designers, and writers were responding to a growing perception that nature and the English rural landscape, as well as the nation itself, were no longer immutable. Darwinism undermined the notion that nature and man existed in a state of harmony dictated by the Creator; industrialization and urbanism changed the face of the countryside. The agricultural depression of the 1870s and 1890s intensified the sense that traditional rural England was passing away. The rise of democracy and the Irish question, as well as increasing resistance to imperialism from all quarters, further challenged the status quo.

Even those who embraced imperialism recognized that the dynamic between core and periphery would forever change notions of Englishness, which many sought to recover from the past. The desire to look to the past for guidance was impelled by uncertainty about the future: now the nation was forced to jostle for the lead in the mounting race for colonial outposts, with its attendant military buildup, and faced increasing economic competition from Germany and the United States. England's sense of self, lulled self-complacent according to critics by an unprecedented period of peace and economic expansion fueled by the spread of industrialization and trade, seemed in doubt. Politicians, writers, and preachers all responded to the felt need to invoke a stable, coherent image of the nation. Many commentators located that image in the garden, with its associations of home and fidelity compounded by sensations of pleasure and beauty. The garden provided a reassuring national image and became both a solace and a bulwark from the vagaries of modern capitalism and imperialism, acting as a physical and imaginative shield.

The garden did not necessarily replace older symbols of national identity, such as Britannia, the Athenalike personification of Great Britain, or John Bull, the hearty country squire who personified England, but it did acquire the trappings of iconicity at a time when alternative tropes no longer proved as compelling. In eighteenth-century cartoons, caricatures, and other images, for example, roast beef often functioned as a symbol of England. These representations were produced at a time of intense international conflict between Great Britain and France. Roast beef stood for English values – honest simplicity and a lack of pretension that still admitted material wealth – in contradistinction to those of the French, whose foreignness and supposedly effete snobbery were connoted by dishes with frog legs or snails. Although the national stereotypes represented by these symbols still operated at the end of the nineteenth century, political and economic circumstances had changed. The issue was less how were the British distinct and superior from their archenemy France, and more how to shore up morale at home in the face of internal conflicts and decline and how to establish a firm sense of national identity in the face of, or perhaps more accurately, at the heart of, the expanding sphere of Empire.

Gardens had long been implicated in machinations of state building and party politics, as can be easily demonstrated with the cases of Stowe, in England, and Versailles, in France. By the mid–eighteenth century, Stowe, home first of the Temple and then the Grenville family (Richard Grenville inherited Stowe from his uncle Lord Cobham – née Sir Richard Temple – in 1749), was recognized as one of the most important landscape gardens in England. The degree to which Lord Cobham's political skirmishes within the Whig Party were explicitly inscribed into the garden has been debated.[1] Nonetheless, to many viewers the patriotic iconography was unmistakable. George Bickham's guidebook of 1750 drew attention to, among other features, the Temple of British Worthies, dedicated to

> those illustrious Worthies, who spent their Lives in Actions; who left Retirement to the calm Philosopher, entered into the Battle of Mankind, and pursued Virtue in the dazling [sic] Light in which she appears to Patriots and Heroes. Inspired by every generous Sentiment, these gallant Spirits founded Constitutions, shunned the Torrent of Corruption, battled for the State, ventured their Lives in the Defence of their Country, and gloriously bled in the Cause of Liberty.[2]

William Mason's poem *The English Garden* (first published 1772–81) underscores how the English landscape garden could be charged with the history of the nation. Early in his poem he instructs his readers, "Ye of Albion's sons/ Attend; Ye freeborn, ye ingenuous few, / who heirs of competence, if not of wealth," to pay attention to the art of proper landscaping and proposes that the garden be carefully composed so as to be "liberal though limited, restrained though free" in order to emblematize Britain's identification with "legal liberty," that is, citizen rights guaranteed by a constitution.[3]

The gardens at Versailles also contributed to the process of state building, as Chandra Mukerji has argued, in the sheer scope of land devoted to royal display, the technical virtuosity of the waterworks and other engineering works, the political iconography of statuary and fountains with their Sun God/Apollo themes and tributes to military victories, and the abundance of precious plants. The order invoked in the formal gardens, with parterres and bosquets organized according to geometrical principles, worked to "show political order as an extension of natural order."[4] At Versailles, designer Le Nôtre was demonstrating how the power of France and the glory of the ruler could be materially represented through controlling and beautifying the earth.

In late-nineteenth-century England, the community for whom the garden functioned as a symbol of national identity widened considerably beyond circles of the landed gentry with expansion of the literate and economically comfortable classes. For this greater audience, gardens continued to function as a means by which to bind together the national community and to articulate what it meant to be English, and they also shaped day-to-day lives. In literature of the period, crises of personal identity were frequently attributed to a perceived loss of a necessary bond between individual and nature. The dirt and contagion of the city, as well as the structures of an increasingly regulated workplace, made access to nature a pressing issue; yet, at the same time, it became increasingly difficult to "get out into nature" as cities swelled outward and railway lines advanced into the countryside. The mounting density of the urban fabric threatened to cut "people off from their rightful world as unnaturally as a cage does an animal from its home in the wild."[5] The solution, prescribed by popular literature such as *Country Life,* was to seek some form of rural living, even if only imaginatively experienced.

Although *Country Life*'s advice was rhetorically aimed at the national community, which was transforming itself, as one article put it, into "a nation of gardeners," in actuality it was delivered mostly to the literate classes, and more particularly, the wealthy middle and upper classes.[6] *Country Life,* first published in 1897, was masterminded by Edward Hudson, who used his knowledge from his family printing firm, Hudson and Kearnes, to turn what originally had been a horse-racing paper into a well-produced journal of rural life featuring extensive illustration by leading photographers. Through romanticizing "the conventional pleasures of country life, gardening, riding and golf," the journal not only enticed the comfortable classes to the countryside, it also epitomized and defined rural England for those classes. Arthur Lee, Viscount Lee of Fareham, recalled how *Country Life* struck a resonant chord with him:

> In January 1897, when serving in Canada, I was turning over the newly arrived English papers in the Montreal Club and was thrilled to come across a new weekly journal of which the outstanding feature, as it seemed to me, was an intoxicating array of temptations in the shape of English country houses – Tudor, Jacobean, Georgian, and what not – which were at the disposal of any homesick exile who could make a fortune overseas and retire to his native land.[7]

This history of *Country Life* points up an important change: growing identification of the wealthy middle classes not with the city, the typical source of their money, but with the countryside. Although they lacked the landed gentry's traditional hereditary ties to rural agriculture, these persons nonetheless (and perhaps because of this) worked to bind themselves to the land and to the English past, thus forging a new identity that obscured their relatively recent emergence in England's class strata. A small country house became a sign of membership in this class; popularization of this housing type gave rise to a wealth of literature on rural pursuits, of which gardening was perhaps the most avidly and widely pursued. The vocabulary of gardens built to accompany these homes was sufficiently multivalent and malleable to suit the needs of this class, borrowing from a wide range of sources, from rural laborers' cottage gardens to aristocratic formal gardens.

It was this very breadth of references, however, that caused the firestorm of debates that swirled about and scorched garden design at the turn of the century. Despite the frequently expressed appreciation of gardens and their ability to signify national virtues, an appropriate style could not be agreed on. From 1870 through 1914, at least four key modes of garden design – the wild or natural garden, the cottage garden, the formal garden, and a fusion of formal and natural styles – were proposed as the leading English style, each claiming roots in the local environment and the past. Like their counterparts in the Arts and Crafts movement in domestic architecture, garden designers and artists often adopted elements derived from medieval or Renaissance styles to provide a correcting counterbalance to modern design, which they believed to be inherently flawed by industrialization and the competitive drive for profit. Although links between the proposed styles and European garden designs were evident, designers, painters, and writers argued that their garden vocabulary was uniquely English. It bore no resemblance to continental developments, they argued; or, if the influence of foreign elements was reluctantly admitted, it proved a case of adapting the foreign to native models and needs.

At stake in these stylistic contestations was the nation's identity, caught in a dialectic between a cozy image of the preindustrial countryside and an expansive image of a commercial empire. This dialectic was ably negotiated by gardens. Sites of a shared cultural identity, gardens contrasted with the increasingly urbanized and industrialized landscape of England and the perceived unfamiliarity and newness of the colonies. They provided a rooted sense of home to which even the most far-ranging imperialist longed to return.

The English Nation at Midcentury: Industry, Horticulture, and Garden Design

Before exploring the construction of England's national identity over the last quarter of the nineteenth century, it is useful to backtrack and pick up the emerging strands of debates that would distinguish the end of the century. Many of these can be located in discussions surrounding the Great Exhibition of the Works of Industry of All Nations, held in London in 1851. This massive undertaking was a public declaration of Britain's self-positioning as world leader in industry, technology, and imperial wealth. The fair's ethos – that ingenuity applied to material resources would result in new and better products – was epitomized in the Crystal Palace (Fig. 1). Composed of glass, metal, and wood, it covered 19 acres of goods. The design and construction of the building was the responsibility of Joseph Paxton, an architect and professional gardener who developed a building based on the garden conservatory he had constructed at Chatsworth.[8] In its use of materials of industrialization, over 3,300 iron columns and 18,392 panes of glass, according to one reporter, and its construction, which utilized prefabricated units, the building was an "exhibition of industry."[9]

From the structure to the displays housed within, the Crystal Palace spoke of the ability to harness and to manipulate nature, bending it to humanity's will and the demands of commercialism. The reference to conservatories reminded visitors that with such garden structures, now readily available because of advances in glass and iron manufacturing, home owners could flaunt the rules of nature by creating microclimates that allowed plant material to be removed from its indigenous habitat, transported to Great Britain, and made part of the decoration of a well-to-do home. Indeed, in the Crystal Palace at Hyde Park, indigenous elms stood alongside imported palms, recalling the structure's roots in the popular Victorian pasttime of cultivating rare tropical plants brought to England from exotic locales.[10] This naturalizing of the exotic within carefully contained spaces emblematizes contemporaneous attitudes to Empire as a storehouse of desirable commodities that could be admitted into the English economy within prescribed boundaries.

Plant collecting was a major impetus behind much British garden design in the eighteenth and nineteenth centuries. The eighteenth-century landscape garden, known as the English garden on the continent, challenged the preceding geometric garden by combining undulating lawns, curving paths, planting arrangements modeled (relatively speaking) after nature, and irregular bodies of water in a pastoral scene. What has often been forgotten, but has been recently recovered by garden historian Mark Laird, is the degree to which the landscape garden accommodated and, indeed, privileged the display of flowering plants, many of which were considered rare and exotic in the British context.[11] The trend toward garden features predicated on the display of imported plants, such as the shrubbery or flower garden, mounted in the early nineteenth century, according to Laird, with the "exponential growth in the range and supply of exotics, the influx of new plants from China, western North America, and the Southern Hemisphere, the development of hybridization, and the swift progress in horticultural technology."[12] The vast increase in new plants is epitomized by the collections at Kew, which grew from 5,500 species to over 11,000 between 1789 and 1813.[13] Clement Markham, a junior clerk in the India Office who oversaw an expedition to transfer Peruvian cinchona trees to India for the purpose of

1. Joseph Nash, Louis Haghe, and David Roberts, "North Transept, Waiting for the Queen," from *Dickinson's Comprehensive Pictures of the Great Exhibition of 1851*, London, 1854. (Source: Photo courtesy of The Newberry Library, Chicago.)

producing quinine to combat malaria, expressed the sensibility of the period in his account of his travels:

> The distribution of valuable products of the vegetable kingdom amongst the nations of the earth – their introduction from countries where they are indigenous into distant lands with suitable soils and climates – is one of the greatest benefits civilization has conferred upon mankind. Such measures ensure immediate material increase of comfort and profit, while their effects are more durable than the proudest monuments of engineering skill.[14]

Attention to new plant introductions in the nineteenth-century garden was facilitated by designer J. C. Loudon and the development of what he called the gardenesque style, the characteristic feature of which, is the display of the beauty of trees, and other plants, individually. . . . [A]ll the trees and shrubs are arranged in regard to their kinds and dimensions; and they are planted at first as, or, as they grow, thinned out to, such distances apart as may best display the natural form and habit of each.

As an example of gardenesque planting, Loudon cited William Harrison's residence, Chestnut Cottage (Fig. 2). There, Harrison had combined the gardenesque manner with the older picturesque style of planting in which "trees, shrubs, and flowers were indiscriminately mixed, and crowded together, in shrubberies or other plantations" in order to "produce as much variety as possible." As Loudon summed it up, the "aim of the Gardenesque is to add all those [charms] which the sciences of gardening and botany, in their present advanced state, are capable of producing."[15] The garden, like the Crystal Palace, thus celebrated the expanding array of resources available in Britain.

The materialistic and mercantilistic associations of the Crystal Palace were underscored by its physical resemblance to a glass-roofed shopping arcade and the panoply of stalls under its roof. Reading from the Crystal Palace back to its host nation, the message of abundance and plenitude registered by the vast array of displayed goods invited viewers to perceive Britain as prosperous and wealthy.[16] It also set in place the notion that the future success of the nation would be judged by its technological progress and capacity to produce material goods. Yet the Crystal Palace contained within it the seeds of an alternative concept of national identity: A. W. Pugin's Medieval Court, a tribute to the past reflective of the historical revivalism that would occupy much of British architecture during the second half of the nineteenth century.

Despite opportunities for self-promotion provided to individual nations, the overall goal of the fair, as announced by Prince Albert, was to reinforce good relations between nations. Karl Marx and Frederich Engels, for example, saw the exhibition as "proof of the concentrated power with which modern large-scale industry smashes national barriers everywhere and increasingly levels out local peculiarities."[17] Throughout the rest of the nineteenth century and into the twentieth, however, industrial development and its attendant competition only reinforced national boundaries and local prejudices. At the Paris World's Fair of 1900, a French observer (Eugène-Melchior De Vogüé) perceived a tension between the proclaimed aims of internationalism and the actual practices of nationalism manifested in the national pavilions ranged along the Rue des Nations,

where each pavilion upholds the ethnic character of its country, of its race. This contradiction of a cosmopolitanism endorsed by all and of a nationalism each day more intransigent, everywhere more jealous of maintaining or restoring the integrity of the race, of the mother-tongue,

2. "View from the Drawing Room Window at Chestnut Cottage, Looking to the Right," from *The Gardener's Magazine,* 1839. (Source: Dumbarton Oaks, Studies in Landscape Architecture, Photo Archive.)

of the laws, the traditions: is this not one of the great unknowns of the problematic legacy our century leaves to its successor?[18]

The practice of reading a nation's character from its cultural expressions had intensified over the course of the nineteenth century. In a series of early essays, "The Poetry of Architecture," written for J. C. Loudon's *Architectural Magazine* (1837–8), art critic John Ruskin, for example, developed the premise that one could "trace in the distinctive characters of the architecture of nations, not only its adaptation to the situation and climate in which it has arisen, but its strong similarity to, and connection with, the prevailing turn of mind."[19] Loudon articulated a similar theory with respect to gardens:

> *The history of gardening* may be considered *chronologically,* or in connection with that of the different nations who have successively flourished in different parts of the world; *politically,* as influenced by the different government [sic] which have prevailed; *geographically,* as affected by the different climates and natural situations of the globe.[20]

In short, gardens manifested their local and national conditions (despite the degree to which plant material had been transported).

The notion that a nation's character was encoded in its architecture was exploited by the Crystal Palace organizers, who decided, because of the building's success, to rebuild it after it closed at Sydenham, a small village south of

London easily accessible by train. The interior was refurbished to contain musi-
cal performance spaces and exhibitions of instruction, commerce, and business
as well as displays of ancient, medieval, and Renaissance architecture and art.[21]
The cumulative effect held modernity – the architectural vocabulary of functional
iron and glass – in tension with historicism.

The extensive grounds at Sydenham, subdivided into a formal Italian garden
and an English landscape garden or park, reflected the partitioning of the interior
by nationality (Fig. 3). The Italian garden, running the length of the building, was
situated on the lower balustraded terrace that surrounded the building and featured a parterre executed in beds of brightly colored flowers set in the lawn and
punctuated by a series of fountains and statues. The grandeur and magnificence
of the formal Italian garden, with its obvious artifice, contrasted with the "natural
grace and freedom" of the English landscape garden beyond, with its "winding
walks, pleasant slopes and gentle undulations" giving way to an expansive view
of "rich wooded country . . . [and] rich corn-fields."[22]

The Italian style had come about with midcentury interest in historicism as
garden designers, like architects, opted for vocabularies redolent with historicist
associations, such as the *Italian Renaissance* or *French* and *English Gothic*.[23]
These terms were relatively imprecisely defined, and treatise writers and critics
occupied themselves with shoring up the boundaries of these relatively perme-
able concepts with extensive discussions that only fueled rather than quelled
stylistic debates. Charles M'Intosh, in *The Flower Garden* (first published
1837–8), attempted to clarify the field, describing an Italian garden as

> characterized by one or more terraces, sometime supported by parapet
> walls, on the coping of which vases of different forms are occasionally
> placed, either as ornaments, or for the purpose of containing plants.
> Where the ground slopes much, and commands a supply of water from
> above, *jets d'eau* and fountains are introduced with good effect (Fig. 4).

The French garden was quite similar, with "parterres, sometimes in very complicated figures," placed beyond the terraces (Fig. 5). The Dutch garden was distinguished by its "rectangular formality, and what may be sometimes be termed
clumsy artifice, such as yew trees cut out in the intended form of statues" (Fig. 6).
The English garden, by contrast, eschewed "the Italian terrace, the French
parterre, [and] . . . the Dutch clipt evergreens" because of their overt artificiality
and instead preferred "an artful imitation of nature" (Fig. 7).[24]

British designer W. A. Nesfield was closely associated with the Italian or French
garden. He worked with leading Victorian architects, such as his brother-in-law
Anthony Salvin as well as William Burn and Edward Blore, and echoed revivalist
forms prevalent in domestic architecture with formal garden forms derived from

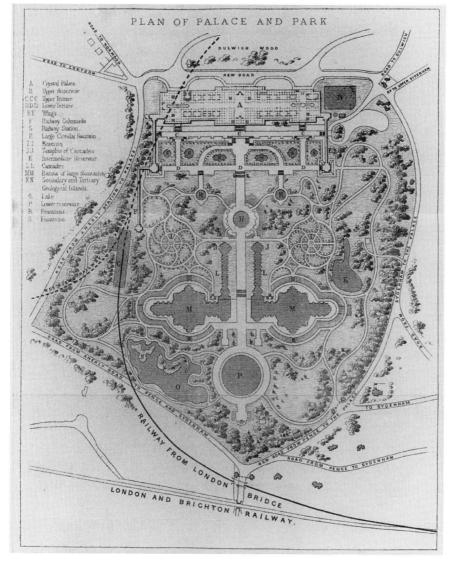

3. "Plan of Palace and Park," from Samuel Phillips, *Guide to the Crystal Palace and Park,* London, 1856. (Source: Dumbarton Oaks, Studies in Landscape Architecture, Photo Archive.)

old treatises, such as Antoine-Joseph Dézallier d'Argenville's *La Théorie et la Pratique du Jardinage* (1709).[25] Although a versatile designer, Nesfield became best known for his parterre designs, elaborately laid out in extensive patterns of contrasting plants and colored gravels or bricks, as in the garden he designed for the Royal Horticultural Society (RHS), laid out in 1860–1 (Fig. 8). The initial response by the press was enthusiastic. But, as Brent Elliott has documented, by 1870 the tide had turned, and the site received heavy criticism for its ornament, artificiality,

4. "An Italian Garden," from Charles M'Intosh, *The Flower Garden*, London, 1839. (Source: Dumbarton Oaks, Studies in Landscape Architecture, Photo Archive.)

5. "A French Garden," from Charles M'Intosh, *The Flower Garden*, London, 1839. (Source: Dumbarton Oaks, Studies in Landscape Architecture, Photo Archive.)

6. "A Dutch Garden," from Charles M'Intosh, *The Flower Garden,* London, 1839. (Source: Dumbarton Oaks, Studies in Landscape Architecture, Photo Archive.)

19

7. "English Garden and Pleasure Ground," from Charles M'Intosh, *The Flower Garden,* London, 1839. (Source: Dumbarton Oaks, Studies in Landscape Architecture, Photo Archive.)

and emphasis on architecture over plants.[26] Calls were made for a new style of gardening that could accommodate the public's fascination with exotics while achieving a more "natural" appearance. Into this breach stepped the proponent of the wild garden, William Robinson, who charged that Sydenham was "the greatest modern example of the waste of enormous means in making hideous a fine piece of garden" and called the RHS gardens "stiff and ugly."[27]

The Meanings of Gardens

Robinson's comments, although ostensibly aimed at correcting the current state of garden design, carried added weight because of the significance attached to gardens in English culture. The values that gardens carried derived both from meanings assigned to their forms and materials and from ways in which the term *garden* was deployed in contemporary discourses in relationship to a complex nexus of other highly charged concepts used to describe England and its landscape. *Garden, countryside, city* (and relatedly industrialization), *nation,* and *Empire* were constantly set into play together by different speakers, who reshuffled the terms to create a variety of constellations. Thus the concepts signified by these words were consistently defined through and against one and other.

The writings of John Ruskin are a useful starting point for tracing these relationships. Ruskin, as an educated man who grew up in the age of the picturesque, was attentive to the representation of nature in English culture as well as the ability of art forms to act on and to shape the beliefs and attitudes of viewers. By the 1860s he increasingly came to believe that England's burgeoning market economy and industrialized society had put nature at risk. The garden became the lens through which he focused many of these ideas in his lecture "Lilies: Of Queen's Gardens" (1864). Here Ruskin takes up the terms *city* and *country,* understood as dichotomies, as well as *nation* and *garden,* conflated and aligned with countryside. He also introduces gender into the equation.

Arising out of Ruskin's educative activities, this lecture addressed the topics of rearing girls and the proper role of women. Women, he argued, in keeping with the prevailing ideology of "the Angel in the House," were intended to rule over the home, relying on their capacity "not for invention or creation [the characteristics of men], but for sweet ordering, arrangement, and decision." To prepare girls for this womanly role, Ruskin spelled out an educative regime "calculated to add the qualities of patience and seriousness to her natural poignancy of thought and quickness of wit; and also to keep her in a lofty and pure element of thought" that would allow the girl "to grow as a flower does." Extending this botanical metaphor, Ruskin insisted that "wild and fair nature" could also exert an important influence on young girls. Indeed, nature was touted as an excellent teaching tool in this period, and numerous children's guides to natural history were published, such as the series *Parables from Nature,* written by Margaret Gatty.[28]

Addressing his remarks to parents in the audience, Ruskin advised that the appreciation and study of nature could begin within the relative safety of the garden attached to the house and then expand outward, provided the landscape could support such activities. Concerned that industrialization would irrevocably blight the countryside and thus prevent such forays into nature study, he turned to mothers, in their capacity as educators of the next generation, and instructed them to extend their supervisory scope from their own home to the countryside as a whole. If they could perceive that "the whole country is but a little garden," he insisted, they would realize their womanly abilities and duties to nurture and to order should be applied to the landscape. At the close of the lecture, Ruskin again used the garden motif to describe women's activities, likening a mother to a gardener in her capacity to create a sheltered space where her children could blossom in the light of Christianity, away from the contaminating chaos and conflict of greater society.

8. Exhibition of 1862. Scaffolding on the East Dome from a corner of the Royal Horticultural Society Garden, 1861. (Source: V & A Picture Library.)

Conceptualizing England as "a little garden" allowed Ruskin to propose that the public landscape be annexed to the private sphere so it could be cleansed and cultivated by virtuous women, who would arrange for its use as a living "schoolroom and playground" for England's children. Once England was remade in the likeness of a garden, with its associated womanly values of "sweet order, arrangement, and decision," values that Ruskin admired – such as appreciation of beauty and nature, Christian love, goodness, and innocence – could flourish. If the nation became a garden, it could then embody "the true nature of home . . . the place of Peace; the shelter, not only from all injury, but from all terror, doubt, and division." Its citizenry would thus be protected from the "peril and trial" associated with industrialization, commercialization, and a laissez-faire economic system.[29] Ruskin would take up again this concept of reconfiguring, through the metaphor of the garden, the nation as the domestic sphere writ large in his introductory "Art of England" lecture, delivered in 1870, in which the concept of nation/home is given added valence by its positioning with respect to the concept of Empire.

Janus-Faced England

The polarizing terms undergirding Ruskin's lecture – city vs. country, industrialization vs. nature, artifice vs. naturalness, Christianity vs. capitalism – derive from a phenomenon observed by numerous subsequent commentators: the Janus-faced nature of late-nineteenth-century England, a leading capitalist economy that clung to traditions associated with its disappearing rural, agricultural-based economy and whose capital city of London contained both the most exuberant displays of wealth and the worst degradations of poverty.[30] The country that had conceived itself as the world's workshop with the 1851's Great Exhibition by 1870 took up what historian Martin Wiener has labeled the "counterimage of an ancient, little-disturbed 'Green and pleasant Land'" as it rejected the cultural trappings of the very trade and industrialization that empowered it.[31]

This counterimage, epitomized by the motif of England as a garden, was compounded by the promotion of the mythic experience of the southern counties – rural and agricultural as opposed to the industrial north – as the epitome of Englishness.[32] The southern metaphor was based on an appreciation of the past and tradition that was tied closely to an ideal of rural life conceived as stable and tranquil. This resulted in a "myth of an England essentially rural and essentially unchanging [that] appealed across political lines both to Conservatives and Imperialists, and to anti-Imperialists, Liberals, and Radicals."[33] Elizabeth Gaskell exploited this cultural and geographic split in her novel *North and South* (1855), which contrasts the bucolic domestic coziness of the rural village of Helston, Hampshire, with the dark dinginess of the manufacturing town of Milton, located somewhere in the north of England.

Whereas Gaskell envisioned Janus-faced England as governed by opposing forces, American expatriate Henry James, in his dissection of British society, revealed a more complicated relationship between concepts such as city and country. In his writings, he articulated how difficult it was to distinguish one term from the next: city blended into country, which melted into nation, and then into Empire. And yet, he noted, the sense of each term still derived largely from its contrast with its neighbor.[34] James anticipates Raymond Williams's cautionary observation that repeatedly setting country against city obscures the inextricable linking of the agrarian and manufacturing bases of the economy throughout the nineteenth century and, likewise, the city's and country's urgent need for and dependence on each other as each was conceptualized in relation to the other.[35] In "An English Easter," James developed a metaphor for this complicated relationship of simultaneously opposing and overlapping concepts. "In England, country-life is the obverse of the medal, town-life the reverse."[36] The medal or coin motif allowed James to describe the contrasting faces of Janus-faced England while insisting on their mutual dependence.

This dynamic of difference and contingency also informed Ruskin's inaugural address as Slade Professor of Fine Arts at Oxford, delivered on February 8, 1870. Here, Ruskin began to spell out how English art could be improved, focusing in large part on landscape painting, in which he claimed the English uniquely excelled. To convince his audience of the value of landscape painting, he promised that if English children could grow up surrounded by paintings of their native country, they would inherit "an intense delight in the landscape of their country as *memorial* . . . the seal and reward of persistence in national life." In other words, landscape painting could inculcate a patriotic and honorific attachment to the nation. The same argument, he added, could be made with respect to physical landscapes; and so it was incumbent on his listeners to improve and to make "more lovely" the countryside by erasing the effects of industrialization and rendering the English landscape into the likeness of a garden:

> The England who is to be mistress of half the earth, cannot remain herself a heap of cinders, trampled by contended and miserable crowds; she must yet again become the England she was once, and in all beautiful ways – more: so happy, so secluded, and so pure . . . and in her fields, ordered and wide fair, of every herb that sips the dew; and under the green avenues of her enchanted garden, a sacred Circe, true Daughter of the Sun.

The impetus behind this remaking of the English landscape, and the solution to how this refashioning could be carried out, was founding colonies. Earlier in his lecture, Ruskin asserted that England must found colonies "or perish." This act would relieve England of its "contending and miserable crowds" and help "to advance the power of England by land and sea." The mandate to reburnish England's image lay not just at the feet of the would-be colonists; Ruskin demanded that those who remained at home give those settled in far-off lands "thoughts of their home of which they can be proud." Hence the need to eradicate the image of a nation covered in cinders in favor of an image of the nation as enchanted garden. In sum, England's landscape, now despoiled by industrialization and urbanization, must be transformed into a garden so it would be an object of pride for far-flung colonists. With this lecture, Ruskin metaphorically charged the garden not just with the domestic well-being of the nation, as he had in "Of Queen's Garden," but also with the well-being of the Empire as a whole.[37]

For readers today, Ruskin's resort to colonies while arguing on behalf of domestic reform might seem like a tangential rhetorical flourish, but for his listeners he was partaking in one of the most pertinent debates of the day. The link between national well-being and the colonies was being explored by popular historian J. A. Froude, for example, who published an essay on the subject, "England and Her Colonies," in *Fraser's Magazine* one month before Ruskin's lecture. In this essay Froude criticized the attitudes of contemporary politicians, particularly Prime Minister William Gladstone, toward Empire. "A powerful school of politicians," Froude warned, claimed "that the colonies as colonies are of no use to us" and even encouraged the dissolution of Empire. Froude attributed this position largely to cultural attitudes, starting with a growing tendency toward cosmopolitanism at the expense of patriotism. The nation's citizenry no longer embraced "that proud belief in England which made men ready to sacrifice themselves and all belonging to them in the interests of their country."

Like Ruskin, Froude believed that patriotic identification required a positive self-image. In casting about for a national icon, Froude chose not the garden but instead its opposite: England as the "emporium of the world's trade and a enormous workshop for all mankind." But then he backtracked and attacked this representation of England, which had been so vividly concretized in the Great Exhibition, by demonstrating the diseased foundation on which this edifice rested. Pursuit of profit, the historian claimed, had morally corrupted the nation. Bubble schemes, proliferation of false weights and measures, the drive for upward mobility, the increasing competitive mind-set, conflicts between labor and employers, increasing division between haves and have-nots, and the deterioration of the living conditions of the country's urban working classes (on which the fate of the

nation and the Empire rested) all pointed to the inadequacy of the great workshop as a national image.

Attention should instead be directed to the colonies, which would, if treated
properly, allow England to slough off its excess population and solve numerous
domestic problems, such as the pressure for land reform, union conflict, and
urban deterioration, while expanding England's markets and thereby its national
prosperity and international profile. This rosy scenario, in Froude's model, all
depended on broadcasting a notion of Englishness that would encompass both
Englanders at home and those in the Empire so that "an Englishman emigrating
to Canada, or the Cape, or Australia, or New Zealand, did not forfeit his nationality, that he was still on English soil as much as if he was in Devonshire or Yorkshire, and would remain an Englishman while the English empire lasted." The
historian drew a picture of a future in which "at great stations round the globe
there would grow up, under conditions the most favourable which the human
constitution can desire, fresh nations of Englishmen," thus ensuring the "indefinite and magnificent expansion of the English [note: not British] Empire."[38]

Ruskin's lecture followed up on many of these points, vilifying the national
self-image as the Great Workshop and pointing to colonies as solutions to problems of urban and industrial blight. As the catalyst to this process, he reintroduced
the notion of England as garden, metaphorically figuring the nation's resuscitation
through spaces that, via their domestic associations, could signify home and give
rise to the patriotic attachment to nation as home in the face of Empire. The
power of the garden metaphor in the hands of Ruskin, James, and numerous other
commentators lay in its ability to signify both the nation and its virtues and to
draw together contested points of town and country, nation and Empire.

Challenging the Status Quo

The promulgation of the garden as a symbol of England's national identity was
fueled, in part, by anxiety generated by suspicion that the status quo could no
longer be maintained.[39] Froude, in 1864, informed an audience at the Royal Institution that "we live in times of disintegration."[40] In short, the appeal of the garden – the frequent evocation of bright sunlight sparkling on emerald lawns and
many-hued flowers and other such tropes – correlated directly with the impression that other aspects of English life faced dark times. The garden, fulfilling its
Edenic promise, was constructed as a retreat and an escape from problems of
modern times.

Between the mid-1870s and mid-1890s the agricultural community was

I.—THE VILLAGE. OLD STYLE.

9. George Morrow, "I – The Village Old Style," from *Punch,* September 11, 1907. (Source: Mary Couts Burnet Library, Texas Christian University.)

plagued by cycles of depression caused by a myriad of factors, including cheap grain imports and bouts of bad weather. The general prosperity enjoyed since the Napoleonic Wars was coming to an end as land values, productivity, and agricultural employment declined. In the 1880s pressure to restructure the rural economy mounted with the land reform movement, which, in response to a survey of 1876 that revealed 24 percent of England's land was owned by 202 individuals, demanded a more equitable distribution of land. The political makeup of the countryside changed further in 1884 with the Third Reform Act that extended the right to vote to male rural laborers over the age of twenty-one. Whereas rural laborers often cast their vote for Liberals, landowners for the most part remained loyal to the Conservative Party.

The countryside was torn apart further in 1885 with the Redistribution Bill that enacted the one person, one vote principle for the first time. As a result, in 1885 the first Parliament was elected in which urban representatives outnumbered rural representatives. The seat of power was gradually shifting away from its traditional base in the countryside to the cities. Limitations placed in 1911 on the powers of the House of Lords, the long-standing base of the great landowning class, was one more nail in the coffin of the political power of this class and the way of life it represented.

This compounded the sensation, recorded by many writers and artists, that the countryside, as it had been understood for decades, was under threat and in

II.—THE VILLAGE. NEW STYLE.

10. George Morrow, "II – The Village New Style," from *Punch*, September 11, 1907. (Source: Mary Couts Burnet Library, Texas Christian University.)

danger of disappearing altogether. Technological developments, such as extension of the railways and introduction of the bicycle in the 1880s and the automobile around the turn of the century, further enhanced the perception that the countryside was undergoing intense change (Figs. 9, 10). The swelling suburbs, with detached and semidetached houses and accompanying gardens, and the later Garden City movement further erased differences between town and country. Much of the increased attention to the rural countryside by writers and artists can be attributed, in large part, to a desire to preserve the countryside, or, more precisely, what the countryside was popularly imagined to be, from erosion caused by the encroaching urban sphere.

The expanding urban domain, for many, characterized the nineteenth century. In 1851 the Census recorded for the first time that more people lived in urban than rural areas. Of England's cities, the capital of London was the largest and most magnificent, rivaling Paris, Berlin, and Vienna. Surveying London, Henry James found that while on occasion it was "anything but a cheerful or a charming city," it could also be "a very splendid one."[41] Money poured into the city at an incredible rate thanks to the circulation of raw materials and finished goods within the Empire, profits earned from Britain's thriving shipping fleet, and London's position as seat of government and financial center of both the British nation and the Empire. Consumerism also drove the London economy. Although the agricultural depression affected pockets of wealthy landowners, and despite a trade depression caused by deflating prices and profit margins, service sectors of the economy, such as shops, blossomed as falling prices made more goods obtainable for greater numbers of buyers.

Consumption patterns were also dictated by changing class dynamics at the end of the nineteenth century. This period, with its infusion of wealth into the middle classes, witnessed the emergence of the upper middle class, described as the "dominant influence of the nineteenth century."[42] The latter was composed in large part of the business and professional classes, whose rising standard of living enhanced the stratification of the middle classes and spurred "competition for status in every field, in dress, housing, and furniture, education, leisure and entertainment."[43] Unlike members of the lower middle class, those of the upper middle class were, according to advice manuals, preoccupied with "keeping up appearances."[44] Many in the upper middle class began to emulate the lifestyle and cosmopolitanism of the wealthy aristocracy through such practices as educating their children at "public schools" and purchasing or building country houses (sheared of their agricultural estates) in imitation of the titled aristocracy. Advice manuals commanded, "Go right away, into a suburb or the country."[45] A country house became more possible for many in this class because of the expanding railway network, which allowed home owners to commute more easily to urban centers, and the selling of older homes and rural tracts by great landowners due to economic pressures of the agricultural depression.

While the upper middle class found itself benefiting from the expansion of capitalism, many sectors of the British economy were nonetheless in decline at the end of the nineteenth century when compared with either midcentury production or that of Britain's competitors. For example, the United States and Germany quickly outpaced British steel production; by 1900 Germany produced 1.5 million more tons of steel a year than England.[46] The quickly changing conditions of British industry hit the laboring classes hard. Many workers were thrown into a desperate cycle of seasonal employment and unemployment that aggravated the already poor living standard of this class. Fears that the underclasses (no longer counted on to produce reliable work because of poor living conditions) would bring down the nation led to numerous social investigations, particularly in urban areas.

One of the most notable of these sociological investigations was Andrew Mearns's "The Bitter Cry of Outcast London" (1883), which focused on the meager lodgings of the poor. Although it echoed accounts of midcentury writers such as Charles Dickens, it was written as a documentary diatribe rather than a novel and it eventually led to the appointment of a Royal Commission on the Housing of the Working Classes (1884). In addition, Mearns reversed conventional wisdom by attributing the immorality of the poor not to moral laxitude but to the filth and overcrowding of their homes:

> Few who will read these pages have any conception of what these pestilential human rookeries are, where tens of thousands are crowded together amidst horrors which call to mind what we have heard of the middle passage of the slave ship. To get into them you have to penetrate courts reeking with poisonous and malodorous gases arising from accumulations of sewage and refuse scattered in all directions and often flowing beneath your feet; courts, many of them which the sun never penetrates, which are never visited by a breath of fresh air, and which rarely know the virtues of a drop of cleansing water.[47]

Mearns's description of the vileness of London's rookeries contrasts vividly with the accounts of glittering shop facades in the West End by Henry James or fresh flower-filled gardens and fields, with their moral and domestic connotations, recounted earlier by Ruskin. Capitalizing on the disgust he aroused in his readership, Mearns argued that the tide of poverty must be stopped or it would sink the nation.[48] Mearns's account, shored up by statistical analyses by other reformers such as Charles Booth and S. Rowntree, as well as statistics on rejected army recruits, led eventually to formation in 1903 of the Inter-Departmental Committee on Physical Deterioration. The report issued by the committee in 1904 determined that the poor were suffering from measurable physical deterioration and concluded that "urbanization of the people" and the deleterious effects of "(i) overcrowding, (ii) pollution of the atmosphere, [and] (iii) the conditions of employment" were "prejudicial to the health of the people."[49]

Such reports exacerbated fears that deterioration of "the physical, intellectual and moral fitness of the nation" would lead, as Froude had predicted, to a decline in England's "competitive position in the world economy."[50] The expansion of democracy with the 1884 Franchise Bill only fostered these fears. Conservatives took alarm at the prospect of the masses possibly voting for the Left. Upper-class voters translated these fears into political action by voting for the Conservative Party, further eroding the already declining Liberal Party. By the outbreak of the Great War, many in England thought the country on the brink of a major crisis that would completely break down the existing social order.[51]

Empire was a solace for many of England's citizens fearful of the loss of preeminence. Yet, as grand monuments to Britain's imperial power were erected in London in the form of the Wren-inspired Admiralty (1895), designed by Leeming and Leeming, J. M. Brydon's classical Government Offices (1898–1912) along Parliament Square, and the Baroque-style War Office, Whitehall (1898), by

William Young, politicians and reformers wrangled over the fate of the Empire. Expansionists faced off against consolidationists.[52] Despite claims that the British eschewed "an increase of territory in tropical countries already occupied by native races," the country participated, alongside the other powers of Europe, in dividing Africa into colonies throughout the 1880s and 1890s.[53] In India, the network of colonial administration grew denser in spite of, and in response to, limited revolts against British rule. The costs of Empire often seemed to out-weigh the benefits, especially with the involvement of British troops in the Sudan, the unpopular Afghan and Zulu wars of 1879, and the Boer War of 1899–1902, as well as the ongoing Irish question. The debates surrounding home rule were particularly intense and changed dramatically the makeup of Britain's political parties, beginning in 1886 with the split of the Liberal Party over Glad-stone's support of home rule. In the same year a Scottish Home Rule Association was founded. Separatist movements formed in Wales in the 1890s, rallying around the question of disestablishment.

On the international front, while prime ministers, such as the Marquess of Salisbury, who led the Tory Party, attempted to maintain a position of "splendid isolation," Britain found itself repeatedly drawn into imperial conflicts and Euro-pean tensions. As the military strength of Germany grew, Britain responded with a military buildup of its own, concentrating on the navy, a rallying point for nationalist agitation particularly in the 1890s and in the period of 1906–11.[54] While some commentators decried Britain's expanding sphere of influence, oth-ers celebrated it, thereby inflating the jingoistic spirit that characterized the turn of the century. Events such as the institution of Queen Victoria as empress of India in 1876, the queen's Jubilees in 1887 and 1897, and the coronation of Edward VII in 1902, functioned as magnets for patriotic fervor.

Threats from outside and internal celebrations may seem to be ingredients for coalescing society, as was the case in the early nineteenth century when a series of wars between Britain and France resulted in a new sense of Britishness; but at the end of the nineteenth century the political landscape had changed.[55] As Gerald Newman has explained, "nineteenth-century nationalism meant much more than support of national military power and of freedom from foreign domination. The idea of national freedom now also carried with it a complex idea of *national soli-darity* in peace as well as war, and, necessarily, of opposition to internal obstacles to this solidarity."[56] Notions of internal solidarity began to form around smaller rather than greater units as romantic nationalism gained force; the United King-dom refragmented into England, Ireland, Scotland, and Wales as each respective group self-identified through language, religion, sport, and culture.[57]

Notions of difference were underscored by the Little England movement, the label attached to those who opposed the Boer War. These anticolonialists set

England against Empire rather than overlaying the two. J. A. Hobson, for example, in his tract *Imperialism: A Study* (first published 1902), argued that if nationalism was the product of "territorial and dynastic" consolidation resulting from resistance to outside threat reinforced by "racial, linguistic, and economic solidarity," then Empire threatened to debase this "genuine nationalism" by forcing it "to overflow its natural banks and absorb the near or instant territory of reluctant and unassimilable peoples." He concluded that "Imperialism is a depraved choice of national life, imposed by self-seeking interests which appeal to the lusts of quantitative acquisitiveness and of forceful domination surviving in a nation from early centuries of animal struggle for existence."[58]

In searching for an appropriate symbol of a "national life," artists, architects, designers, and writers latched on to the garden. It became a unifying symbol of national identity that promised internal solidarity while assimilating the exoticism of Empire. It also connoted maintenance of the status quo in the face of quixotic change and fears of degeneration. But despite such agreement about the garden's significance, the form it would take was sharply contested.

The Glory of the Garden

The garden's unifying potential, as well as its position at intersection of town and country, home and Empire, and past and present, is brought home by two texts that prominently deployed the garden as a symbol of national identity: Henry James's "Gardens and Orchards," an essay written to accompany an exhibition of Alfred Parsons's garden paintings at the Fine Art Society in 1891, and Rudyard Kipling's poem "The Glory of the Garden," which first appeared as the conclusion to *A School History of England* (1911).

The American writer Henry James had taken up residence in England in the early 1880s and became friends with Parsons through a network of American artists, including E. A. Abbey and F. D. Millet, living in the rural town of Broadway in the Cotswolds region.[59] Parsons, for his exhibition at the Fine Art Society in 1891, assembled a collection of watercolor and oil paintings of rural orchards and gardens, many of which were executed *en plein air*. In type, the gardens ranged from cottagers' plots – such as Mrs. Hopkin's Cottage, Broadway – to small manor-house gardens – the vicarage garden at King's Langley or the garden at Russell House where Millet lived – to grand estates – such as Holme Lacey or Stourhead.[60] Also included were several views of the gardens at Gravetye, home of garden writer William Robinson, for whom Parsons also worked as an illustrator (Fig. 11).

In the opening paragraph of the exhibition catalog, James quickly established that Parsons's paintings carried meanings beyond literal representation of gardens. First, and most significantly, he equated Parsons's "numerous and delightful studies of gardens, great and small" with "happy England." Then, slying digging at his English readers and with the twisting ease of his prose, James submitted that Parsons's paintings "might easily minister to the quietest complacency of patriotism" because they provide "a kind of compendium of what, in home things, is at once most typical and most enviable" of England. Capitalizing on the iconic and symbolic value of Parsons's paintings, James then proposed that they "be carried by slow stages around the globe, to kindle pangs in the absent and passions in the alien." Playing (rather sarcastically) to the assumed patriotic sentiments of his audience, James added, "as it happens to be a globe that the English race has largely peopled, we can measure the amount of homesickness that would be engendered on the way." One can imagine Froude, who hoped for "great stations round the globe" where "fresh nations of Englishmen" could flourish, delighting in this proposal to bind together the imagined community of English citizens through viewing portable representations of English gardens.

James, writing from the declared position of a Colonial (i.e., American), then detailed the distinguishing characteristics of English gardens: their look of great age or character, a quality unique to England because of the country's long, stable history, and their owners' devotion to them. This mixture of veneration and age led James to refer to gardens as "pious foundations" of the nation, thus implying that nationalistic sentiment might fill the vacuum created by the-post-Darwinian demise of religion. Continuing the religious metaphor, the author described Parsons's "quest" for subjects as "pleasant pilgrimages" and recommended that exhibition goers embark on their own "*trouvailles.*"

The remainder of the catalog describes individual paintings in richly evocative prose and underscores the Englishness of each depicted site. With respect to a portrayal of a Somersetshire garden, for example, James called attention to "that peculiarly English look of the open-air room . . . produced by the stretched carpet of the turf and the firm cushions of the hedges."[61] Critics were repeatedly struck by how accurately the author had delineated their community. *The Spectator,* as if listing the writer's credentials, called attention to James's "intensified sense for English characteristics," and *The Times* declared his prose to be colored by the "almost despairing love for the Old World that is felt by some at least of the natives of the New."[62]

Several other reviewers adopted this paradigm of old and new, but for different purposes. Picking up on James's point that English gardens "have had a history," several described how gardens could be a vehicle to the past and a means by which to bind it to the present. This was the case in the *Illustrated London News*'s review, which claimed that "in looking on the yew hedges, the grass walks, and the ancestral elms and twisted apple trees, we feel the continuity of our national life, and recognize how each succeeding generation or family has been linked together by a love of flowers and nature."[63]

This reviewer's evocation of endless chains of ancestors worshipping the same yews, elms, apple trees, and grass walks is a sharp reminder of Benedict Anderson's argument that nationalism insists that nations "always loom out of an immemorial past."[64] As in the eighteenth century, gardens gave the English landscape a past that the community could draw on to construct their identity. James's contemporaries recognized the power of the past for creating a sense of nationhood. Mandell Creighton, Lord Bishop of Peterborough and honorary fellow of Merton College, insisted, in his 1896 Romanes Lecture, that "national character is the abiding product of a nation's past."[65] Pointedly, the character and past to which Creighton referred was that of the English, whom he asserted "were the first people who formed for themselves national character" by withdrawing "from the general system of Europe" and building their own traditions through "assimilating what was in accordance with the national temper, and rejecting what was not."[66] The reception of Parsons's exhibition indicates that "a love of flowers and nature" was a vital component of the national character that Creighton had illuminated.

11. Alfred Parsons, *The Terrace Wall, Gravetye*, n.d. (Source: Collection of Mr. Peter Herbert, Gravetye Manor Hotel.)

The notion that "continuity of our national life" could be expressed in a garden was again articulated in an article on the history of gardening in England written a few years after Parsons's show. The author of this article praised, for example, "an old yew hedge [that] links us in unbroken chains to those who planted for others and not for themselves," and thus captured an appreciation of land in England being passed, undisputed, from generation to generation thanks to primogeniture and a continuous nation-state. The garden, in other words, becomes the nation's heritage. Respect for gardens, the article continued, would also provide a sense of constancy in the face of change: "So much in modern democracy is necessarily new and self-assertive, we pull down much merely for the sake of asserting our own especial taste," but "nature," in the form of the garden, "survives" such transformations.[67] The context for this assertion was the expansion of the franchise and the sense of volatility attendant on the new politics of democracy: the lack of a track record for the bulk of the voting population created an atmosphere of unpredictability. But what remained the same, what was essential to Englishness, insisted this article, was the garden.

The act of defining the nation that James performed not only helped Englanders, or at least reviewers, to see themselves as a common community bound together by shared interests but also distinguished that community from those outside it. This is a crucial rhetorical maneuver often employed in travel writing, for without difference there is no point in traveling. As both an occasional tourist and a writer about tourism, James was well aware that the passionate desire to experience objects and scenes distinctive to a place fueled travel, or what he called pilgrimages.[68]

Although guidebooks of the period were rarely as poetic as James, they set forth itineraries, sites, and monuments by which England could be best understood by outsiders. In keeping with the long-standing practice of country-house visiting in England, which grew tremendously at the turn of the century with the increasing participation of the middle classes, tourist guides emphasized country houses, particularly those of the Elizabethan period, such as Berkeley Castle, Haddon Hall, Hardwick Hall, Hatfield House, Loseley, and Penshurst, all of which possessed notable gardens.[69] What made these country houses so compelling, according to guidebooks, was that they made the past, embedded in the very structures and grounds, accessible to the present.[70] Overgrown vegetation, marks of decay, and styles of design assigned to the premodern age all became signs of the authentic, truly English experience so desired by the tourist. And that authenticity was even more appreciated from the vantage point of modernists, who despaired of ever experiencing genuineness in an age defined by the emergence of mass commodity culture and the pursuit of the new, ever changing, and disposable.[71]

As doubts about the future and notions of progress mounted, the past increasingly appeared as a safe haven in the storm. Within the garden, as described by James, a sense of place and past commingled to produce true Englishness. Parsons's painted gardens could become portable icons of that living past, thus collapsing the distance between past and present, as well as between the local, the nation, and the Empire. They allowed each viewer to partake in a sense of community generated by the circulation of travel writings and images.[72]

Whereas James's text revolved around the metaphorical equation of gardens as English, Rudyard Kipling, in his poem "The Glory of the Garden," reversed the positioning of the terms and built his prose on the metaphor of England as garden:

> Our England is a garden that is full of stately views,
> Of borders, beds, and shrubberies and lawns and avenues,
> With statues on the terraces and peacocks strutting by;
> But the Glory of the Garden lies in more than meets the eye.
>
> For where the old thick laurels grow, along the thin red wall,
> You'll find the tool- and potting-sheds which are the heart of all,
> The cold-frames and the hot-houses, the gundpits and the tanks,
> The rollers, carts and drain-pipes, with the barrows and the planks.
>
> And there you'll see the gardeners, the men and 'prentice boys
> Told off to do as they are bid and do it without noise;
> For, except when seeds are planted and we shout to scare the birds,
> The Glory of the Garden it abideth not in words.
>
> And some can pot begonias and some can bud a rose,
> And some are hardly fit to trust with anything that grows;
> But they can roll and trim the lawns and sift the sand and loam,
> For the Glory of the Garden occupieth all who come.
>
> Our England is a garden, and such gardens are not made
> By singing: – 'Oh, how beautiful,' and sitting in the shade,
> While better men than we go out and start their working lives
> At grubbing weeds from gravel-paths with broken dinner-knives.
>
> There's not a pair of legs so thin, there's not a head so thick,
> There's not a hand so weak and white, nor yet a heart so sick,
> But it can find some needful job that's crying to be done,
> For the Glory of the Garden glorifieth every one.
>
> Then seek your job with thankfulness and work till further orders,
> If it's only netting strawberries or killing slugs on borders;

And when your back stops aching and your hands begin to harden,
You will find yourself a partner in the Glory of the Garden.

Oh, Adam was a gardener, and God who made him sees
That half a proper gardener's work is done upon his knees,
So when your work is finished, you can wash your hands and pray
For the Glory of the Garden that it may not pass away!
And the Glory of the Garden it shall never pass away![73]

Written in England, where the British poet had settled after extensive years in India, Europe, and the United States, the poem reflects both a toning down and shoring up of his earlier proimperialist rhetoric. Around the period of the Boer War and shortly after, Kipling began to express doubts about the spirit of jingoism that flooded Great Britain and colored descriptions of its imperial accomplishments. In "The Islanders" (1902), he had chastised his readers: "And ye vaunted your fathomless power, and ye/flaunted your iron pride . . . Idle – openly idle – in the lee of the forespent Line."[74] Kipling feared that years of an expanding empire and economy had inculcated a sense of self-satisfaction and had led Englanders to rest on their laurels and to abdicate the principles of duty, moral responsibility, service, and sacrifice that had previously driven their accomplishments.

In "The Glory of the Garden," Kipling employs the metaphor of England as garden to reinvigorate the value and benefits of hard work. Like Ruskin, he incites readers to care for the country so it could be an object of pride. He casts a wide net for caretakers: he implicitly acknowledges that gardens were typically the property of the landed classes labored by the working classes, but closes the poem by instructing readers that no one is above or exempt from the labor necessary to maintain England as garden. The poem was originally published in *A School History of England* (1911) and was highly appropriate for this context because at this time one of education's primary roles was to instill civic and imperial values. Contemporaneous pedagogical texts sought to establish the parameters of Englishness (as opposed to Britishness) through recourse to what were believed to be shared racial or national characteristics and virtues, such as hard work, loyalty, and sacrifice, and Kipling's textbook was no exception.[75]

Kipling practiced what he preached, creating a garden at his home. A seventeenth-century manor house situated in an East Sussex valley, Bateman's offered the Kiplings a physical and mental retreat because of its relative isolation.[76] The respect Kipling held for the past manifested itself in his treatment of his home; *Country Life* described the house, built of local sandstone with roof tiles and chimney bricks made of local Weald clay, "an unspoilt survival of a good architectural age."[77] Elements of newness, however, crept in with the planting, which

Country Life described as reflecting "modern horticultural development," suggesting that it included hybrids and/or exotics.[78]

Kipling's garden was an amalgamation of the formal and natural styles prevalent at the turn of the century. The author may have gained the input of two of the great lions of garden design of the period: William Robinson, a proponent of natural or wild gardening whose West Sussex home of Gravetye was a short distance away, and architect Reginald Blomfield, an advocate of the formal garden who worked at Bateman's, converting an oasthouse (for drying hops) into a cottage.[79] But the plan of the ornamental garden, located largely off the southern front of the house, was by Kipling, who used the proceeds from the £7,700 he received with the Nobel Prize in 1907 to add a pond garden, rose garden, and framing yew hedges, as well as an orchard and a wild garden, to the already planted avenue of pleached limes (Plate I; Fig. 12).[80] The alley, pond garden, rose garden, and yew hedges were features specifically mentioned in Blomfield's treatise on formal gardening and a wild garden, laid out below the pond garden and informally planted

37

12. Bateman's from the Southwest, 1998. (Source: Author's photograph.)

flowering trees and shrubs set amid meadow grass and flowering spring bulbs, was a mode of design heavily promoted by William Robinson.[81]

In its use of natural and formal garden styles, and local and imported materials, as well as its links to the past and rural England, Bateman's embodies styles, materials, and themes that would occupy English gardening over the years 1870–1914 as designers, patrons, and critics debated what form could best give expression to their desired image of the English nation. While designers and commentators were preoccupied with defining Englishness through the garden, the Empire nonetheless maintained a constant presence in their debates, sometimes acknowledged and sometimes denied just as Empire remained ever present in Kipling's imagination even as he increasingly turned to rural England as the subject of his writings. Although the discourse of garden design constantly turned inward, to define self-consciously what was English, the outside world was never forgotten. It provided designers with materials and ideas at the same time they set the English garden in opposition to it.

Chapter 2

Re-presenting the Countryside
William Robinson and the Wild Garden

The first full articulation of the wild garden type came with publication of William Robinson's *The Wild Garden* in 1870 (Fig. 13), in which the author explicitly rejected prevailing garden styles and claimed to look back "to the time of Shakespeare" and its old-fashioned flowers. The wild garden, nevertheless, was very much of its time, partaking of recent explorations of nature conducted by natural scientists and artists and reflecting the ongoing importation of plant material into England, and, somewhat paradoxically, a growing desire to resurrect or to preserve distinctively English rural culture. Robinson's colleagues credited him with instigating a revolution in garden design, and English audiences affirmed that wild gardens suited their social and aesthetic needs. The wild garden claimed to be natural, and that was its most potent weapon in the battle of styles in which it eventually figured. Its rustic associations also allowed it to participate in the ongoing construction of the English countryside as the antithesis of the polluted city.[1]

The Wild Garden (1870) and Contemporary Garden Practices

Born in Northern Ireland (a fact that he reportedly concealed later in his life) of Protestant parents in 1838, Robinson came to England in 1861 to take a position at the Royal Botanic Society's Garden in Regent's Park after having been employed as a private gardener and at the National Botanic Garden in Dublin.[2] At Regent's Park, where he worked under Robert Marnock, an important nineteenth-century landscape designer known for his "seminatural" style, Robinson was placed in charge of the herbaceous ground where he specialized in British wildflowers. In 1866 he left Regent's Park to take up writing full time, becoming a correspondent for *The Gardeners' Chronicle* and *The Times.* In expanding his purview to writing, Robinson astutely positioned himself to take advantage of the exploding growth of publishing in this period. Industrialization made printing both text and images, typically woodcut illustrations, cheaper and quicker by the last quarter of the nineteenth century, and with these advances a burgeoning market for garden-related publications developed.[3] Treatises, aimed at polite society in the seventeenth and eighteenth centuries, became more widely available to the middle classes; gardening magazines, directed at a wide range of amateur enthusiasts and dedicated professionals, flourished.

Robinson took advantage of this emerging market by founding his own journal, *The Garden, an Illustrated Weekly Journal of Horticulture in All Its Branches* (1871–1927), which merged into *Homes and Gardens* in 1927. He also ventured into more short-lived, heavily illustrated (and thus more costly) publications with *Gardening Illustrated* (1879) and *Flora and Sylva* (1903–6). Even before launching his journal, Robinson had considerable experience in garden writing through his books, beginning with *Gleanings from French Gardens* (1868), *The Parks, Promenades, and Gardens of Paris* (1869), followed by *Alpine Flowers for Gardens* and *The Wild Garden* in 1870.[4] He published two expanded, illustrated editions of *The Wild Garden* in 1881 and 1894, as well as numerous editions of his equally famous book *The English Flower Garden,* which first appeared in 1883.[5]

With money made from his publications, which he partly invested in London real estate, Robinson purchased, in 1884, Gravetye Manor, an Elizabethan stone house in Sussex set on a 1,000-acre estate. Robinson was just one of many of the wealthy middle classes who established rural residence at this time. As Horace Townsend explained in an 1895 article in *The Studio,* modern businessmen felt overburdened by stresses of the modern marketplace and needed "some country *pied-à-terre* to which they can run down for weeks or months . . . and feel themselves free from society or business cares."[6] This return to the land was considered a self-consciously, typically English phenomenon:

> There is nothing that gives greater gratification to the average Englishman than to be the possessor of a plot of ground, no matter how small, where he may enjoy the felicity of seeing something of nature's way of working, helped on by his own labour and attention. This is, of course, specially applicable to those who are often long-time confined to crowded cities, where streets and buildings form the chief attraction; for, after a hard day's or week's or perhaps even year's work, what can give more pleasure than a summer visit to the country.[7]

"I wish it to be framed, as much as may be, to a naturall wildnesse."
LORD BACON.

13. "Frontispiece," from William Robinson, *The Wild Garden,* London, 1870. (Source: Reproduced from the collections of the Library of Congress.)

With the purchase of Gravetye, Robinson, who also argued that nature could be a soothing retreat from modern urbanism, could put his beliefs into practice.

Robinson's theory of wild gardening, as set forth in his book *The Wild Garden,* brought him his first brush with fame, largely owing to his persuasive promise that wild gardens were both easy and beautiful. Despite implications of unplanned fecundity that the name "wild garden" suggested, Robinson's text set forth a very specific gardening method and aesthetic. His object in *The Wild Garden* was

> to show how we may, without losing the better features of the mixed bedding or any other system, follow one infinitely superior to any now practised, yet supplementing both, and exhibiting more of the varied beauty of hardy flowers than the most ardent admirer of the old style of garden ever dreams of. We may do this by naturalizing or making wild innumerable beautiful natives of many regions of the earth in our woods, wild and semi-wild places, rougher parts of pleasure grounds, etc., and in unoccupied places in almost every kind of garden.[8]

In these two sentences, Robinson declared his intention to overturn existing gardening practices by realizing a new garden form based on naturalizing exotics and wildflowers in underutilized areas of garden or park.

Robinson's campaign to reform English garden design had begun at least a year earlier with his publication *The Parks, Promenades, and Gardens of Paris.* Impressed by the "varied collection of the finest shrubs and trees tastefully disposed" he saw on islands in the Parisian Bois de Boulogne, Robinson wondered why English gardeners could not adopt this practice of permanently establishing hardy plants instead of following the prevalent method of bedding out.[9] The latter referred to the practice of transplanting South African and South American annuals, such as calceolarias, lobelia, and geraniums, in summer months from greenhouses to specially designated flower beds, typically executed in geometric patterns achieved by tightly knit rows of contrasting or massed plants (Fig. 14).[10] "Naturally grouping hardy plants" in staggered, varied arrangements offered many benefits, Robinson argued.[11] First, it was less expensive than bedding out. Second, it offered far more variety than bedded-out gardens, which utilized a limited range of plants to create vast swaths of color. Third, it purported to be directly after nature, the sole source of all true design according to Robinson and aestheticians whom he admired, especially John Ruskin.[12]

Emulating the changeful variety of nature in gardens was a pressing issue for Robinson. Like many of his contemporaries, Robinson feared that increasing urbanization was loosening Englanders' ties to nature and the rural countryside, long considered a source of national strength. In *The Parks, Promenades, and Gardens of Paris*, Robinson chastised garden designers for creating monotonous, artificial gardens and thus denying Englanders an opportunity for, quoting Ruskin, "fellowship with nature."[13] "Natural" gardens, Robinson promised, would allow gardening, in both "the private and public place," to "be nearer to proving the 'greatest refreshment to the spirits of man' than it has ever been in any era."[14]

In *The Wild Garden*, Robinson expanded this brief outline for a new gardening

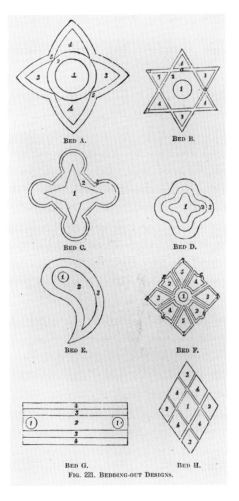

BED A.   BED B.

BED C.   BED D.

BED E.   BED F.

BED G.   BED H.

FIG. 221. BEDDING-OUT DESIGNS.

14. "Bedding-Out Designs," from George Nicholson, ed., *The Illustrated Dictionary of Gardening*, vol. 1, London, n.d., c. 1884–8. (Source: Dumbarton Oaks, Studies in Landscape Architecture, Photo Archive.)

43

scheme. His attention shifted from parks to owners of country and suburban gardens, but his goal – adoption of a more natural garden design in underutilized spaces of the pleasure ground – remained the same. Robinson did not advocate replacing bedded-out gardens, often located just outside the house or conservatory; instead, he focused on such areas as shrubberies, open places between plantings, ditches, hedgerows, brooksides, and bogs, leaving the "garden proper" intact.[15] These zones suited his concept of the natural, which referred not, as the appellation *wild* might suggest, to uninhabited tracts, but to woodlands, meadows, roadsides, and other fringes and edges of the worked, agrarian, and settled landscape of southern England. In honing in on this particularized aspect of the landscape – the rural scene as it was commonly described – Robinson was engaging with a motif already heavily freighted in English culture with nationalistic value.[16]

Incorporation of bogs and hedgerows into the ornamented landscape was particularly meaningful in the decades following the onset of the agricultural depression, which led to increases in fallow land, conversion of wheat fields to grazing or horticulture, and sales of tenant farms and estate property. Naturalist Alfred Russel Wallace claimed in 1885 that the amount of "bog, waste, etc." increased by 457,930 acres between 1872 and 1882.[17] The depression, according to historian P. J. Perry, hit the lowland zone first: counties such as Essex were unable to make the transition from unprofitable farming to more profitable grazing. Regions around London and Middlesex, such as the county of Surrey, experienced agricultural failure at a rate of 16 to 20 percent of the farming population from 1871 to 1873.[18] Although Robinson never directly addressed the depression, his theories accommodated the appearance of the depressed countryside that he must have witnessed around him. The wild garden offered the possibility of turning the detritus of the depression into an aesthetic statement that could erase the unsettling effects of the financial collapse of English farming.

In recasting wasteland as aesthetically promising, the wild garden was like other preservation movements at the end of the nineteenth century. The Commons Preservation Society, for example, was founded in 1865 in order to prevent enclosure or "improvement" of public spaces formerly dedicated to grazing and other practical purposes so they might continue to be enjoyed by the public, increasingly desirous of open spaces for leisure activities. Proponents of radical land nationalization movements celebrated the victories of the Commons Preservation Society, arguing that enclosure deprived the public of its rights and "one of the greatest enjoyments of country life – the power to wander freely under the shade of trees, in places where the choicest wild flowers blossom, and where the living denizens of the woods may be seen in their native haunts."[19] But unlike the commons preservation movement, Robinson had no public agenda in mind. His precepts were aimed at the landowning class and were intended to guide private enjoyment of landscape. Indeed, although Robinson supported retaining commons, he opposed any restriction on private property.[20] In 1888 he was embroiled in a court case, opposing public access to a footpath running through his estate.[21]

Although Robinson clearly admired such passages of the rural landscape as hedgerows and roadside banks and used them as models for the wild garden, his gardening style required much more intensive planning than these intermittently maintained spaces. Within the liminal zones occupied by the wild garden, plants and shrubs of different foliage and blooming schedules were carefully placed in graduated arrangements, from lowest to highest, to permit "the beauty of individual species" to "proclaim itself when at its height" and then be "succeeded by other kinds" when "passed out of bloom."[22] Yet, when compared to the bedded-out garden, less labor (at least in theory) was required by the wild garden. According to Robinson, as plants died back in the wild garden, they should not be tied, cut, or replaced as in the bedded-out garden; instead, their foliage should be absorbed into the garden to create a suitable background for the next succession of blossoms. This planting scheme, with its irregular disposition of plants within massed groupings or smaller groupings dotted over the landscape, was intended to emulate nature but nonetheless owed much to developments in designing Victorian shrubberies and flower beds.

Midcentury landscape architect Edward Kemp, who had worked with Joseph Paxton early in his career, for example, had advocated an irregular outline for planting beds in his popular book *How to Lay Out a Small Garden* (1850). "The outside plants in a mass," he explained, "should stand forward or recede in a most irregular fashion, approaching nearest to the front of the bed at the prominent parts, and towards the middle or one of the sides of the recesses, but retiring a good deal in other places."[23] Kemp also insisted, as would Robinson, that spaces between the lawn and planting features be softened by the introduction of "showy or early-flowering 'British' flowers," such as "snow-drops, violets, squills, ficaria, primroses, lychnis, and wood anemones," some of the very species later recommended by Robinson.[24] Robinson's aesthetic dovetailed with these practices, although it, overall, emphasized variety and contrast in placing plants, whereas Kemp advocated harmony and unity punctuated with "episodes" of contrast.[25]

Robinson rarely acknowledged his reliance on his predecessors. For example, with respect to the eighteenth-century landscape or picturesque garden, which some critics believed was a model for the wild garden and had been the crucible for developments in shrubbery design, he pointedly rejected this influence.[26] Disparaging the eighteenth-century model, he claimed that "a garden may be highly picturesque, and yet in every part the result of ceaseless care."[27] This blindness to history may be due, in part, to differing overall conceptions of the nineteenth-century wild garden and the eighteenth-century landscape garden. The eighteenth-century landscape garden, in the hands of landowners such as Earl Temple, writers such as Alexander Pope, and designers such as William Kent and Capability Brown, was said to be based on nature, but the result, as at sites such as Stowe, was nonetheless highly idealized. Alexander Pope, in his epistle to the Rt. Hon. Richard Boyle, 3rd Earl of Burlington, may have proclaimed, "In all, let *Nature* never be forgot. /Consult the *Genius* of the *Place* in all," but he also approved introducing classical temples, columns, arches, grottoes, and other structures into the landscape.[28] His own garden at Twickenham contained a temple, an amphitheater, and an obelisk dedicated to the memory of his mother in addition to other classical allusions. Robinson's wild garden was bereft of hallmarks of the landscape of antiquity; his notion of nature was more insistently local, and the poets and painters he admired were those that described primarily English fields, woods, and streams.

Robinson's scope of vision, moreover, was not as broad or sweeping as his eighteenth-century predecessors, who reworked the landscape into the desired ideal of naturalness on a grand scale and took into account and even modified distant views.[29] Although ambitious in his desire to change English gardening systems, Robinson's framing of the garden was more modest and appropriate to his middle- and upper-middle-class readers. Unlike circuits of views set up in eighteenth-century gardens, his chosen scene could be encompassed within a single frame as in the case of "a common ditch shaded with trees" transformed into "a perfect paradise" by the introduction of "plants that love, and thrive in, shady sheltered spots, and by so arranging them that no two parts of the scene shall present the same aspect of vegetation."[30] The wild garden was on a scale pragmatically suited to the times: realizable for even a suburban home owner, it was a more attainable landscape than its eighteenth-century forebear. Indeed, Robinson was more anxious to establish links between the wild garden and gardens that predated the eighteenth century.

In the frontispiece to the 1870 edition of *The Wild Garden*, Robinson quoted from Francis Bacon's 1625 essay "Of Gardens," in which the philosopher described an ideal garden as "divided into three parts: a green in the entrance; a heath or desert in the going forth; and the main garden in the midst." The heath, Bacon stipulated, should "be framed, as much as may be, to a natural wildness," meaning it should resemble an uncultivated landscape, which he described as thickets of shrubs intermixed with wild vines and shade-loving flowers.[31] Robinson repeated this phrase in the caption for his frontispiece engraving (Fig. 13), which depicts a woman and child gazing at a landscape dominated by evergreen shrubs underplanted with peonies, yuccas, irises, and other flowers set among the grasses. The inclusion of the well-dressed woman and girl in the wild garden makes it clear that Robinson did not envision the wild garden as an unruly, unregulated wilderness, but rather as a space appropriate for the "angel in the house" and her offspring.

The presence of the woman and child in the garden also made a case for the fashionableness of the wild garden, which was a crucial point in Robinson's campaign against the bedded-out garden. The latter garden type was in vogue and, with its tender exotics and substantial related costs, easily registered as "high class." By contrast, the wild garden required less maintenance, used hardy exotics, cottage flowers, and native plants that Robinson acknowledged were "not . . . so showy as those usually considered worthy of a place in gardens" and, in fact, could be regarded as common or weeds.[32] He needed to assure readers that the wild garden would prove, as he asserted, "far superior" to other garden forms.[33]

His frontispiece reinforced his contention that if "a poet, with an eye for natural beauty, or an artist, or any person of taste" were to come upon a wild garden, he or she would recognize the home owner's accomplishment and the visitor

> would acknowledge that you [the home owner] had indeed caught the true meaning of nature in her disposition of vegetation, without sacrificing one jot of anything in your garden, but, on the other hand, adding the highest beauty to spots hitherto devoid of the slightest interest.[34]

The sight of the well-dressed couple contemplating the garden underscored this rhetoric and gave readers figures with whom they could identify. They could, vicariously, imagine themselves looking upon the new beauty they had brought forth in the garden and enjoying compliments by poets, artists, and "people of taste."

Throughout his text, Robinson championed plants that were currently out of favor. He began his 1870 edition of *The Wild Garden* with a despairing account of the disappearance of hardy flowers, dating from the time of Shakespeare, from English gardens over the previous twenty years. Although hardy flowers had actually never totally disappeared from English gardens, Robinson nevertheless polemically argued for bringing back such "old favourites" as lilies, marigolds, wild roses, foxgloves, and columbines.[35] They had been unfairly dismissed, he argued, in response to the prevailing fashion for bedded-out exotics and should be revived because they required less care than tender plants. To illustrate the charms of hardy flowers, subject of tributes from such writers as John Milton and Bacon, Robinson pointed to cottage gardens of "Kent, Sussex and many other parts of England," which he characterized as "little Elysiums, where the last glimpses of beautiful old English gardening may yet be seen."[36] The appeal of the cottage garden was not only its use of hardy plants but also its ties to the past and a perception that it represented an authentic form of folk culture that had been handed down for generations.[37]

This figuring of the cottage as a model for a distinctly English form of garden reflects what has been called "romantic nationalism" – the adaptation of folk and other indigenous cultures to express a country's identity. Both a nostalgic reaction to industrialization and a means to negotiate the rapid and abrupt transmutations of modernity, romantic nationalism swept through much of Europe at the end of the nineteenth century. In England, it arguably began in the 1860s with the Arts and Crafts movement.[38] Indeed, William Morris, a leader of the movement, addressed garden design in the context of his ongoing critique of modern manufacturing. He condemned bedded-out gardens because they privileged masses of brightly colored florist flowers, which he associated with commercialism and industrialism.[39] As part of his plan to reform modern design through close study of nature and honest use of materials, Morris called for a return to "old-fashioned" flowers, such as columbine, China asters, and snowdrops.[40] Morris put his words into practice: his textiles, tiles, and wallpapers featured "old-fashioned" flowers, such as daisies, primroses, marigolds, lilies, columbine, and wild roses. At his home, the Red House at Upton, near Bexley Heath, Kent, he planted sweet-briar or wild rose, lilies, and sunflowers.[41]

In like manner, Ruskin, in his discussion of the Elizabethan villa in "Poetry of Architecture" (1837–8), had condemned the modern flower garden, with its hybrids and exotics:

> an assembly of unfortunate beings, pampered and bloated above their natural size, stewed and heated into diseased growth; corrupted by evil communication into speckled and inharmonious colours; torn from the soil which they loved, and of which they were the spirit and the glory, to glare away their term of tormented life among the mixed and incon-gruous essences of each other, in earth they know not, and in air that is poison to them.[42]

Effectively preparing the way for Robinson's essay, Ruskin instead had recom-mended that "everyone who is about to lay out a limited extent of garden, in which he wishes to introduce many flowers, should read and attentively study, first Shelley, and next Shakespeare" for flower choices.[43]

Using the literature of Shakespeare to select garden plants was quite popular during the second half of the nineteenth century when the playwright's reputa-tion as the leading figure in the history of English literature was being formed by both the popular press and academia.[44] Henry Ellacombe, in his *The Plant-Lore and Garden-Craft of Shakespeare* (first published in *The Garden* in 1877), pro-moted the study of Shakespeare's plants because of the

> thoroughly English character of his description. . . . This is certainly true of the plants and flowers we meet within the plays; they are thor-oughly English plants that (with very few exceptions) he saw in the hedgerows and woods of Warwickshire, or in his own or his friends' gardens.[45]

Robinson was well aware of the poetic and romantic associations of "old-fash-ioned" flowers and called on such associations in his polemic. In his text, he briefly quoted Tennyson and described how the wild garden would promote plants "of the highest order of beauty and fragrance, and clothed with the sweetest associations."[46] In keeping with the developing notion that rural culture was older and more pure than urban culture, Robinson advised obtaining plants from the "country or other places where many good old border flowers remain in the cot-tage gardens."[47] This advice dovetailed with the late-nineteenth-century back-to-the-land movement, when the wealthy urban classes left the increasingly crowded and polluted cities to find retreat and solace in the countryside.[48] Gleaning flowers from rural cottage gardens, thought to be untouched by vagaries of modern fashions, allowed owners of country houses and suburban plots to take part imaginatively in this return to the land by naturalizing signifiers of rural England within their grounds. Seed companies responded quickly to the growing appreciation for "old-fashioned" flowers and by the early 1870s introduced older species, such as asters, stock, wallflowers, sweet pea, phlox, and sunflowers, to their seed lines. Sutton's, for example, sold "English" flower seeds, such as delphinium, heartsease, hollyhock, larkspur, marigold, phlox, and sweet pea.[49]

Robinson's instructions to cull "old-fashioned" flowers from cottage gardens related closely to his interest in native plants, formed at his post at the Royal Botanic Society's gardens. In the first edition of *The Wild Garden,* Robinson included a chapter on "The Garden of British Wild Flowers," in which he proposed making "a charming little hardy garden" composed of "pretty flowers . . . selected from wild places in various parts of the British isles."[50] Other contemporaneous writers, such as J. T. Burgess, author of *Old English Wild Flowers* (1868), also urged readers to explore the significance of common wildflowers. Burgess based his promotion of wildflowers, in part, on their ties to the past, claiming that they "carry us into the homes of our ancestors . . . [telling] us of bygone festivities, of well-dressing, decking of town crosses, of weddings, and of funerals."[51] The nature writer Richard Jefferies often discoursed on the beauty of wildflowers in his descriptive tributes to the English countryside: "Before I had any conscious thought it was a delight to me to find wild flowers, just to see them. It was a pleasure to gather them and to take them home."[52]

In his discussion of plants, Robinson also appealed to science, interspersing his text with references to eminent botanists such as Hewett Watson.[53] Ironically, although Robinson mentioned Watson's research in reference to collecting British wildflowers, Watson eventually claimed,

> there is no "species" . . . peculiar to the British Isles. True, during the past hundred years, nominally new species have been named and described as British specimens only, from time to time. But these have gradually come to be identified with species described elsewhere under other names.[54]

Indeed, as Robinson's selective use of Watson should suggest, his polemic in favor of British plants lacked scientific precision. He failed, for example, to distinguish between *wild* and *native* plants, using the terms interchangeably.[55] His scholarship on native plants was also faulty; a number of the species he mentioned, such as pinks or peas, had been introduced into Britain.[56] In addition, although he spoke of gathering plants from the entire British Isles, most of his discussion focused on "English" trees, shrubs, and plants, and particularly on plants with which he was familiar, such as woodruff, which he had witnessed "flowering very abundantly among the trees and shrubs round some of the Colleges of Oxford," or traveler's joy *(clematis vitalba),* which he described as cascading in "graceful folds from many a low tree in many parts of the south of England."[57]

This is not to suggest, however, that the wild garden was completely insular. In addition to cultivating native and "old-fashioned" flowers, with their myriad associations, Robinson also employed judiciously selected hardy exotics of the "highest order of beauty" that could be easily naturalized and that had been, according to Robinson, dismissed from "our 'trim gardens.'"[58] The gardener advocated introducing exotics in woodlandlike settings rather than transplanting them into manicured beds as in the bedded-out style, so that *scilla hispanica* could be intermingled with native wood hyacinth.[59] Arranging exotics according to the "varied, indefinite, and changeful" disposition of plants in "nature," so that they could grow and appear like native plants, obscured their artificial introduction by the gardener.[60] Robinson developed this argument further in his subsequent book *The Subtropical Garden* (1871), in which he advised against segregating subtropical species within sharply delineated flower beds and instead advocated judiciously disposing them in irregular groups or singly within the landscape in the manner of nature.[61]

For the repertoire of exotics for the wild garden, Robinson sharply discouraged selecting those from countries that were the source of plants for bedded-out gardens. He insisted that "we are infinitely more interested" in plants from Italy, North America, Europe, Greece, Spain, the hills of Asia Minor, and the Arctic regions. To shore up these choices, he added that these areas were most likely to be "interesting to the traveller," who could bring home seeds or plants and thus "establish round his home the pleasantest souvenirs of the various scenes he has visited." Like other remembrances of travel, these souvenirs would be best enjoyed from the vantage point of home. "By taking the best hardy exotics and establishing them with the best of our own wild flowers . . . we may produce the most charming results."[62] If the home owner could not travel to these sites, plants from these regions were relatively accessible in Britain, thanks to the nation's highly developed trade network and state and private support for plant exploration and exchange.

Artfully arranged, yet seeming natural, the wild garden, with its combination of exotic and vernacular, naturalized the presence of Britain's trading partners within the English landscape at the same time it seemed to recover a disappearing English rural landscape. Robinson's aesthetic owed a great debt to the landscape of southeast England, and, in particular, the Weald, a heavily wooded region running through Surrey, Kent, and Sussex, where Robinson spent most of his mature career. Arguably, the wild garden was an attempt, as geographer B. F. Brandon describes it, "to reproduce the Wealden vestigial semi-wilderness." The Weald – "underwoods managed on the coppice system, ferny banks, heathery hillsides and hedgerows full of dog roses – and the way in which woodland slowly gave way to cultivation" – provided ample suggestions for gardens emulating nature.[63]

By promoting the local Sussex landscape, the wild garden also participated in the dialogue between North and South that shaped much of the debate about what defined Englishness. Richard Jefferies, in *Wild Life in a Southern County*, visualized the southern region, outside the perimeters of the city, as a landscape of hedgerow, copse, and stream where "old manners and customs linger."[64] Such writings helped recover and even invent rural culture, then threatened by the spread of urbanism and the decline of agriculture, and concomitantly insisted that rural culture was essentially English, representing English values and practices.

The wild garden likewise promised to revive rural culture, idyllically remembered as natural and "old fashioned," in reaction against the advances of technology that had encouraged the dissemination of the bedding-out style with its hothouse-raised exotics. But, at the same time, the wild garden was very much of its moment as it suited the increasing interest in the minutiae of nature manifested in the developing sciences of botany, geology, and natural history, in which the case study, as opposed to abstract laws or principles, was emerging as the paradigm through which knowledge of the world was systematized.

The Wild Garden and Science

The wild garden was firmly grounded in post-Darwinian natural science, which offered rational, empirical explanations for climatic determinism and close links between species and local environment. Robinson knew Charles Darwin, who sponsored him for membership in the Linnean Society in 1866, and it is likely that Robinson heard Darwin's lectures on plant physiology given to the Linnean Society in the 1860s. Even without this personal connection, it would have been difficult to be unaware of Darwin's writings, particularly his *Origins of the Species* and *Variation of Animals and Plants,* published in 1859 and 1868, respectively. These texts overturned the Enlightenment vision of nature as a regularized system governed by natural laws, verifiable by empirical evidence, which produced rational, ordered taxonomies. This mechanistic view of the world had been successfully married with notions of divine Providence, that is, the ordered workings of the universe revealed the presence of an omnipotent deity. By contrast, Darwin's theories rested on accident and thus undermined the notion of a divine purpose guiding all development.

Nature, according to the scientist, was organic and ever changing. To explain the process of development and progress Darwin observed, he arrived at his theory of natural selection, which attributed a species's adaptation to its environment to chance variation. To this he added the notion of competition, that is, the struggle for survival, which eliminated those species ill adapted to their circumstances. Thus environmental conditions, according to Darwin, produced variation in organisms.[65] The latter theory underpinned Robinson's wild garden, influencing the plants he chose and his creation of specialized gardens reflecting different soil and water conditions. Echoing the findings of the evolutionists, for example, Robinson argued that "the beauty" of wild gardening was "that, carried out well, the plants are adapted to the site, climate, and trees or other permanent vegetation."[66] Under the rubric of the wild garden, Robinson recommended creating brookside, water, bog, and rock gardens (earlier championed by Loudon) to meet better "the wants of the plant."[67]

To validate further his inclusion of plants formerly excluded from bedded-out gardens, Robinson turned to writings by late-nineteenth-century naturalist Alfred Russel Wallace. Wallace collaborated with Darwin on his theory of evolution and published his own *Contribution to the Theory of Natural Selection* in 1870. Robinson was intrigued by Wallace's 1869 account of his extensive travels in the Amazon region and the Malay Archipelago, especially Wallace's statement that "during the twelve years spent amidst tropical vegetation, I have seen nothing comparable to the effect produced on our landscapes by Gorse, Broom, Heather, Wild Hyacinths, Hawthorn, and Buttercups."[68] Wallace's admiration for these plants, which were often eschewed in contemporary flower borders, led Robinson to promote them, drawing his readers' attention to both indigenous and foreign varieties.[69]

Rules regarding relations between organisms and their environment set forth by Wallace also informed Robinson's gardening practices. In an early essay, "On the Law Which Has Regulated the Introduction of New Species" (1850), Wallace first developed his principles governing the distribution of organisms. His fourth stipulation – that "in countries of a similar climate, but separated by a wide sea of lofty mountains, the families, genera, and species of the one are often represented by closely allied families, genera and species peculiar to the other" – underlies Robinson's theory that plants from climates similar to England's could be naturalized in the wild garden.[70] In his later work, Wallace, along with Darwin, continued to elucidate the influence of habitats on organisms. Although botanists, gardeners, and natural historians had long known of close ties between plants and their environments, these new investigations into evolutionary theory profoundly changed the direction of natural science as Wallace explained in his 1881 book *Island Life:*

So long as it was believed that the several species of animals and plants were "special creations," and had been formed expressly to inhabit the countries in which they are now found, their habitat was an ultimate fact which required no explanation. . . . But so soon as the theory of evolution came to be generally adopted, and it was seen that each animal could only have come into existence in some area where ancestral forms closely allied to it already lived, a real and important relation was established between an animal and its native country, and a new set of problems at once sprang into existence.[71]

Fundamental to Wallace's and Darwin's studies was the investigation of methods and structures by which plants adapted to changes in their environments.[72] Knowledge of plants' mutability, Darwin explained, allowed man to "select, preserve, and accumulate the variations given to him by the hand of nature in any way he chooses" and thus "produce a great result."[73] Robinson adopted Darwin's dictum to his own enterprise, claiming that gardeners could remove a plant from its original climate and naturalize it in a new climate and soil, where it would thrive. In the 1881 edition of *The Wild Garden,* for example, Robinson advocated creating waterside wild gardens in which "little colonies of hardy flowers" were introduced along the waterside. By punctuating the water's edge with clusters of plants from northern and temperate regions, such as day lilies, phloxes, and irises, one could create "charming garden pictures" filled with more variety than could be had by allowing plants found naturally along the water to dominate.[74] In establishing these new juxtapositions of vegetation, Robinson added, he was augmenting or assisting nature rather than working against its laws.[75] Theories of natural selection also influenced Robinson's preference for freely grown plants as opposed to the staked and tied plants of bedded-out or gardenesque gardens. According to Robinson, a freely grown plant acquired strength and beauty from learning to "take care of itself" and "overcome weeds" in its struggle to survive.[76]

Robinson should not be considered a strict Darwinist, however. Underlying much of his writing was a spiritual reverence for nature as opposed to the vicious competition figured in Darwin's texts. For example, in a passage regarding true taste in garden design, Robinson argued that the highest taste in garden design was exhibited by gardens showing "a real love of the beautiful in Nature."[77] Unlike botanical gardens, which coldly named and classified each plant, natural gardens, by displaying the unplanned abundance of nature, were in "accordance with the true gardening spirit," which brought forth "the life we want."[78]

This focus on spirit and life suggests links between Robinson's wild garden and vitalism, a late-nineteenth-century response to Darwinism which advocated that every organism possessed an innate vital spirit pushing it to survive. Put forth by such authors as Charles Kingsley, vitalism offered a way to draw together the theories of natural selection with older theological philosophies which insisted that nature was direct evidence of God's handiwork and spiritual munificence. Vitalism, according to David Allen, led logically to "the conviction that all life is equally deserving of reverence."[79] In the view of Joachim Wolschke-Bulmahn, Robinson's abhorrence of cut or trimmed trees, shrubs, and grass was not just a rejection of earlier gardening styles but also an indication of his respect for life.[80]

Robinson's plan to naturalize British and foreign plants, shrubs, and trees into cohesive communities also relates to the vitalist conception of vegetation as part of a dynamic, cooperative community. At the same time Robinson was writing *The Wild Garden,* amateur biologists such as Kingsley and the Reverend E. A. Woodruffe were studying various plant communities found throughout England, focusing on "disentangling . . . the broad relationships between vegetation and the environment."[81] The work of these early vitalists was, like Robinson's, characterized by expressions of "solemn wonder and joy" at the "inexhaustible fertility and variety" of nature and her "significances, harmonies, chains of cause and effect endlessly interlinked."[82] Such commentary demonstrates how the forces of romanticization and scientific inquiry commingled and mutually influenced each other in the nineteenth century. For many naturalists, the impulse to analyze nature was closely related to their appreciation of nature as restorative scenery untouched by the corruption of urbanism and indicative of the power of the divine.

The Wild Garden and Art

The twin desires to study and to valorize nature helped shape nineteenth-century art. Understanding nineteenth-century art practices is crucial for analysis of Robinson's wild garden, because he often turned to art both to generate and to validate his notions of good garden design. Many of his writings reveal the influence of Ruskin, whose theory of vital beauty, first articulated in volume 2 of his series *Modern Painters* (1846), shared many premises with natural scientists' theories of vitalism.

In the section devoted to "Ideas of Beauty" in *Modern Painters,* Ruskin distinguished between different forms of beauty; he identified vital beauty as that expressed by living organisms. He contrasted, for example, the "impression of loveliness" one received from a "slender, pensive, fragile flower" growing on the edge of an ice field with the lack of beauty and feeling generated by "the dead ice and the idle clouds." The flower's beauty was due to its "appearance of healthy vital energy." In addition to providing a glimpse of loveliness, the flower enabled the viewer to reach a state of happiness by contemplating the plant's energy and how every aspect of the organism efficiently serves a function. This state of happiness, for the Christian viewer of sound moral judgment, would eventually lead to a better appreciation and understanding of God's laws, love, and charity. It was insights into spirituality, according to Ruskin, that one should derive from nature rather than principles of utilitarianism or mechanization. Pointedly, the author insisted that viewers neither transfer to nature "our own human passions and predilections," such as a fascination with swiftness, strength, cunning, animosity, or cruelty (ingredients in the Darwinian struggle for survival), nor alter nature by developing new strains or varieties of plants and animals.[83]

55

Robinson likewise argued that the gardener should respect the life and beauty of plants (he apparently considered transplanting plants compatible with this advice). He also echoed Ruskin's advice to artists to depict the "specific, distinct and perfect beauty" of each plant. According to Ruskin, observation of beauty distinguished the artist's approach to plants from that of a botanist, who saw the plant as a specimen and nothing more. The task of the landscape painter, Ruskin asserted, was to recognize that "every herb and flower of the field has its specific, distinct, and perfect beauty . . . its peculiar habitation, expression, and function." Thus, Ruskin explained, "the highest art is that which seizes this specific character, which develops and illustrates it, which assigns to it its proper position in the landscape."[84] Robinson's wild garden, whereby "plants . . . of the highest order of beauty and fragrance . . . may be seen to greater perfection, wild as weeds," extends Ruskin's principles of painting to gardening.[85] Following out this logic, Robinson claimed that wild gardens were akin to landscape paintings, creating "distinct effects" and "beautiful pictures."[86]

Using art to describe or to represent nature was a common trope in the nineteenth century, and Robinson's equation of wild gardens with pictures or paintings should be considered within this larger pattern. Many nineteenth-century English artists privileged scenes of naturalistic or pastoral beauty and erased the effects of industrialization or the agricultural depression. They brought the countryside to the urban art market, helping define nature for nineteenth-century viewers and shaping a growing taste for rural scenery, outings to the countryside, and gardens. Their images tended to be tightly framed scenes of nature, rather than the broad panoramas or prospect views popular in the eighteenth century. These vignettes, or "bits" of nature encouraged the perception that the rustic scene could be easily replicated in grounds of limited scope, as in the case of James Aumonier's *A Nook in Nature's Garden* (1879), which portrays a group of small children at play in a flowery meadow backed by a thin woodland, a scene remarkably akin to images of the wild garden proposed by Robinson (Fig. 15).[87]

Indeed, Robinson acknowledged the influence of paintings on his theories of wild gardening. Throughout his career, Robinson amassed a small collection of nineteenth-century French and English paintings. His paintings by English artists included works by Peter De Wint, then considered one of the old masters of English landscape painting, as well as contemporary landscape painters, such as Cecil Lawson and Alfred Parsons, regarded as among England's leading landscape painters.[88] Robinson's collection of French paintings focused on landscape paintings by artists of the Barbizon school, such as Jean-Baptiste Corot, Narcisse-Virgile Diaz de La Peña, and C. F. Daubigny, and still lifes of "old-fashioned" flowers by the flower painter H. Fantin-Latour, all of which were extremely popular in London at the time.[89] A common thread linking many of these painters was the sincere and honest representation of nature.

Although the influence these paintings had on Robinson's day-to-day thinking cannot be pinpointed because their exact dates of purchase are unknown, in general, Robinson's art collection provided a powerful model for imitating nature in the garden. The gardener derived artistic principles from these images, and he clearly wanted the rusticity and naturalness associated with their paintings to be transferred to his garden designs. For example, in the 1894 edition of *The Wild Garden,* Robinson referred to Corot and J. M. W. Turner when explaining his decision to eliminate an iron fence in favor of a sunken fence garlanded with roses: "such a visible tangible fence," he claimed, "will last for many years and might come in the foreground of a picture by Corot or Turner."[90] The artist Mark Fisher, a prominent *plein air* painter who belonged to the Royal Academy and the New English Art Club, reportedly directed Robinson's decision to cease cutting and trimming shrubs: while painting at Gravetye, Fisher complained to Robinson that a yew hedge separating the flower garden from the Alpine Meadow created a "hard black" line instead of a more desirable free line, and Robinson removed the yew the following autumn, replacing it with "the noble rose Bouquet d'Or, mixed with the claret coloured Clematis, both formed a charming line for years. The lesson I never forgot; we abolished the shears and clipped no more."[91] In his later book *The English Flower Garden,* Robinson held up Corot and Turner again, along with the English watercolorist John Crome, the leading painter of the Norwich school, and the painter Alfred Parsons, as artists whom gardeners should emulate if they wanted to create true art based on beauty and nature.[92]

Of all these artists, Alfred Parsons played the most crucial role because he provided illustrations for Robinson's books and magazine articles. As an illustrator, Parsons was highly involved in contemporary developments in natural his-

15. James Aumonier, *A Nook in Nature's Garden,* 1879. (Source: Birmingham Museums & Art Gallery.)

tory and the late-nineteenth-century nostalgia for old rural England.[93] In his illustrations for *The Wild Garden,* Parsons turned his knowledge of the English countryside and flowers to good use, creating images that Robinson insisted were "after nature."[94] Such comments reinforced the impression that wild gardens were simulacrums of the idealized pastoral countryside. In addition, Parsons's images established that excellent examples of wild gardens had already been executed and thus implied that they were attainable for any reader.

Moreover, Parsons's illustrations clarified many of Robinson's principles, which were vaguely described and, as Robinson himself admitted, easily misunderstood.[95] In illustrated editions of *The Wild Garden*, the writer frequently pointed to Parsons's vignettes to explain his theories, especially artfully grouping and massing plants.[96] Robinson's claim that plants set among "some . . . graceful wild spray" were "more attractive than any garden denizen" was also substantiated by Parsons's artwork.[97] Stark illustrations of botanical specimens placed against a white background, such as those Parsons produced for rose connoisseur Ellen Willmott, would have seriously undermined Robinson's argument. Parsons instead provided Robinson with images of plants in situ, thus demonstrating the significant role the greater environment played in highlighting each plant's particular beauty and implicitly reinforcing the connections between wild gardens and Darwinism.

Parsons's illustrations were especially important in disseminating the design principle for which Robinson is perhaps best known – naturalizing spring bulbs.[98] For the frontispiece of 1881 edition of *The Wild Garden*, Parsons depicted a group of narcissus planted underneath a flowering rhododendron ensconced in a wood (Fig. 16). This image exemplified Robinson's principle that spaces between bushes, formerly "garden graveyards," should be "embellished" with "rare exotic wildlings."[99] Perhaps even more importantly, the image illustrates how art reaffirmed the supposed naturalness of the wild garden. By utilizing nineteenth-century landscape painting practices, Parsons was able to present the wild garden as an integrated whole. A highly detailed foreground composed of densely planted flowers gives way smoothly to a middle ground of shrubs and trees that blends easily into a wooded background. There is no evidence of the gardener's hand, such as worked soil or staked flowers. The rhododendron and daffodils, artificial introductions, are treated as commonplace elements within a woodland scene. Parsons's image, in effect, naturalized the wild garden. Furthermore, the illustration literally supported Robinson's theory that introducing hardy exotics into English landscapes would result in "beautiful pictures."[100]

Parsons's images were well received by art critics, who argued that the wild garden offered scenes of idyllic nature and thus could provide the respite desired by jaded urban dwellers.[101] *The Art Journal*, for example, feared that Englanders were "rapidly becoming a town-loving people" and "our devotion to country life and country pursuits . . . seems to be dying out" or so "overlaid with town prejudices" that even commercializing nature, as in the growing florist trade, had become acceptable. The author found the "commercial aspects of flower growing" particularly reprehensible because it threatened to taint a long-standing "national enthusiasm" for "our love of flowers and their cultivation." In other

≈§ 59

16. Alfred Parsons, "Colonies of Poet's Narcissus and Broad-Leaved Saxifrage," 1880, from William Robinson, *The Wild Garden*, London, 1881. (Source: Dumbarton Oaks, Studies in Landscape Architecture, Photo Archive.)

words, modern urban culture threatened a national pastime. Hence the reviewer's delight in Robinson's book as it made "an earnest appeal in favour of a return to our former ways," meaning a greater appreciation of flowers found in nature as opposed to hybrids touted by florists. The critic was particularly drawn to Robinson's admonition that London parks could be improved by adopting principles of wild gardening. Introducing a wide variety of flowers and shrubs and allowing these to grow freely, the reviewer predicted, "would gladden the eyes of us weary Londoners . . . [and] might by degrees lead us and our country visitors back to those simpler joys of nature and her offerings, on which for so long we have seemed to turn our backs."[102] Even those who had never seen a wild garden could enjoy its benefits through Parsons's illustrations, which lifted local examples of wild gardening out of their original context and circulated them in the public sphere where they could be read as models for a national aesthetic that could serve as a panacea for those suffering from the stresses attendant on industrial capitalism.

Robinson's contemporaries clearly welcomed his representation of nature. The ardent gardener S. Reynolds Hole (later Dean of Rochester), who believed a wild garden should be part of any ideal garden, dedicated his book *Our Gardens* (1899) to Robinson. A number of books emulating Robinson's were published, such as Frances Jane Hope's *Notes and Thoughts on Gardens and Woodlands* (1881), which included a chapter entitled "A Plea for Wild Flowers," and S. W. Fitzherbert's *The Book of the Wild Garden* (1903), which offered correctives to popular misconceptions about the wild garden.[103]

But at the same time, these authors cautioned that careful planting and arranging were required to achieve the look of uncultivated nature. Although Robinson had assured readers that the success of the wild garden did not depend on money, extensive plant collections, or the size of the grounds but only on "true taste" and "knowledge of the enormous wealth of beauty which the world contains,"[104] garden writer C. W. Earle, author of the highly popular *Pot-Pourri from a Surrey Garden* (1897), insisted that "in spite of all the charming things Mr. Robinson says about it, 'wild gardening' is, I am sure, a delusion and a snare." A wild garden, she reported, "requires endless care and is always extending in all directions in search of fresh soil." Moreover, it requires "the most judicious planting, with consummate knowledge and experience of the plants that will do well in the soil if they are just a little assisted at the time of planting."[105] Indeed, Robinson's daybook reveals that he himself devoted much of his own time and energy, as well as resources of his estate, to tending his wild gardens, which, in addition to points raised by Earle, required protection from such menaces as rabbits and deer.

Wild Gardens

Despite difficulties in cultivating wild gardens, a number of significant wild gardens were established, and these sites give the best evidence for acceptance of Robinson's ideas. Professional garden designers and even landscape architects affiliated with more formal modes, such as Italian revivalist H. A. Peto, adopted

17. "On the Slope near the Cottage," from "Heatherbank and Oakwood, The Residence and Garden of Mr. G. F. Wilson, F. R. S." (Source: *Country Life,* September 8, 1900.)

the style.[106] And although Robinson's gardening practices were shaped by and took place within discourses of Englishness, he was not opposed to wild gardens beyond the bounds of England; in fact, he delighted in any evidence of wide-spread adoption of his ideas. Ireland proved a particularly hospitable climate for wild gardens, and David Ottewill has discussed the Robinsonian gardens erected there by Lord Lansdowne, Samuel Heard, and the 4th Earl of Dunraven.[107] Readers of Robinson's journal, *The Garden,* submitted numerous descriptions of their wild gardens, as in the case of Tewensis, who gave several accounts of his 8-acre wild garden.[108] Robinson, in later editions of *The Wild Garden,* praised wild gardens at the estates of Crowsley, Brockhurst, Longleat, and Tew Park (probably the home of Tewensis) as well as those planted by Mr. Hewitson and G. F. Wilson. Wilson was a businessman and Royal Horticultural Society trea-surer who began a series of experimental gardens at his 60-acre Surrey estate, Oakwood, in 1878. After passing through the hands of Sir Thomas Hanbury, Oakwood came to the Royal Horticulture Society in 1903 as part of the Wisley estate. Wilson was best known for arranging plants after nature and for planting exotics in habitats closely resembling their indigenous situations (Fig. 17).

Wilson's garden is a reminder that although Robinson's writings encouraged widespread dissemination of the wild garden, the strongest area of his influence was in his own corner of southeast England, where soil conditions were optimum and home owners could establish a network for exchanging ideas and plants. According to Peter Brandon and Brian Short, "most affected was the triangle bounded by Horsham, Lewes and Tunbridge Wells where wealthy business people modified entire parishes into one continuous 'wild' garden."[109] The Loder family was at the heart of many of these gardens. Sir Robert Loder bought High Beeches, in the High Weald region of Sussex, in 1859; High Beeches passed to the second son and then, in 1906, to his son, Colonel Loder, who developed much of the present landscape garden, known for its rhododendron collection, and exchanged plants with Arthur Soames at Sheffield Park and the Messels at Nymans.[110] The eldest son of Sir Robert took up residence at Leonardslee and was responsible for the landscape gardens there; another son became Lord Wakehurst and developed the botanical collection of exotic trees and shrubs at Wakehurst Place.

Robinson's own gardens of Gravetye Manor, which he supervised from 1885 to 1935, still offer a living example of wild gardening. The original outlying grounds, over a thousand acres, were largely woodland and were bequeathed to the Forestry Commission upon Robinson's death.[111] The areas of the garden most in keeping with the precepts of wild gardening are found a short distance from the house, creating gradations from the more formal plantings around the house to the woodland beyond. Robinson's heath garden, located high on the slope north of the house, included "common heaths of England and Western Europe" (Fig. 18).[112] The effect of an open wood was gained here, with low shrubs set among grasses under pines, the branches of which Robinson trimmed (despite his own advice against cutting) to open views "both to and from the house."[113] South of the house, on the lawn, Robinson removed the fir trees and "little beds of wired-in rhododendrons" that were there when he arrived in order to create more "breadth of effect" and then planted flowers, such as daffodils, crocuses, grape hyacinths, and winter aconite, that would bring color into this area in springtime while allowing it to be mown for hay in the summer (Fig. 19). This landscape scene thus provided for both aesthetic pleasure and agrarian utility.

The notion that a landscape could be both productive and beautiful evokes the georgic mode more popular at the turn of the previous century and links Robinson's designs to these older ways of viewing the landscape. Robinson, however, was loath to make such connections, and, indeed, his discourse eschews the intellectual underpinnings that often distinguished that of his predecessors and instead offered pragmatic advice about where and when to plant. Nonetheless, it can be seen that Robinson's lawn meadow also partakes of the early-nineteenth-century picturesque and recalls the advice of aesthetician Richard Payne Knight:

18. "Heath Garden." (Source: William Robinson, *Home Landscapes,* London, 1914.)

> The usual features of a cultivated country are the accidental mixtures of
> meadows, woods, pastures, and cornfields, interspersed with farm
> houses, cottages, mills, &c. and I do not know in this country that bet-
> ter materials for middle grounds and distances can be obtained, or as to
> be wished for.[114]

In combining the georgic and the picturesque, much like the landscape
painter John Constable, whom he admired, Robinson thus reinforced the
impression that the wild garden offered the possibility to aesthetize land formerly
or partially worked.[115] But, whereas Constable began to undermine his georgic
message in later paintings, such as *The Cornfield* (1826), by introducing motifs of
neglect and dilapidation, such as the sheepherder who turns his back on his task
to take a drink at a nearby stream,[116] Robinson reversed the process by taking a

scene that had been rendered nonproductive by the introduction of firs and rhododendrons and transforming it into a scene of successful husbandry.

Robinson also introduced a great deal of new plant material around the lakes situated below the meadow. By the upper lake, for example, he planted a myriad of daffodils (Fig. 20), and closer to the waterside he placed a combination of indigenous and foreign plants, including flag, reed, loosestrife, buttercup, cat-heads, bulrush, rush, Siberian dogwood, and iris; and daffodils were also introduced around the lower lake, which he filled with waterlilies and bounded with willows and fences to keep out the rabbits.[117] Orchestrated naturalness carried over to other features as well; the upper lake once contained an island that Robinson removed because it was "too prim and too evidently artificial."[118] Beyond the lakes and the pleasure ground proper lay woods and fields; the former Robinson managed on both aesthetic and utilitarian grounds, clearing away "ill-placed timber trees" to improve the view while adding material, such as hazel, European and Japanese larch, cedars of Lebanon, varieties of firs, sitka spruce, and willows, to improve the composition.[119] He also deliberately retained cultivated fields on his property.[120] A working, rustic landscape thus framed the wild garden and encouraged the aesthetic conflation of the two.

19. "South Lawn in Haytime." (Source: William Robinson, *Home Landscapes*, London, 1914.)

20. "View by Upper Lake in Spring." (Source: William Robinson, *Home Landscapes,* London, 1914.)

The popularity of the wild garden lay in its promise of a richly planted rural landscape scene that could revive Englanders' rustic traditions and counteract the destructive effects of urbanization and industrialization while accommodating the riches made available by Britain's network of worldwide trade. Word and image circulating in the public sphere, and designers, gardeners and home owners working on the ground put the wild garden to work in constructing a national identity that put the rural scene at the heart of an Englishness that both denied and desired the exotic.

Chapter 3

Domesticating the Nation

The Cottage Garden

Robinson bolstered the authenticity of the wild garden by linking it to cottage gardens. Many of his contemporaries regarded the cottage garden as a remnant of England's vernacular or folk culture, untouched by modernity or continental influence. The notion that the cottage signified an unsophisticated rusticity admired by the more cultured outsider was not new; late-eighteenth- and early-nineteenth-century writers, such as Oliver Goldsmith and William Wordsworth, had paid extensive tribute to the cottage in this manner. What was new was the breadth and depth of this discourse as numerous articles and books were published, particularly by the Batsford firm and *Country Life,* carefully delineating rural cottages of various districts and commending these structures to the public's attention because they were "essentially English in design and workmanship" and thus constituted a national "heritage." Cottages became a site for collective national identity.

Appealing to what a community has deemed folk culture is a major building block of modern nationalism. Although "nationalism is, essentially, the general imposition of high culture on society," Ernest Gellner proposes that it arrives in a different guise. It "usually conquers in the name of a putative folk culture. Its symbolism is drawn from the healthy, pristine, vigorous life of the peasants, of the *Volk,* the *narod.*" Then, "if the nationalism prospers . . . it revives, or invents a local high (literate, specialist transmitted) culture of its own, though admittedly one which will have some links with the earlier folk styles and dialects."[1]

This process is precisely what happened to the cottage garden. Through the writings of specialists such as William Robinson, cottage gardens were transformed from local practices of the rural working classes to potential source material for middle- and upper-class gardens. This transformation occurred, in large part, because the cottage garden was conceptualized within the frame of an idealized vision of rural life desired by middle- and upper-class home owners. The preservation, or "invention," of the cottage ideal became a pressing issue for turn-of-the-century English culture because at the same time the cottage and its garden were idealized, they were also elevated as icons of national identity. This took place in the context of domestic turmoil produced by late-nineteenth-century transformations of the national economy and a developing dynamic between homeland and Empire.

⋙ 67

The Cottage Garden as Design Source

The significance that cottage gardens held for turn-of-the-century English gardening practices was well summarized by an article entitled "English Ideals of Gardening" that appeared in *The Times* in 1907. It established both key characteristics that professional designers would adopt from this amateur art form and its reading as a national folk tradition. This article opened by arguing that just as German folk music had reintroduced simplicity and sincerity in German music, so had the cottage garden in English garden design. Following this logic, it concluded,

> And the English cottage garden has provided the same kind of standard for the art of gardening and in the same way has redeemed that art from exotic perversities. When the bedding-out system was at its height, it was the spectacle of cottage gardens, with their beauty that seemed as natural to the English countryside as the very meadows and hedgerows, which gave people a disgust for their rows of Calceolarias and Geraniums and Lobelias. But for the cottage gardens they would never have been even aware of the existence of all the beautiful old plants which have been banished so long from the gardens of the rich; still less would they have been aware of the right manner of growing them. It was because gardening was a national art practised by the poor for love, and not as a fashionable amusement, that it recovered so suddenly from those perversities of taste which infected nearly all arts of the 19th century. But it would not have so recovered unless the tastes of the rich had found in the gardens of the poor what they desired in their own gardens. This is the great difference between gardening in England and in other countries, that in England the cottage garden sets the standard, whereas in other countries the standard is set by the garden of the palace or the villa. . . . We remain at heart a country people, unlike the French, or the Italians, and more even than the Germans. . . . The English love of the country has already delivered us from the worst errors of gardening.[2]

The cottage garden, as described by this discourse, was unspoiled and "unperverted," exemplifying vernacular or indigenous practices sought and praised by Arts and Crafts designers and others in search of honest, authentic, and high-quality art, as opposed to the artificiality and cheap gaudiness attributed to industrial goods.

The cottage garden was both a mythic ideal and a specific gardening practice. Mentioned by countless commentators and enlisted in numerous causes, but rarely defined, the term *cottage* referred to a broad range of structures from small cramped houses leased to agricultural laborers or smallholders to larger scale, more substantial homes built by craftspersons, tradesmen, and farmers, and to decorative *cottages ornées* built by the middle and upper classes as accoutrements to their estates. Likewise, a cottage garden could encompass a variety of forms and plants.[3]

Although nineteenth-century laws attempted to quantify the cottage garden – the Allotments and Cottage Gardens Compensation for Crops Act of 1887 defined a cottage garden as an allotment ("any parcel of land of not more than two acres in extent held by a tenant under a landlord and cultivated as a garden or as a farm, or partly as a garden and partly as a farm") "attached to a cottage" – its appearance is far more difficult to pin down.[4] Anne Scott-James, in her study of the cottage garden, insists that "it is difficult to find even the flimsiest record of a good cottage garden before the second half of the eighteenth century" and that the cottage garden, "with its mixture of flowers and neat rows of nourishing vegetables," was "largely a Regency and Victorian conception."[5]

Researching the cottage garden is complicated further because it was not the stylistic product of any one designer, like Robinson's wild garden, but rather a collective practice. Moreover, accounts of cottage gardens, including those drawn on for this study, were typically undertaken by outsiders: well-to-do writers and designers who observed cottage gardens through relatively brief visits to the countryside. The sense of distance between the cottager and the observer is clear, for example, in a 1900 *Country Life* article in which the author, whose voice is marked with privilege and who came to a rural village for "rest and quiet," describes her dismay at the disorderly layout of a cottage garden: "the rows and groups of various vegetables showed no clearly marked boundaries; one ran gaily into another, and the weeds filled up any possible gap," a point of view not necessarily shared by the cottage owner.[6]

This sense of distance is also suggested by accounts of the moral associations of cottage gardens that commonly featured an enlightened and educated commentator reporting delightedly that the cottage owner had set aside his former vices in favor of gardening, which had a soothing influence on him. J. C. Loudon, for example, praised cottage gardens because they could "attach" the cottager to his home and induce "sober, industrious, and domestic habits."[7] This rhetoric was repeated again nearly seventy years later in an article that appeared in the *Spectator,* which asserted, "the love that a cottager has for his garden is the most purifying influence which can be brought to bear upon him."[8] To determine the character of a cottager, one need look no further than the garden:

> a tangled wilderness of weeds conjures up a vision of a neglected wife and children, and a hard-earned wage wasted in wanton drink. While a gay garden plot – with herbs and rose bushes, sweet-peas running riot over bushes, covering them with their butterflies, white and red, and white and violet – betokens thrift and care and thoughtfulness.[9]

Nonetheless, this uneven historical record is indicative of the period, for much of the widespread discussion of cottage gardens as a key mode of English garden design is owed to middle- and upper-class commentators seeking, just as Robinson had done, to reform English garden design by locating a solution in vernacular practice.

Although cottage gardens were rarely designed by professional landscapists, Loudon provided a specific account of a cottage garden in the context of his typology of gardens. The typical cottage plot, according to Loudon, should be square or rectangular in form and no less than an eighth of an acre. It should be enclosed with a fence, wall, or hedge. Just inside the enclosure should be planted a border for "early and late culinary crops, as early potatoes, pease [sic], turnips, kidney beans, etc." and another border should be planted around the house for "savoury pot-herbs, flowers, and low flowering shrubs." The space in between could be planted with fruit trees, such as plums, which could also be planted among the hedge. Utilitarian considerations dictated the layout and plants.[10]

Although Loudon's definition, published in the early nineteenth century, is generally prescriptive, it accords with many late-nineteenth-century accounts of cottage gardens in which vegetables were given pride of place, as in a description by writer Richard Jefferies, who had been raised on a smallholding. In his 1874 essay on the laborer's daily life, Jefferies described a cottage garden demarcated by high hedges, with flowers near the doorway, and vegetables and fruit trees beyond arranged in regular order for ease of maintenance.[11] Flora Thompson, who was born and raised in a small village near Oxford (dubbed Lark Rise in her memoirs), gave a similar account. Cottagers' gardens, she explained, were "reserved for green vegetables, currant and gooseberry bushes, and a few old-fashioned flowers. Proud as they were of their celery, peas, and beans, cauliflowers and marrows, and fine as were the specimens they could show of these, their potatoes were their special care, for they had to grow enough to last the year round."[12] An exception in her village was a cottage occupied by a couple with some savings, who possessed a flower garden filled with "wallflowers and tulips, lavender and sweet william, and pinks and old-world roses. . . . It seemed as though all the roses in Lark Rise had gathered together in one garden. Most of the gardens had only one poor starveling bush or none."[13] Most cottages, Thompson later explained, only had a narrow border near the front entrance devoted to flowers, such as "pinks and sweet williams and love-in-a-mist, wallflowers and forget-me-nots in spring and hollyhocks and Michaelmas daisies in autumn. Then there were lavender and sweetbriar bushes, and southern-wood," with the occasional rose bush.[14] Surveying evidence for late-nineteenth-century village gardens, Stephen Constantine has concluded that they were primarily economic in function, filled with fruit and vegetables and with only a few flowers.[15] Period manuals on cottage gardens likewise emphasized fruits and vegetables.[16] Photographs published in turn-of-the-century surveys of cottage architecture bear this out, showing enclosed plots with plants such as cabbages arranged in rows (Fig. 21).

Most commentators from outside the rural economy, however, rarely noted the utilitarian productivity of cottage gardens, preferring instead to elaborate on their aesthetic qualities, and, in particular, the contrast they offered to middle- and upper-class garden design practices, such as bedding out. Mrs. Lisbeth

21. "Front of Cottages at Farncombe," from W. Curtis Green, *Old Cottages and Farmhouses in Surrey*, London, 1908. (Source: This item is reproduced by permission of *The Huntington Library, San Marino, California*.)

22. "Rank Luxuriance." (Source: *Country Life,* April 14, 1900.)

Gooch Strahan (writing as L. G. Seguin), for example, praised a farmer's garden because it was

> old-fashioned, unpretentious . . . not cribbed, cabined and confined within modern rules and regulations, not laid out in geometrical patterns of dingy reds and browns, the beds crammed with a thousand plants all taught to bloom and bend after the same pattern, but a wild, irregular unconventional garden . . . where the flowers have all the sociable, home-bred English names that one has known from childhood.[17]

Lucy Hardy, writing in *Country Life,* echoed these points:

> To wander round the cottager's plot is to come upon perpetual horticultural surprises. Cabbages and roses jostle each other in one bed; sunflowers beam benignantly above vegetables. Pinks – the old-fashioned white cloves, so fragrant, but so rarely seen in modern fashionable gardens – run riot all over the place, and the lavender bush is never wanting. . . . Cabbages and potatoes are the favourite cottage vegetables, grown chiefly for home consumption (Fig. 22).[18]

Here are the main characteristics of the cottage garden as configured in the

discourse of garden design. Old-fashioned, as opposed to exotic, flowers dominate, and sufficient fruits and vegetables are grown to sustain the cottager and
family, but not enough for market gardening. The garden lacks apparent order,
with plants arranged in masses or drifts, but is nevertheless fecund and productive. Both lack of evident arrangement and choice of plant material marks this
garden type apart from "modern fashionable gardens," that is, elaborate parterres
of the bedded-out style. William Robinson's desire to resurrect cottage gardens
was based on just such a perceived antipathy between cottage plants and certain
exotics, on the one hand, and the disordered profusion of cottage gardens and
the tidy arrangement of fashionable country-house gardens, on the other. His
description of the cottage garden, "embowered in fruit trees and forest trees,
evergreens and honeysuckles rising many-coloured from amid shaven grass
plots, flowers struggling in through the very windows," fits the terms of this discourse with its implications of luxuriance and floral beauty. By characterizing
these plots as "little Elysiums," Robinson underscored a key element in cottage
garden discourses – the construction of a cottage ideal.[19]

72

The Cottage Ideal

The cottage ideal is used here to denote notions of pleasure, "of visionary plenti-
tude, of Golden Age fecundity," attached to homes of rural laborers despite, or
because, cottages were often poor hovels or even empty ruins – the detritus of the
growing lure of urban centers and the enclosure movement (the early-nineteenth-
century process by which open fields and commons were consolidated and
brought under individual ownership, often forcing out small farmers, cottagers,
and squatters).[20] George H. Ford argues that idyllic visions of the cottage persisted, despite evidence to the contrary, because the cottage came to signify the
preindustrial and preurban past, the supposed innocence of which was used to
measure the perceived corruption of the urban sphere in the Victorian period.
He concludes "cottages served in Victorian times as metaphors . . . for those who
dreamed of them as felicitous spaces."[21]

The garden was an essential ingredient in the formulation of felicity. Signs of
this can be seen in William Shenstone's poem *The School Mistress* (1748), which
Raymond Williams argues reflects a doubled contrast between city and country,
and past and present:

> And here trim Rosmarine, that whilom crown'd
> The daintiest garden of the proudest peer;
> Ere, driven from its envy'd site, it found

A sacred shelter for its branches here;
Where edg'd with gold its glitt'ring skirts appear.
Oh wassel days; O customs meet and well!
Ere this was banished from its lofty sphere:
Simplicity then sought this humble cell,
Nor ever would She more with thane and lordling dwell.[22]

The theme continues in Oliver Goldsmith's poem *The Deserted Village* (1770), an elegy to a rural village lost to the enclosure movement that includes a loving description of a parson's flower garden, praised as an exemplification of virtue, charity, and a love of community.[23] Mary Burrow's poem *Sketches from Our Village* (1852) likewise posits the cottage garden as a signifier of a moral, industrious community:

◄§ 73

Scatter'd round the verdant village green
The peasants' humble cottages are seen;
Some almost hidden by the clust'ring flowers,
The produce of their evening's leisure hours,
Within these small abodes the eye may see
The neat and careful hand of industry.[24]

The image of the cottage ensconced in a flowery garden disguised the disrupting dislocations that occurred as British agriculture lurched from one stage of capitalistic development to the next. Its emergence as a symbol of the national community also correlated with the gradual, yet pronounced, shrinking of the rural agricultural economy, the changing nature of which is encapsulated in the statistic that by the 1880s more of England's populace lived in towns than in rural villages. In this context, the flowery cottage garden functioned as an "invented tradition," to borrow Eric Hobsbawm's phrase. It represented what Englanders were in their minds – domestic, home loving, and in touch with nature – if not in practice.

Yet, despite the many attractions of the cottage ideal, many commentators at the end of the century sought to peel back its sugary coating to reveal its rotted core. In 1862 art critic Tom Taylor wrote a poem on the old cottage that acknowledges the patent falseness of the cottage ideal and critiques the garden for masking intolerable living conditions:

The cottage homes of England: Yes, I know,
    How picturesque their moss and weather-stain,
Their golden thatch, whose square eves shadows throw
    On white-washed all and deep-sunk latticed pane
. . .

The guelder roses, snow on emerald green,
   The ivy twining o'er grey post and pale,
The white-starred jessamine, whose fragrant screen
   Clothes the rough walls and scents the passing gale;

. . .

All these I know, – know, too, the plagues that prey
   On those who dwell in these bepainted bowers:
The foul miasma of their crowded room,
   Unaired, unlit, with green damps moulded o'er,
The fever that each autumn deals its dooms
   From the rank ditch that stagnates by the door;
And then I wish the picturesque less,
   And welcome the utilitarian hand
That from such foulness plucks its masquing dress,
   And bids the well-aired, well-drained cottage stand,
All base of weather-stain, right-angled true, –
   By sketchers shunned, but shunned by fevers too.[25]

Taylor's poem was just one of many indictments of conditions prevailing among the rural working classes that appeared in the wake of increased immigration of rural laborers to cities. This influx reportedly swelled the already overflowing pool of unemployed, dissatisfied urban poor. Moreover, current theories in genetics proposed that without a constant reserve of "country stock" the quality of the British race, already seriously undermined by urban living, would rapidly deteriorate.[26] E. J. Urwick, for example, in his *Studies of Boy Life in Our Cities,* voiced the common concern that the only chance of survival for the "town type" "is in the constant reinforcement of his vigour by fresh blood from the country, or in his own return to an agricultural life."[27] The agricultural population was regarded as the "backbone of the nation," and it was of utmost importance to "stem the 'rural outflow' and return laborers to the soil."[28] This issue cut across political lines as each of three major political parties – Liberal, Labour, and Conservative – proposed campaigns to restore laborers to the land.[29]

How to return or to retain laborers in the countryside, especially when faced with diminished prospects for employment caused by the agricultural depression? To solve this problem, inquiries were instigated on a variety of levels from local county officials to national royal commissions. Their reports all employ firsthand accounts of wretched living conditions intended to shock readers into action.[30] Some investigators, such as Seebohm Rowntree and May Kendall, even registered surprise that cottages they encountered did not fit with the idyllic myth, or what they called "the Christmas almanac cottage, with its old-fashioned borders and ivy-clad walls, its roses climbing round the porch," with which they were so familiar. What they found were dark, damp structures, and "the old-fashioned flowers which we associated with village life had apparently, to a very great extent, yielded precedence to potatoes."[31] In such reports, in contradistinction to poetic accounts of cottage life, structural age and decrepitude lost their pleasurable aesthetic frisson and registered instead as indexes of national conflict and decline.

Although incontrovertible reports of degradation and deterioration issued by governmental agencies, nascent social scientists, and journalists undermined the cottage ideal, it persisted. In fact, it gained strength at the end of the nineteenth century and into the twentieth century as can be seen by returning to the article by Lucy Hardy:[32]

> The gardenless cottage is happily a rare, indeed almost an unknown, spectacle in many rural places, where we find HUMBLE HOMESTEADS, built, perhaps, some two or three centuries ago, surrounded by typical old fashioned cottage gardens, where the humbler flowers and vegetables seem to attain a degree of perfection unknown in more aristocratic parterres. Surrey, Sussex, Devonshire, and many other localities still boast charming specimens of peasant gardens, such as Herrick, Shenstone, Gay, and Goldsmith have described.[33]

The gardens that rendered the village into such picture postcard perfectness were the products of moral laborers who, according to Richard Jefferies, posed no threat to the existing political order:

> These men are the real true peasantry, quiet and peaceful, yet strong and courageous. These are the class that should be encouraged by every possible means: a man who keeps his little habitation in the state I have described, who ornaments it within, and fills his garden with fruit and flowers, though he may be totally unable to read or to speak correctly, is nevertheless a good and useful citizen, and an addition to the stability of the State.[34]

Perhaps artists were even more responsible than writers for perpetuating the myth of idyllic rusticity. The history of representations of the cottage in the late eighteenth and early nineteenth centuries begins with the development of the picturesque. The cottage was favored as an artistic subject in the picturesque mode because its uneven, rugged outlines and contrasting textures and passages of light fit with a developing appreciation for rural variety. Numerous drawing manuals of the period used the cottage as a model subject for the artist learning how to sketch, define masses, and to lay in tints, lights, and shadows. In these manuals, as well as in images by professional artists, the picturesque cottage was typically shown in a dilapidated and near ruinous state. In his treatise on land-scape design, John Varley, a founding member of the Old Water-Colour Society and one of the leading watercolorists of the early nineteenth century, instructed students to learn how to make "the cot more lowly; its tenants more simple and homely," because

> the great interest which is excited by cottage scenes originates in the facility of finding so many of those subjects in nature subdued in all their primitive and formal eccentricities and offensive angles; where age and neglect have both united to obliterate the predominance of art, and to blend them with nature by irregularity of lines and neutrality of colour; [and] with growth of weeds.[35]

Varley's aesthetic was carried out by numerous watercolorists, including his apprentice William Henry Hunt, whose view of cottages seen from the back exemplifies the decrepitude exhorted by his teacher (Fig. 23). Through such images and texts, writers and artists thus naturalized the neglected cottage.

By the mid-nineteenth century, however, a new strain in cottage representa-

23. William Henry Hunt, *Old Farm Buildings*, c. 1815–20. (Source: Yale Center for British Art, Paul Mellon Collection.)

24. Myles Birket Foster, *The Cottage Garden,* n.d. (Source: By permission of the British Library.)

tions can be detected in watercolors by Myles Birket Foster, Helen Allingham, and their followers. Not only are these images brightly colored, in response to a rising interest in realism and local color, but they also include flowery gardens. Such images represent a coming together of picturesque appreciation of age with the literary myth of the cottage idyll. Foster, a wood engraver turned watercolorist, was credited with modifying the motif of the ruined cottage by adding, or putting greater stress on, the garden, including both utilitarian plants, such as cabbages, and plants associated with pleasure, such as roses (Fig. 24).[36] Increasingly, late Victorian viewers' enjoyment of cottage representations lay in contemplating flourishing gardens and not the melancholy passage of time as with the picturesque.

Helen Allingham adopted, adapted, and popularized the model provided by Foster, focusing even more closely on gardens and developing a method of painting with short, feathery brush strokes well suited to representing the varied textures and colors of masses of densely packed flowers. Although she insisted that her subjects were taken directly from nature, she felt entitled to edit.[37] In the case of her depiction of Unstead Farm, a favored subject of local amateur photographers, when her image is compared to photographs (Plate II; Fig. 25), it is clear that she displaced cabbages, suggestive of laborer's subsistence gardening, with an extensive flower garden, with masses of lavender, lilies, and pansies. The more well-to-do connotations of the garden are reinforced by the female figure, whose gloves and ornamental hat suggest gentility. Allingham's images were among those that Ruskin praised for protesting "against the misery entailed on the poor children of our great cities, – by painting the real inheritance of childhood in the meadows and fresh air."[38] Ruskin's criticism positioned Allingham's work as rural and antiurban, thus inserting her watercolors into the developing dialogue between city and country. Audiences responded favorably. The critic for *The Times* reported of her watercolors in 1898: "the large educated public finds them more and more charming and shows the most constant and unfailing desire to possess them. We do not wonder at it for everyone loves old cottages and gardens."[39]

Cottage Tourism

Part of Allingham's popularity stemmed from her depiction of a region that was becoming increasingly familiar to London art buyers through tourism. The critic for the *Illustrated London News,* referring to her exhibition "On the Surrey Border" (1889), explained that "Witley, Haslemere, the Hindhead, and even the Isle of Wight, are now so accessible that is not necessary to refer to the special points which Mrs. Allingham has once more recalled with so true a sympathy with their local beauty and natural adornments."[40] The rural villages mentioned had become tourist destinations with the expansion of the railway network and became even more popular with the introduction of the automobile. Once viewed aesthetically by the small circle of those initiated into the picturesque, villages such as Witley had become part of the official tourist circuit.

For those unable to take the physical journey to visit these rural villages, publishers such as Batsford and *Country Life* offered numerous publications catering to the armchair traveler. The Batsford series began in the 1880s, when Herbert Batsford entered the family business and developed a series intended to appeal to "the average Englishman," who was, Batsford presciently observed, "beginning to care for the story of his Island and the buildings of it."[41] With titles such as *Old Cottage and Domestic Architecture in South-West Surrey* (1889), *Old Cottages and Farmhouses in Kent and Sussex* (1900), *Old Cottages, Farmhouses, and Other Half-Timber Buildings in Shropshire, Herefordshire, and Cheshire* (1904), and *Old Cottages, Farmhouses, and Other Stone Buildings in the Cotswold District* (1905), Batsford led the reader into numerous hamlets, villages, and rural byways in search of authenticity in rural architecture, taking care to point out what was distinctive to each region. Publishers took advantage of the new medium of photography and amply illustrated their accounts of rural England, although the images provided did not always accord precisely with poetic descriptions found in the texts.

The cottage of the tourist imagination was a fairly consistent type: small scale, perhaps with a tiled or thatched roof, walls of half-timbering, stone or stucco, and a flowery garden:

> It is a small house, of odd, irregular form, with various harmonious colouring, the effects of weather, time and accident, the whole environed with smiling verdure. Old English flowers – roses, pansies, peonies, sweet williams, and London pride – adorn the strips of ground on each side of the path. . . . Such is the cottage which the poet and the painter loves, a type which is happily not extinct in modern England.[42]

79

Literature, art, and tourism collaborated in the ongoing construction of the cottage ideal, making the garden into a locus of desire for the literate classes anxious to partake in the supposed purity and simplicity of rural life and the felicity it promised.

Part of the desirability of cottages lay in their ties to the past and in their antiurban character. An article on Shere, a village located between Guildford and Dorking, claimed that it "completely retains its old-world appearance and air of

25. S. R. Verstage, Unstead Manor House, 1904. (Source: Reproduced by permission of Surrey History Service.)

sleepy repose," encompassing the visitor in a "feeling of rest and repose. . . . [T]he great city, with its hurry and bustle and harassing cares, becomes a thing of the past and fades from the mind like a bad dream."[43] According to the essay Allingham's poet husband William wrote for her 1886 exhibition, she depicted only those cottages that had escaped renovation and looked much as they did when first built. Much of the catalog is a diatribe against "improvement," which Mr. Allingham described as "trees getting cut down, roadsides enclosed, footpaths stopped up, obtrusive fences raised, pretentious mansions built, [and] ancient cottages destroyed or spoilt." Improvers were, according to Allingham, rubbing out "a piece of old England."[44]

Cottage Preservation

William Allingham's sentiments reflect the developing preservation movement. Like the practices of tourism, preservation or heritage movements were crucial for nurturing national identity: preserving a site often hinged on arguing its value for the nation and its history. In England, preservation movements were institutionalized at the end of the nineteenth century with the formation of organizations such as the National Trust and the passage of laws to protect the material past. These activities reflected a number of compounding insights: one, a sense of divide between past and present, exacerbated by the rapid change accompanying the Industrial Revolution; two, a belief that the past could be embedded in material remains; three, a conviction that the history of each nation unfolded in unique ways and monuments.[45] To chronicle this history and to give voice to the nation's distinctive identity, the material past had to be saved. The urge to preserve became particularly intense at the end of the nineteenth century when the ideology of progress and improvement came into doubt. William Morris, expressing an increasingly vocal point of view, castigated efforts at restoration. In the manifesto for the Society for the Protection of Ancient Buildings, which Morris founded in 1877, he argued that older buildings should be left unrestored so they could serve as instructive lessons to future generations. He called for "protection in the place of restoration."[46] In his lecture "The Beauty of Life" (1880), Morris asserted that preservation was every citizen's concern because "these monuments of our art and history[,] . . . whatever the lawyers may say, belong not to a coterie, or to a rich man here and there, but to the nation at large."[47]

Cottage preservation had become a pressing issue, ironically, because of numerous social investigations, which brought pressure on landlords to improve estates, and because of increased enforcement of the Housing Act of 1890. This act allowed rural authorities to condemn neglected houses; to issue bylaws concerning sanitation, stability, and security of new buildings; and to buy land for new housing.[48] This legislation did not transform the countryside wholesale, however, as it was difficult to enforce and was unevenly applied; nonetheless, enough rebuilding took place for an art critic to complain that old cottages were "being demolished as fast as the sanitary reformer can contrive, or modernized out of all their picturesqueness and historical significance.[49]

The reference to modernizing hints at another reason for the transformation of cottages: the back-to-the-land movement. Ironically, the very constituency that was most enamored with the rural countryside altered its appearance. Countless examples were noted of well-to-do middle-class professionals purchasing or leasing rural cottages in the Home Counties, which were available in increasing numbers because of the agricultural depression:

> We know that within the last few years there has been observable a tendency towards the leading of a "double life" as regards the professional and other men of moderate means . . . we are want to class as belonging to "the upper middle class." By this double life I [mean] . . . the combination in one individual of the habitudes of both town and country mouse. His workaday world lies in London; the more pleasurable and more restful of his days are spent in some quiet Surrey, Sussex, or Kent village.[50]

The village of Farnham in Surrey, for example, quadrupled in population during the last quarter of the nineteenth century. Numerous books, such as C. R. Ashbee's *A Book of Cottages and Little Houses* (1906) and George Morris's *The Country Cottage* (1906), exhibitions of model cottages such as that sponsored by the *Daily Mail* in 1913, and articles explained how to renovate or create "new old" cottages:

> The demand for inexpensive houses as headquarters for country holidays increases daily. We have already suggested how this need may be met, either by restoring the pretty old "cottages," so called, which were really small farm-houses . . . or by building modern cottages of special design, like those shown in the number of *Country Life* published February 19th last. As an example of what may be done to make new homes in old houses we give a view of one of these old tenements RESTORED AND INHABITED, with its garden set with roses, its windows formerly stopped up with plaster, reopened, reglazed, and filled with flowers (Fig. 26).[51]

Gardens, as this account suggests, were an essential component of the renovated or new cottage. Architect M. H. Baillie Scott argued that home owners should adopt plants from rural laborers' homes, using hardy perennials rather than tender exotics favored in bedded-out gardens.[52] According to these discourses, gardening not only improved the physical appearance of the home, it also improved the physique of the home owner. A writer who leased a farmhouse found that "the glory of the house" was "the spacious garden, and health and enjoyment come in the tending of it. . . . What more can brain-weary man, or children pining for country air, desire in the world?"[53]

When calling for preserving rural cottages, most authors did not insist on it in the name of their class, but instead in the name of the nation, promoting it as a national art form. Gardener Gertrude Jekyll argued that if the English citizenry was willing to support institutions such as the British Museum or the National Gallery, they should be willing to preserve old cottages, which were the "precious heritage" of the nation.[54] The Arts and Crafts journal *The Studio* articulated a similar line of argument in a 1906 editorial stating that improving cottages was destroying "that old-world atmosphere which has inspired so many generations of our greatest artists" and concluded that older cottages were "a national asset" that should be preserved at all costs.[55] An art critic for the *Illustrated London News* hoped Allingham's 1896 exhibition of cottage paintings would "excite the energy of some Ancient Buildings Preservation Society to apply its theories to these humble but characteristic expressions of English national life."[56] The first building ever purchased by the National Trust, founded for "the permanent preservation for the benefit of the nation of lands and tenements (including buildings) of beauty or historic interest," was a fourteenth-century vicarage, the Clergy House, Alfriston, that displayed key characteristics of cottage building: thatched roofing, timber-frame architecture, and plaster walls.[57] Once the symbol of the tightly controlled, paternalistic relationship between landowners and rural laborers, cottages were now recast as ideal symbols of the nation's rural heritage.

When justifying their actions on behalf of the nation, reformers, preservationists, and back-to-the-landers seemed little concerned with complaints of their detractors. Yet friction, perhaps inevitable, arose between new settlers and "natives." A 1908 article on the Home Counties in the quasi-socialist journal *World's Work* described "a feeling of resentment against the invaders" who only came for the summer and then disappeared again.[58] Another article criticized the weekenders for bringing their servants with them from town and thus failing to help the local economy.[59] Much of local resentment against middle-class excursionists stemmed from their ability to live in the countryside and yet be unaffected by the rural social order. That holiday seekers could stand outside the existing hierarchy made up of "squire, parson, the farmer and the labourer" infuriated both the lower classes, who resented the climbing real estate prices caused by tourism, and the gentry, who felt threatened by the outsiders, who often "directly challenged or replaced old owners."[60]

26. "Restored and Inhabited." (Source: *Country Life,* May 7, 1898.)

Instituting Gardens

Landowners' resentments also may have been prompted by the increasing regulation they faced as a result of reformers' efforts. Not only cottages, but also gardens were subject to legislation. In belief that if cottagers had more of a stake in the land they would remain in the countryside, the Agricultural Holdings Act of 1883 forced the landowner to provide compensation to the tenant for improvements executed during his tenancy. It was followed by the Agricultural Holdings Act of 1900, issued in response to recommendations by the Royal Commission on Agricultural Depression, that expanded improvements for which the tenant could seek compensation upon leaving his holding, including gardens not exceeding one acre. Possession of such land was still largely at the discretion of the landlord, although acts throughout the end of the nineteenth century and into the twentieth legislated for provision of allotments by trustees of charity land and rural sanitary, district, or parish councils.[61]

Where the law failed, popular opinion often tried to succeed. Sutton's seed company, for example, offered seeds for free or for a reduced price to clergymen and others if they were to be distributed to cottagers so that they could encourage "industrious habits."[62] *Country Life* reported enthusiastically about a landowner who encouraged gardening among his tenants through prizes:

> Mr. Hudson is offering two silver cups, one for farm servants' gardens and one for the other men employed on the estate. Not a weed is visible, and the rows of beans and peas, the drills of potatoes, the cabbages and other homely vegetables, are planted with commendable neatness. It adds to the attractive appearance of the cottages.[63]

84

Here the garden operates on many different levels: it aestheticizes the appearance of the cottage, it offers an incentive for laborers to remain on the land, and it absorbs the laborer into a culture of discipline, order, and industry. This became of particular concern in those areas affected by the Agricultural Labourers Union, founded by agricultural laborer Joseph Arch in 1872. Although relatively short lived, the union, through strikes and the public media, was able to bring attention to agrarian laborers' worsening work and living conditions, which appeared even more egregious in comparison with slowly gained reforms in industry.

The notion of achieving personal improvement and respectability through gardens clearly informed the Garden City movement, which was shaped by the belief, emerging in response to debates about rural emigration, that gardens were a key means by which to address the condition of the working classes. An important antecedent to the garden cities, Port Sunlight, was built by William Lever to provide housing for workers at his soap manufacturing plant. Lever, a strong believer in Ruskin's notion that one's surroundings influenced behavior, explained his aesthetic choices in a 1915 lecture, "Art and Happiness." This businessman, who owned paintings by Allingham, stipulated that beautiful art could induce "happiness and pleasure" as well as "civilize and elevate" through the depiction of enlightened and ennobling themes. To illustrate his notions, Lever cited a "picture of a cottage crowned with a thatched roof, and clinging ivy and a small garden foreground suggesting old fashioned perfume of flower and a home in which dwell content and happiness."[64] Lever modeled his corporate housing after a rural village, echoing the picturesque, ornamental villages built by eighteenth- and nineteenth-century estate owners to ameliorate the conditions of their tenants and to aesthetize their estates.

Begun in 1888, Port Sunlight was designed largely by local architect William Owen, working in close cooperation with his employer. The early houses, half-timbered and tile-hung with latticed windows, were resolutely English in their architectural vocabulary and based on local examples of vernacular architecture. They were arranged in an intentionally bucolic setting. A large irregular dell served as a public common, with schools, a church, an inn (serving nonalcoholic

27. Nos. 89–97 Bebington Road, Port Sunlight, c. 1902. (Source: Board of Trustees of the National Museums and Galleries on Merseyside, Lady Lever Art Gallery, Port Sunlight.)

beverages), and blocks of cottages around it. The large portion of the site devoted to greenery earned the village its posthumous label as the first garden city.[65] Each house possessed its own garden in keeping with Lever's declaration that "A home requires a greensward and garden in front of it, just as much as a cup requires a saucer (Fig. 27).[66]

Gardening was likewise mandated at Bournville, the planned village of chocolate manufacturer George Cadbury begun in 1895 and based on "quaint and picturesque" examples of the "best traditions of country architecture" (Figs. 28, 29).[67] Cadbury, a devout Quaker with paternalistic leanings, believed gardening to be the "most natural and healthful of all recreations"; lectures and classes were organized to encourage gardening, particularly in young men.[68] Gardens were laid out even before tenants moved in; maintenance was compulsory due to a "clause in every contract which says that every tenant must keep his place up to a certain standard of neatness and beauty."[69] These employers were clearly seeking ways to ensure a reliable and harmonious work force, one that would be physically fit and undeterred by alcohol; and the power of the cottage ideal was such that Cadbury and Lever believed their goals could be achieved by giving it a physical manifestation.

Garden cities were intended also to prevent rural laborers from flocking to larger urban areas and to encourage city dwellers to leave the decaying urban core, thus solving problems of both city and country. In 1903 the first garden city proper, Letchworth, based on theories laid out in Ebenezer Howard's *Tomorrow: A Peaceful Path to Real Reform* (1898), was begun. As in Port Sunlight and Bournville, the architects, Barry Parker and Raymond Unwin, designed houses based loosely on vernacular examples in the manner of Arts and Crafts architecture. Each was provided with a garden, replete with roses and herbaceous borders filled with old-fashioned cottage plants.[70] Although intended for the working classes, Letchworth eventually became a middle-class suburb of London because many workers could not afford the housing or resisted the regimented regularity of the community.

The failure of the garden cities has often been commented on; nonetheless, they are noteworthy for the significance they attached to the cottage ideal and its supposed ameliorating qualities. Whether in its physical or painted form, the cottage ideal offered a seductive civic model, promising domestic bliss and productive labor.[71] Architects, tour guides, and others often praised how cottage architecture and gardens were adapted to local circumstances, and they concomitantly believed that the vernacular could be severed from its soil and transplanted to another site. This liberty is indicative of how the cottage and its garden, although still admired as a local phenomenon – a practice of laborers located in small rural communities – had become, through images and accounts of the countryside circulated by the press, an icon available to and constitutive of the national community without regard to station or locale.

Shared appreciation of the cottage ideal functioned not only to bring together England's varied populations but also defined England in the international arena, and in particular, in the context of Empire. It defined homeland, both for those within England's shores and those posted to the colonies, and thus fulfilled what Ruskin called for in 1870 – a sense of England that could instill pride in colonists. A useful introduction to this discourse is provided by Stewart Dick's *The Cottage Homes of England* (1909), illustrated by Helen Allingham. Dick opens the book by inquiring what signifies modern England. In response he invokes and rejects several potential national symbols, such as John Bull – too out of date – and the shopkeeper – indistinctive and "hardly an article in his shop is native produce" – before settling on the cottage, claiming that its homeliness reflects the English devotion to family, and its simple organic plan, like that of its garden, reveals the national character.[72] Sidney Jones echoed such sentiments in *The Village Homes of England* (1912) when he claimed that cottages "stand for much that is peculiarly and characteristically English. They are records of lives well spent; they tell of contented possession, of love of home and country . . . of order, of security, and

28. "Every Front Yard in Bournville (near Birmingham) is as Good as This." (Source: Wilhelm Miller, *What England Can Teach Us about Gardening*, Garden City, 1911.)

29. "Every Back Yard in Bournville is as Neat and Productive as This." (Source: Wilhelm Miller, *What England Can Teach Us about Gardening*, Garden City, 1911.)

comfort ... [and] of settled stability," qualities prized in an age that believed itself to be engulfed in widespread, detrimental change.[73] Whereas hints of this discourse can be located in the picturesque, if not earlier, it gained particular momentum at the end of the nineteenth century. As Elizabeth Helsinger has pointed out, not until this period did John Constable earn his reputation as a national painter, which rested largely on *The Cornfield* and *The Valley Farm,* images that located national greatness in an idealized rural community.[74]

In nationalizing the rural scene, and, in particular, the cottage, purveyors of this discourse had to convince their audience that these motifs, largely associated with southern England, referenced all of England. This Marcus Huish did in *Happy England* (1903), a collection of Allingham's paintings. Allingham painted mostly in Surrey, Sussex, Kent, and Hampshire, yet Huish evaded mention of these sites in the title of the collection and insisted (against the author's wishes) on grouping her paintings under the label 'Happy England'. So, just as the wild garden took the indigenous landscape of the High Weald and offered it as a national model, the cottage garden, as configured by such sources as *Happy England,* promoted the rustic landscapes of southern England as characteristic of the nation as a whole.

By the early twentieth century, the ubiquity of the cottage ideal enabled it to displace or subsume other metaphors of Englishness rooted in the landscape. The Lake District, for example, was regarded as a "sort of national property" in the early nineteenth century; and through Wordsworth's writings the cottage helped register the area's arcadian associations.[75] In late-nineteenth-century discourses, however, the cottage was typically severed of its Lake District connections and firmly rooted in the southern agrarian landscape. The Lake District, as well as the Wye Valley, and parts of Wales and Scotland, were also valued for their rugged variety, a quality prized in the picturesque as well as the sublime. Yet although the picturesque and the sublime suited the late-eighteenth- and early-nineteenth-century need for an aesthetic that could rival the decaying ruins and craggy carapaces prized in European view making, it did not suit the late-nineteenth-century interest in more domesticated, ordered landscapes. For the same reasons, the wild, heaving moors of Yorkshire described prominently in the Brontës' fiction were not taken up to the same degree as Thomas Hardy's Wessex villages at the end of the nineteenth century.

The motif of the flowery cottage was also distinguished from other national types. Ruskin argued that the whitewashed thatched cottage covered with roses found in England signified "finished neatness" as opposed to the "general air of nonchalance" associated with the French peasant's home with its peeling whitewash and absence of garden.[76] Ruskin's vision of the English cottage was also distinguished from those in Ireland. The latter rarely included a garden because the land on which the cottage was typically located was common land, devoted to grazing, and brooked no boundaries between neighbors. The Irish cottage, especially in visual representations, was typified as set in "wild, uncultivated land" in contrast to the English cottage, whose garden signified "cultivation and orderliness."[77] William Robinson contributed to this discourse, emphasizing the southern metaphor:

> The bare cottages of Belgium and North France are shocking in their baldness and ugliness. Even in Ireland and Scotland we do not see the same pretty little gardens. And these are not so good in some parts of England. In Surrey, Kent, and the Southern counties we find the prettiest cottage gardens.[78]

That the English cottage ideal offered a sense of national identity, particularly for those returning home or imagining England from overseas, is demonstrated by the emphasis in cottage literature on the uniqueness of the English cottage and its garden. E. T. Cook insisted that "nothing, nowadays, is more characteristic, as we know of our English countryside, and there is nothing that strikes a foreigner more forcible than the cottage gardens, with their aspect of homely comfort."[79] In *Rural England* (1881), L. G. Seguin queried readers about what "after . . . years of exile in some far-distant continent, our thoughts revert" when thinking of England? Not "smoke-begrimed metropolis, or . . . fashion-crowded thoroughfares." Thoughts turned to rural England, a country home and a cottage with a "bit of garden-ground attached."[80] Stewart Dick employed a similar rhetorical maneuver, inquiring "what is the most typical thing in England," and answering "the old English cottage": "A little cottage nestling amidst the green, and a bower of roses round the door . . . these are the pictures of England that are carried away to other climes."[81] That this was literally done is demonstrated by a copy of *Old English Country Cottages* (1906), with illustrations by Helen Allingham, which was sent to someone in Calcutta, India, for Christmas in 1906.[82]

Cook's reference to "homely," shared by other writers, hints at the national character implied by the veneration of cottage gardens. It was a national character framed by moral labor and domesticity. An article in *Country Life* perceived a link between the virtuous pursuit of labor in leisure hours and the future of England: "When gardening releases its hold upon the affections of English men and women, then will the national character of our sturdy race go too."[83] The home was at the core of gardening practices, both physically and imaginatively; the activities demanded by the garden, such as nurturing plants, had evident parallels to domestic tasks such as child rearing. Men were not contaminated by this link with domesticity; rather, gardening was described as invigorating physical exercise and was the subject of fierce competition as home owners vied for the most splendid plant specimens in local fairs and exhibitions.[84] These activities were, in fact, encouraged as a means of driving away vice in the lower classes and as a means of relieving stress in the middle classes. This was healthy competition as opposed to the supposedly draining conflicts and strife of the capitalist marketplace.

The rural village community signified by the cottage and its garden was likewise sheltered from the public sphere of business and politics, both physically – with walls and hedges – and metaphorically – through its ties to the past.[85] Implicit in the model of the rural village was a sense of sentimental domesticity. Allingham's images reinforced such notions with their depiction of healthy sweet-faced children and young mothers standing in their front gardens, leaving the safety of their walls and hedges only to tend to domestic tasks. None of the overcrowding, dirt, or contagion reported by social investigators taints this depiction of rural England.

This vision of the nation exists in complex relationship to Empire. Whereas certain strands move across the discourses of national and imperial identity, such as moral rectitude and physical exercise and stimulation, marked differences nevertheless distinguish the two. England's cottage ideal, in text and image, implied respecting boundaries, with its focus on the circumscribed space of home, and promoted turning one's attention inward, to the decoration of one's domestic sphere. In rhetoric and in practice, British Imperialism advocated pushing frontiers, disregarding physical and metaphorical boundaries in the pursuit of material resources, and conquering mental and physical challenges. War, hunting, sport, adventure stories, histories shaped by heroic narratives, and jingoistic music-hall ballads were the vehicles that expressed and defined Imperial identity.[86]

The ways in which the cottage ideal and imperialist rhetoric were defined against each other should not be overstated, however. The cottage ideal can also be seen as the mirror image of imperialism as back-to-the-landers colonized the countryside. It also enabled imperialism by creating the notion of home that sustained expansion overseas. Similarly the economic benefits of imperialism, particularly in the case of Port Sunlight and Bournville, which were built as part of domestic-imperial manufacturing enterprises, spurred and sustained the cottage ideal at home.[87] But unlike the wild garden, the cottage ideal erased any traces of its relationship with Empire, signifying resolutely a sense of homeland rooted in southern English rural villages and the practices of the rural working class. In the popular imagination, the cottage garden was an unchanging, rural tradition, binding together England's generations and fortifying its citizenry.

Chapter 4

Ordering the Landscape

The Art Workers Guild and the Formal Garden

In 1910 *The Architectural Review,* a journal founded by the circle around the Art Workers Guild, published an article entitled "Modern Garden Design."[1] Although the article opened with an extensive quote from *The Times*'s essay on cottage gardening that had appeared several years earlier, the modern garden referred to in the title was not the cottage or wild garden, but formal gardens in which "attempts at imitating nature have been thrown aside as both foolish and futile" and the gardener has been superseded by the architect.[2] That the author of this article could refer to yet another style – the formal garden – as the leading manner of garden design underscores the aesthetic rivalry that distinguished English garden design at the turn of the century. This rivalry also reveals competing notions of traditional Englishness then available in English culture. The formal garden, with its orderly arrangement and emulation of country-house architecture of the highest social class, created a very different national image than that evoked by either the wild garden or the cottage garden.

According to architect Reginald Blomfield, the formal garden united house and landscape as it extended the "principles of design which govern the house to the grounds which surround it" and thus harmonized the house with its surroundings and "prevent[ed] its being an excrescence on the face of nature."[3] The formal garden, he added, could also be called architectural treatment of gardens because its orderly layout should be the responsibility of the architect, rather than the gardener.[4] The latter was an important point, for the rise of the formal garden paralleled the development of the landscape architecture profession. Thomas Mawson, the featured architect in *The Architectural Review*'s 1910 discussion of modern garden design, was the first university lecturer in landscape architecture – appointed to the Liverpool Department of Civic Design in 1909 – and became the first president of the Institute of Landscape Architects in 1929.

To underscore the need to wrest the design of the space surrounding the house away from gardeners and nurserymen, Blomfield insisted that only architects understood a garden should be "treated specifically as an enclosed space." Features such as terraces with straight and wide paths, broad masses of shorn grass demarcated by trimmed hedges and alleys, and clearly defined box-edged beds filled with "sweet old-fashioned flowers" would achieve the desired sense of architectural arrangement.[5] Rather than the seemingly unplanned disorder and profusion of the wild or cottage garden, plants were framed or hemmed in by green walls so the garden came to resemble an out-of-doors room, with flowers as paintings and garden seats and ornaments resembling interior furnishings.

These spaces were not just for promenading and studying nature, as in the wild garden: with their close-shaven lawns framed by hedges they suited newly fashionable sports, such as badminton, croquet, and lawn tennis. The latter, with its origins in the fifteenth and sixteenth century, was enthusiastically resuscitated in the 1870s and was taken up the middle and upper classes so that "no afternoon party was complete without it."[6] In fact, it can be said that the fashion for lawn tennis and croquet shaped garden design as the need for large areas of level, smooth lawn was met by reviving such features as the bowling green (Fig. 30). These sports were taken up enthusiastically by both men and women and allowed for new rituals of courtship to develop within the protected sphere of the garden.[7] Bowling also enjoyed a revival at the turn of the century, spreading, like tennis and croquet, through amateur clubs. The lawn thus became the favored locus for upper-middle- and upper-class leisure activities.[8]

The formal garden functioned like reception rooms of the house. It was available to the family and to invited guests and thus broached the public and the private spheres. Formal gardens easily lent themselves to entertaining as a 1907 article in *The Spectator* explained:

> the best garden for a garden-party is an old one, – walled, enclosed, subdivided, trim, and suggestive everywhere of shelter and limitation. Here the flutter of muslin and the sheen of bright silks are altogether in place. This is no escape for wild spirits, but the abode of peace. . . . Here we see Nature thoroughly disciplined. The most civilized thing in the world is a well-kept garden.[9]

The aspects of the formal garden that made it appropriate for entertaining – enclosed, ordered, peaceful, civilized – also rendered it a symbol of a desired sense of Englishness. These qualities were said to have disappeared in the modern age, and thus the formal garden came to offer a way to recover a lost past – the past of country houses as opposed to untouched heaths of the Weald or the

30. "Lawn Bowls, or Bowling on the Green." (Source: Wilhelm Miller, *What England Can Teach Us about Gardening*, Garden City, 1911.)

cottages of rural villages. The emphasis on the appearance of great age in formal gardens, achieved through quoting from the past as well as modern techniques of simulating weathered effects, also provided an instant heritage for the newly emergent upper middle classes. Older or pseudo older gardens also underscored differences between nations of supposedly great age, whose roots could be traced to time immemorial, and brash newcomers, such as the United States, or colonial regions that lacked the status of nationhood. In particular, the formal garden was seen as a means by which to revive the lost values of the English Renaissance. It was a style that therefore communicated a certain sense of cosmopolitanism – of participation in highest, most refined circles of art and architecture within England and the continent; of membership in an elite predicated on good taste, in contrast to the peasant associations of cottage gardening.[10]

The cosmopolitanism associated with the formal garden points up a paradox that lay at the heart of the enterprise to encode the formal garden as the English garden. While British architects were feverishly establishing the historic roots of formal gardens in the English landscape in order to legitimize the style as English, a revival of architectural or formal gardening was taking place in other places, including France, where restoration of Le Nôtre's Vaux-le-Vicomte paved the way for a renewed interest in the principles of geometry, symmetry, and balance associated with this designer. In Germany, a band of young architects and garden designers, dubbing themselves *Gartenarchiteckten,* brought a new focus on formalism to garden and park design. Even in the United States, which lacked the historic precedents of Britain or the continent, formalism took hold. Frederick Law Olmsted, perhaps more commonly associated with the pastoral scenes of

New York City's Central Park, designed a garden in the manner of Vaux-le-Vicomte for George Vanderbilt at Biltmore House, North Carolina. A younger American generation continued the interest in gardens designed as a series of outdoor rooms; Charles Platt, for example, dedicated his career to gardens laid out in an architectural manner.[11] His designs relied heavily on principles he observed in Italian gardens, which he had also described and illustrated in his book *Italian Gardens* (1894). This text was just one of many tributes to Italian gardens published in this period; Edith Wharton's *Italian Villas and Their Gardens* (1904) and Sir George Sitwell's *An Essay on the Making of Gardens* (1909) are perhaps the best known of these.

Given the design world's growing familiarity with and admiration of Italian garden design, particularly that associated with Renaissance villas, British garden designers arguing on behalf of the inherent Englishness of the formal garden were often forced to walk a fine line. On the one hand, they wanted to signal their knowledge of the design vocabulary of the Italian Renaissance, which was undergoing a general revival throughout the architectural community. In the United States, for example, the architectural firm of McKim, Mead, and White brought motifs from Italian Renaissance palazzi to bear on such commissions as the Henry Villard houses in New York and the Boston Public Library. The World's Columbian Exposition, held in Chicago in 1893, brought this "American Renaissance" to international attention with its obvious references to classical, Italian Renaissance, and French École des Beaux-Arts architecture. The latter was a particularly important influence, because this school, with its strong roots in classicism, had helped to initiate a Renaissance revival earlier in the nineteenth century.

On the other hand, the British architects, rooted in the Arts and Crafts movement and schooled in the Gothic revival, were anxious to continue to uncover and to revive architectural traditions regarded as indigenous to Great Britain, particularly England. The ways in which British architects attempted to strike a balance between arguing on behalf of the significance of Italian Renaissance architecture and identifying a uniquely English tradition is illustrated by architect Reginald Blomfield's *A History of Renaissance Architecture in England, 1500–1800* (1897). The author, who was anxious that English Renaissance architecture be considered as important as the Gothic architecture championed by Ruskin, opened his text by defining Renaissance architecture as "the art that derived its first impulse from the revived interest in scholarship at the end of the fifteenth century; – particularly in the remains of Roman architecture in Italy; – and which ran its course . . . until the original inspiration was superseded by other motives." Blomfield, therefore, began his study with the first attempts by Italian workmen in England, and closed it at the end of the eighteenth century, when architects abandoned the models of Roman and Italian architecture. But throughout his text he often discounted the influence of imported ideas and argued on behalf of a strong national tradition. The language Blomfield used to summarize Inigo Jones's contribution is revealing:

> His extraordinary capacity is shown by the success with which he freed English architecture from the imbecilities of the German designers, and started it on a line of fresh development, borrowed it is true from Italy, yet so successfully adapted to English traditions, that it was at once accepted and followed by the best intelligence of the country for the next hundred and fifty years.[12]

The Art Workers Guild

Much impetus for the formal garden movement came from members of the Art Workers Guild. In particular, it stemmed from Reginald Blomfield, who wrote a seminal treatise, *The Formal Garden in England,* in collaboration with F. Inigo Thomas, a wellborn country-house artist and architect.[13] Blomfield, after graduating from Oxford University, took a position with his uncle, Arthur W. Blomfield, and began attending the Royal Academy School in the evenings, where he was exposed to the work of leading British architects, such as G. E. Street, Alfred Waterhouse, and Richard Norman Shaw.[14] In 1884, following a study tour of Gothic and Romanesque architecture in France and Spain, Blomfield launched his own practice. His new office was above that of E. S. Prior, an architect who had trained with R. N. Shaw and was engaged with the emerging Arts and Crafts movement. Through Prior, Blomfield entered the circle of architects associated with R. N. Shaw.

Shaw had helped launch the so-called Old English style, characterized by tile-hung roofs, leaded windows, and brick chimneys, developed from study of sixteenth- and seventeenth-century vernacular architecture in the Weald of Sussex.[15] Like Robinson, whose wild garden translated the landscape of the Weald to a national aesthetic, Shaw transported the architecture of the Weald throughout England, building, for example, Cragside in the Old English style in Northumberland for Lord Armstrong. Shaw impressed on his apprentices looking to the local landscape for examples of good craftsmanship and design, a sensibility that accorded with the developing Arts and Crafts movement.

In 1884 a group of Shaw's apprentices and colleagues formed the Art Workers Guild, which Blomfield joined in 1887.[16] First convened by Ernest Newton, E. S. Prior, Mervyn Macartney, and E. G. Horsley, the group proposed "a new society for promoting more intimate relations between Painters, Sculptors, Architects, and those working in the Arts of Design, and with a view to advancing the Arts of Painting, Sculpture, Architecture, and of design."[17] In attendance at this meeting were a number of revivalist architects, such as J. D. Sedding, who had trained with Street and became master of the guild from 1886 to 1887, as well as a handful of artists, including Alfred Parsons. Its activities included monthly meetings featuring expositions of different artistic techniques, exhibitions of examples of excellent workmanship, and scholarly papers on topics of general interest to the membership – for example, on May 3, 1889, papers were read on the theme of the architectural treatment of gardens. Occasional "country meetings" were organized, the first to the medieval moated manor house Ightham Mote, Kent, on July 22, 1884. Through studying the past and integrating the arts, the guild intended to reform British architecture, interior design, and landscape design. The new style would not strictly copy the past; rather, pre-eighteenth-century precepts and examples would be studied in order to establish a modern form of design sensitive to local historic practices and suggestive of a close sympathetic relationship between the building and its surroundings.[18]

Roots of many of the ideas of the Art Workers Guild can be traced to the writings of William Morris, who included garden design in his charge for reforming the arts of England and repairing the damage that industrialization and modernity had wrought on the English landscape. In his lecture "Making the Best of It," for example, Morris poked fun at town gardens for attempting to imitate larger landscape gardens within limited grounds and for adopting the carpet bedding fashion. But he did not go as far as to espouse the wild garden; he insisted that the garden should not imitate "either the wilfulnesss or the wildness of Nature" but "should, in fact, look like part of the house" and appear "both orderly and rich."[19] Whereas Morris never promoted a particular style, his own gardens suggest how his ideas could be put into practice. At the Red House at Upton, near Bexley Heath, Kent, the garden, located within the embrace of the two arms of the house, was, according to Lady Burne-Jones, "spaced formally into four little square gardens making a big square together; each of the smaller squares had a wattled fence around it with an opening by which one entered, and all over the fence roses grew thickly"; a bowling green and an orchard were also included (Fig. 31).[20]

A number of the guild architects took Morris's advice to heart and included garden design in their professional repertoire. Financial concerns may have spurred this interest: many of these architects were beginning their careers and saw garden design as a foot in the door – a way to meet important clients and eventually obtain substantial commissions. To this end, they published on garden design. In his autobiography, Blomfield observed that writing about the history of the formal garden led him to a number of clients he met while researching historic houses or who sought him out after publication of his writings.[21] The guild architects' publications addressed several themes: the history of English garden design and architecture, particularly that of the Renaissance, which many in the guild thought had been unfairly overlooked in favor of the Gothic revival; the vocabulary for formal garden design; and the benefits of formal gardens as opposed to other styles. Most major statements on the formal garden rarely appeared in the horticultural literature aimed at gardeners, nurserymen, and botanists; instead, they were published in journals favorable to progressive architecture, such as *The Studio*, or those aimed at a wealthy, educated readership, including *Country Life* and *The Portfolio*. Architects thus reached their target audience: owners of small country houses, who typically supervised the garden with assistance of hired labor, as opposed to large estate owners who typically left their gardens in the hands of professional gardeners to whom much horticultural literature was directed.

❧ 97

Writing the History of the Formal Garden in England

Blomfield's interest in the formal garden resulted from trips he undertook to southern England in the 1880s when he, following the model of Shaw, used time between occasional architectural commissions to travel the countryside in search

31. "Example of an Orchard Garden, Originally Laid Out by William Morris," from Edward Prior, "Garden-Making," *The Studio*, 1900. (Source: This item is reproduced by permission of *The Huntington Library, San Marino, California*.)

of evidence of a distinctive English tradition in sixteenth- and seventeenth-century architecture.[22] Blomfield soon became aware of the role gardens played in providing a setting for houses of that era. In the last of a series of articles he published about his Kent trip, he concluded that to recover the unity of the arts deemed necessary by the guild, architects should take charge of the house and garden, as they had, he believed, in the sixteenth and seventeenth centuries.[23]

J. D. Sedding, who, through his studies of the past, became convinced that older means of garden making – the formal style – constituted a uniquely English form of garden design well suited to the modern age, shared this position.[24] For Blomfield and Sedding to move forward in reforming garden design they had to move backward to recover traditions on which modern design should be based. F. Inigo Thomas articulated this notion more fully in 1900:

> when tradition in architecture has been broken, what has started it afresh on reasonable lines has always been a careful adaptation of past methods to modern requirements. So the writer has felt the necessity of drawing attention to examples of old work to form some intelligible starting point for what may be done in the future.[25]

These architects' notion of modern architecture rested on a fusing of the old and new, a paradigm that became a guiding principle in garden design at the turn of the century.[26]

Thus these architects became among the first modern scholars to tackle the problem of the history of the formal garden of the English Renaissance. Although flaws mar their scholarship, their treatment of the issue is nevertheless admirable in scope, presenting close examination of treatises of the time and referencing extant examples of Renaissance design. These efforts distinguished the guild architects' revival of the formal garden from that of their predecessors, such as W. A. Nesfield and Charles Barry, who also espoused an architectural treatment of gardens executed in a revivalist manner. The accounts of Blomfield and his colleagues were set apart by their almost single-minded pursuit of a purely English form of garden design, whereas Nesfield had been more admittedly catholic in his range of references, using a French parterre design, for example, at Worsley Hall and an Italianate-based design at Grimston Park.

Unfortunately for guild architects, many sites from which they derived their principles of design did not date in their entirety to the sixteenth or seventeenth centuries. Blomfield, for example, admired Montacute greatly as an exemplar of pre-eighteenth-century design. He visited in 1889, and his notebooks reveal careful sketches, notations, and measurements he took of the site, including the lower or north garden and its architectural ornament (Fig. 32). Nothing in the notes indicates that Blomfield was aware the lower garden had been redesigned in the 1840s and the east court had been reworked in the 1850s: the wall connecting the

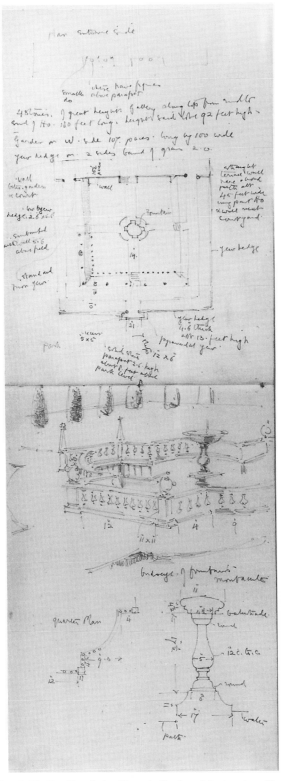

32. Reginald Blomfield, Details of the Formal Garden, Montacute, 1889. (Source: RIBA Library Drawings Collection.)

two corner pavilions was reinstated, a matching fountain placed in the center, and flower beds and Irish yews planted on either side of the garden walks running alongside the terrace and garden walls.[27] Blomfield was not the only one to be misled. When *Country Life* profiled the house in 1898, no mention was made of the nineteenth-century renovations. Architect H. Inigo Triggs began his survey of formal gardens, published in 1902, with Montacute and claimed it "remains to-day in a practically unaltered state."[28] This should not suggest, however, that Blomfield was sloppy in his research. He was aware, for example, that the formal gardens at Arley Hall, built in the revivalist fervor of the 1840s, and Penshurst (Fig. 33), restored by George Devey in the nineteenth century to its early-eighteenth-century appearance, were modern. Two points should be noted here: garden history was in its infancy, and Blomfield was driven by a desire to furnish the style that he came to espouse with historical legitimacy.

In his treatise *The Formal Garden of England*, Blomfield clearly used the past for such ends, referencing historical examples to construct an English tradition in formal garden design. Through his history, he disengaged the formal garden from its frequent association with Italy, justified his aesthetic, and instructed others. He divided his account into roughly eight phases, beginning with the medieval period when enclosed formal gardens, typically executed in geometrical layouts with hedged or walled squares divided into quarters ornamented with knots or interlaced bands of vegetation, were attached to the residence. Decorative objects, such as fountains, statues, and heraldic devices, placed along walkways lured the promenader through the garden. Terraces along the house or mounts in the garden provided views out of the garden to the landscape beyond. This constituted the core of the English tradition onto which, according to Blomfield, layers of outside influence were lacquered.

In the second phase of development, in the sixteenth century, English gardens were "plainly inspired by Italian examples," Blomfield admitted, but one could not "import an exotic style wholesale into the midst of a people with a strong indigenous tradition."[29] In his discussion, Blomfield eschewed reference to extant examples of Italian work and instead relied on ancient Roman Pliny's account of his gardens, which he argued had inspired Italian Renaissance examples. Glossing over the significance of Italian designs shored up Blomfield's thesis that the formal garden constituted a uniquely English tradition. Indeed, he argued as much in his discussion of the sixteenth-century garden. Referring to Francis Bacon's essay "Of Gardens," Blomfield insisted,

> the only specific importations from Italy appear to have been the use of
> terraces and balustrades and great flights of stairs, and the free use of
> statuary; a habit of mythological allusion in various parts of the garden;
> and the practice of clipping trees into various shapes and distributing

PENSHURST PLACE : KENT : A MODERN GARDEN

33. F. Inigo Thomas, "Penshurst Place: Kent: A Modern Garden," from Reginald Blomfield, *The Formal Garden*, London, 1901. (Source: Dumbarton Oaks, Studies in Landscape Architecture, Photo Archive.)

> them symmetrically. The alleys, green walks, and covered walks . . . the arbours, the knots or figures, labyrinths and mazes, the conduits, tanks, and fountains, and particularly, the enclosing walls and definite boundary lines, were only the development of features which had existed already in the mediaeval garden.[30]

Other features described by Bacon, such as "little Figures with broad plates of round coloured glasse gilt for the sunne to play upon," were dismissed by Blomfield for their extravagance. "Caprices of this sort obtained no permanent hold in England," he explained, because "the national tradition was too sober to accept them."[31] Blomfield thus continued to build a case for a national tradition built on simple geometric designs with little ornamentation. Echoing arguments made by proponents of cottage gardens, Blomfield insisted simplicity was a leitmotif of the authentic English tradition.

In tracing the history of the English formal garden into the early seventeenth century, a period of dynamic interaction between England and Europe, Blomfield reiterated the presence of the core tradition he had already identified: "the distinction of all these earlier seventeenth-century garden plans is the extreme simplicity of their arrangement."[32] These plans, he pointedly explained, were the product of architects, who had been responsible for garden design up until the eighteenth century (and should, he implied, be restored to this function). Blomfield mentioned such figures as Isaac de Caus, Inigo Jones, and André Mollet (who did much to introduce a new vocabulary based on Italian and French models into English garden design), but downplayed their influence by failing to draw any significance from their designs. Turning to the period from the Civil War to the Restoration, Blomfield claimed that little was accomplished, save for John Evelyn's treatises.

With the Restoration, the fifth phase in Blomfield's history, garden design was reinvigorated largely through the Francophile interests of Charles II, who helped initiate a fashion for the designs of André Le Nôtre, perhaps best known for Versailles. Le Nôtre's predilection for long avenues, broad plats of grass, and reflecting canals was picked up in English gardens, albeit on a smaller scale, as at Hampton Court and Melbourne.[33] But in Le Nôtre, Blomfield also found seeds of the coming decline of the formal garden. Grand avenues drew designers' atten-

34. F. Inigo Thomas, "Topiary Work at Levens Hall: Westmoreland," from Reginald Blomfield, *The Formal Garden*, London, 1901. (Source: Dumbarton Oaks, Studies in Landscape Architecture, Photo Archive.)

LANDSCAPE GARDENING.

Mr. Intrim D. Scoop. "Well now, that's what I call Real Art!"

35. "Landscape Gardening," from *Punch*, January 28, 1903. (Source: Mary Couts Burnet Library, Texas Christian University.)

tion away from the garden proper to the parkland beyond and invited gardeners "to manipulate the face of an entire countryside."[34]

With the installation of William and Mary came the sixth phase, which incorporated the Dutch tradition of elaborate parterres, statuary, waterworks, and trimmed plant material (Fig. 34). Although Blomfield espoused the use of topiary and insisted it had become popular in England because of a prexisting tradition of pleaching and trimming vegetation, he observed that topiary contributed to the further decline of the formal garden as "the clipping of yew and box trees was carried to an excess that made it an easy prey for the sarcasm of Pope in the following century."[35] Yet Blomfield's contemporaries admired topiaries, which were extremely labor intensive, perceiving them as signifiers of wealth and status (Fig. 35).

Returning to Blomfield's history, he explained that formal designs persisted into the early eighteenth century largely through London and Wise, who brought French and Dutch ideas to England. The final decline of the formal garden came in the mid-eighteenth century with the birth of the landscape garden, when designers lost the "fundamental principle of the relation between the garden and the house . . . though that principle had been accepted as a matter of course throughout all the greatest periods of English art."[36]

The eighteenth-century landscape garden was the bane of Blomfield's existence. Slipping from his previous empirical tone, he launched a direct attack on this style. He disputed Joseph Addison's assertion that nature is the measure of any work of art. He found the work of William Kent duplicitous for destroying nature in order to emulate nature, and he ridiculed Kent's efforts at natural allusion by jesting "he might as well have nailed stuffed nightingales to the boughs."[37] The aphorism "Kent leapt the fence and saw that all nature was a garden" was claptrap. Gaining steam, he charged that Capability Brown "took the judicious line that knowledge hampered originality."[38] He thus demolished the reader's perception that the landscape garden had the sole proprietary claim to the title of English garden.

Blomfield's treatment of the nineteenth century was equally acerbic. Humphry Repton, who did much to reinvigorate formal garden design in the early nineteenth century, was dismissed with the offhand comment that he and other professors of landscape gardening "between them destroyed some of the finest gardens in England."[39] Sir Charles Barry, who championed Italianate architectural garden design at midcentury, was said to "show a misapprehension of the intention of the formal garden as a matter of design," because, according to Blomfield, he advocated a gradual transition from the garden to the parkland, whereas in Blomfield's opinion, "there should be no question where the garden ends."[40] In terms of recent design, the only sites that earned the author's praise were the revivalist gardens of Penshurst and Arley, and the only contemporary designers he found worthy were George Devey (associated with Penshurst) (Fig. 33) and William Eden Nesfield (son of William Andrews Nesfield and partner with Richard Norman Shaw).

On the whole, Blomfield's book was held together by a conceptual framework which stipulated that architecture reflects the key characteristics of the peoples who construct it. This idea was not new to garden design; Loudon had embraced this principle in his *Encyclopedia,* and, indeed, at the time Loudon was writing, in the early nineteenth century, numerous participants in the romantic revolution held to the notion that an intrinsic relationship among national identity, art forms, and their historical moment existed. This belief gained sway as the nineteenth century advanced; in 1842 Thomas Leverton Donaldson, for example, asserted in the context of a series of university lectures on architecture that "no architect can fully appreciate any style of art, who knows not the history of the country, and the habits of thought, the intelligence, and customs of the nation."[41] Thus, when Blomfield asserted that "a garden is perhaps the most legible evidence of national character. In it may be seen traces of its reticence or van-ity, of its love of soberness or of its passion for display, of its patient ingenuity or of its loose thought and carelessness of execution," he was folding garden design into a well-established discourse.

To support his point with regard to the relationship between national character and garden design, Blomfield cited the contrasting examples of Montacute and Versailles: "The quiet lawns of Montacute," he insisted, "are as eloquent of the well-ordered life of an English gentleman as the gardens of Versailles of the fatuous ambition of Louis Quatorze."[42] The conclusion to *A History of Renaissance Architecture in England, 1500–1800* (1897) developed more fully the architect's theory that "the art of the English people can only be understood by the help of some insight into the past history and character of the English people themselves."[43] Blomfield ascribed this character or "instinctive preferences" to racial origins.[44] More specifically, he argued that the Saxons, although defeated by the Normans who stamped the countryside with their Romanesque architecture, "in the long run gave to English art its peculiar bias." It is to the Saxons that he attributed a "simplicity of taste and directness of purpose" that shaped the taste for "sober dignity" throughout English architecture.[45] Thus an Englishman could not fully "get in touch with" the architecture of countries such as Spain or France, where "one finds a certain expansiveness, an irresistible impulse to let himself go," as it failed to correspond with his appreciation for "self repression" and "sanity and reticence in art."[46] The latter constituted the sense of tradition in English architecture according to Blomfield, and he closed his book with a pessimistic assessment of whether this sense of tradition could be recovered in the modern age. The Gothic revival had failed to do so, he claimed, because of its excesses and capriciousness. Without reinforcement of tradition, Blomfield warned, "distinctions of national character" might disappear in the face of an international diaspora.[47]

Blomfield's assumptions with regard to ethnicity seem problematic today, but we should regard them seriously as an important index of cultural arguments made at the turn of the century. Theories that racial or ethnic background guided behavior gained strength with backing of supposedly irrefutable scientific findings in anatomy, anthropology, ethnology, natural history/science, and history. The cosmopolitanism of modernity and the ever-expanding marketplace led many to search for untainted examples of national characteristics, which were typically located in the past.[48] In seeking to reinstate a strong sense of Englishness, many turned to the sixteenth and seventeenth centuries, popularly associated with the reign of Queen Elizabeth and nostalgically remembered as a time of nation building; it was then, it was believed, that a strong domestic sensibility, based on the harmonious workplace culture fostered by guilds, enabled the country to defend its interests with impunity. In historian J. A. Froude's analysis, the triumph of Elizabeth over her foreign enemies was made all the more poignant by his belief that present-day England faced potential social and political decline caused by the immoral effects of capitalism and a lessening appreciation of the benefits of Empire.[49]

The formal garden, as figured in Blomfield's account, was an English tradition rooted in the Elizabethan past and expressed the moral values of the age in its prizing of sobriety, reticence, and order. It, as opposed to the natural garden, was the true English garden and thus should be called on in the quest to reform garden design. Blomfield's version of history gave both authority and authenticity to the style of design he and his colleagues were to practice in coming decades. Yet we should remember that the formal garden, like the cottage garden, was largely an invented tradition. It arose in a particular moment of perceived cultural crisis and was intended to reverse the supposed decline in the national arts, to reinvigorate English values and character, and to create a sense of community that could be sustained on the national level, legitimated and strengthened through its connectedness to the past. In the conclusion to his treatise, Blomfield summed up the need for the formal garden, hinging his argument on his readers' desire to shore up an implicitly diminishing sense of Englishness:

> It is nothing to us that the French did this or the Italians did that; the point is, what has been done in England, what has been loved here, by us and by those before us. The best English tradition has always been on the side of refinement and reserve – not the obvious beauty of the south, but the charm and tenderness, the inexpressible sweetness of faces that fill the memory like half-remembered music. This is the feeling that one would wish to see realised in the garden again, not the coarse facility that overwhelms with its astonishing cleverness, but the delicate touch of the artist, the finer scholarship which loves the past and holds thereby the key to its meaning.[50]

Blomfield's theory that the formal garden constituted the English tradition in garden design was shared by many of his colleagues. F. Inigo Thomas articulated a like argument in the context of explaining why Sir Charles Barry's gardens did not constitute the formal garden tradition Thomas hoped to revive:

> Sir Charles Barry made one or two formal arrangements to the houses he built, but they were a good deal borrowed from Italian instances, and not in all in harmony with English traditions. . . . There is a popular superstition that all formal gardens in England were either Italian or Dutch. . . . Now Italy, no doubt, supplied us with many ideas on this subject, as she did in architecture, but the buildings that rose under Italian influence in Tudor times were so English in feeling that we have to call them "Elizabethan." And so it is with gardens, the English tradition coming out so strongly as to render them markedly different from Italian examples.[51]

Little over a decade later, Sir George Sitwell attempted to refute Thomas by claiming that the revival he and Blomfield had spearheaded "falls short of the great examples of the Italian Renaissance" and by insisting that Englanders should turn to Italy for lessons. But arguments to the contrary mounted at the turn of the century.[52] J. D. Sedding's *Garden-Craft Old and New* (1891) was more sympathetic to Sitwell's position in that he readily recognized the influence of France and Italy on English gardens; nonetheless, he argued in favor of an English tradition of garden design, subscribing to the belief that "The character of the scenery of a country, the section of the land generally, no less than the taste of the people who dwell in it, prescribes the style of the type of garden."[53] With respect to taste and scenery, the English were defined by a love of nature, which reflected an inherent appreciation of liberty and freedom.[54] Ironically, Sedding insisted that this love of nature and freedom dictated a formal garden, in which nature was idealized and transformed by art, as opposed to a landscape garden, in which nature was wild and barbaric.[55] Like Blomfield, he held that English formal gardens were distinguished from European ones by their simplicity and disavowal of overt public display, which again expressed an English appreciation for rusticity and nature:

> For an English garden is at once stately and homely – homely before all things. . . . The convention is broad, dignified, quiet, homogenous, suiting alike the characteristics of the country and of the people for whom it is made. Compared with this, the foreign garden . . . is overwrought, too full.[56]

The formal garden also reflected the nation's virtues because of its sixteenth-century roots. Like Froude, Sedding believed the sixteenth century had witnessed the "making of England" and, therefore, that the gardens of this time were "the handiwork of the makers of England, and should bear the marks of heros."[57] Like others of the period, Sedding painted an idealized image of this age, neglecting inequalities of power associated with feudalism in favor of an image of a golden age based on the chivalry of knights.[58]

The modern age, Sedding bemoaned, had lost touch with this vibrant and instructive past, but it could be made to live again by building formal gardens.[59] Once built, the garden could inculcate "kindly social virtues." Even capitalistic pursuit of profit could be forgotten:

> Here [in the garden] friend Smith, caught by its nameless charm, will drop his brassy gabble and dare to be idealistic; and Jones, forgetful of his main chance and "bulls" and "bears" will throw the rein to his sweeter self, and reveal that latent electation of soul and tendency to romance known only to his wife![60]

The formal garden formed a necessary counter to modern existence: "its tranquil grace is a boon of unspeakable value to people doomed to pass their working-hours in the hustle of city-life."[61] The seclusion of the formal garden was secured largely by its enclosed character and clearly demarcated boundaries that provided a screen and buffer from the outside world (Fig. 36). Hedges helped "to conceal villadom and the hulking paper-factory beyond."[62]

Sedding's account firmly placed the garden at the center of an ideal home, as described by the rhetoric of Victorian domesticity, and linked the sense of privacy, morality, and purity prized in Victorian domesticity to reviving the styles of the sixteenth and seventeenth centuries. But certainly Sedding was not the first designer to tie the manner of gardening he espoused to creating a space that could be a haven from the rough and tumble marketplace. Earlier in the century, Humphry Repton, in his *Fragments on the Theory and Practice of Landscape Gardening* (1816), for example, had explained to readers how he "improved" his cottage, set in the midst of the turnpike village of Hare, by appropriating land from the adjacent common and then planting hedges, bushes, and flower beds that allowed him "to control the appearance of the village." From his "improved" vantage point, nearby shops appeared less commercial (the displayed goods were hidden by roses entwined on a planter), traffic on the roadways was obscured (by hedges, shrubbery, and flowering vines), and Hare became a scenic backdrop. The cottage thus fulfilled its promise as Repton's retreat "from the pomp of palaces, the elegancies of fashion, or the allurements of dissipation."[63] The notion that home should be a "retreat from industry" cut across modern industrialized nations. The late-nineteenth-century development of the suburbs, featuring single-family detached dwellings, in nations including the United States and Germany, rested on the belief that home should be separate from the public sphere of business, industry, and debauched entertainment.[64]

Attention paid to arts of the home in the nineteenth century was a logical by-product of an ongoing critique of contemporary society as it was shaping up under the impact of capitalism. Sedding, like many of his contemporaries, positioned the garden as both antithetical and an ameliorating counterbalance to the modern condition. William Morris's utopian fantasy *News from Nowhere* (1890) also used the motif of the garden to critique the alienation of the individual by industry and urbanism. In this tract, Morris imagined a future – twenty-first-century England – that is an idealized recreation of the past – fourteenth-century England, nostalgically remembered as a golden age in which men and women lived in harmony with each other and nature and were joined together in pursuit of beauty. The hero of the novel goes to sleep one night in a western suburb of London and awakens the next morning to find that it is now 2003 and along the

36. W. R. Lethaby, "A Garden Enclosed, 1889," from J. D. Sedding, *Garden-Craft Old and New*, London, 1891. (Source: Dumbarton Oaks, Studies in Landscape Architecture, Photo Archive.)

Thames, instead of "soapworks with their smoke-vomiting chimneys" were lines of "very pretty houses, low and not large, standing back a little way from the river. . . . There was a continuous garden in front of them, going down to the water's edge."[65]

Fellow guild member Walter Crane offered his interpretation of the formal garden as a vehicle to the romanticized past in *A Floral Fantasy in an Old English Garden* (1899). The reader is drawn into the story of a modern Englishman who suddenly finds himself imaginatively transported to the bygone days of knights, squires, and dames. The formal garden (Fig. 37) – "with its peacock hedges of yew/ . . . [and] formal knot and clipt thicket, /And smooth green sward so fair to see" – becomes the setting for this medievalizing fantasy world where old-fashioned flowers come to life.[66] Through a formal garden, Crane's text implied, home owners could escape the chaotic world of modern existence for a world ordered by principles of art and architecture and decorated with the grace of flowers. These sentiments could be carried over into the interior of the home with Crane's wallpapers (Fig. 38). Around the turn of the century, for example, Crane created "The Formal Garden" pattern for the firm of Messrs. Jeffrey, of Islington, featuring key decorative elements – hedges, old-fashioned flower borders, and smooth lawns – prescribed by Sedding and Blomfield.[67]

In making a case for the formal garden in the modern age, architects were both implicitly and explicitly condemning the natural or wild garden. Yet, although treatises often insisted on differences between the two forms of design, significant similarities marked both. Both Blomfield and Sedding, with their attention to extant examples of formal gardens, were working within the developing paradigm of elevating local practices to national models of good design. Like Robinson, they also reinforced the transmutation of the southern metaphor – the rural, archaizing landscape associated with the southern counties – into the national metaphor, displacing the modern landscapes of industrialization and urbanization. And all were convinced that problems of the present could be solved by recourse to the past.

Designing the Formal Garden

The history constructed by Blomfield and Sedding, above all, established key principles governing the design of the formal garden. A generally shared aesthetic emerges from reading across texts on formal garden design written by members of the Art Workers Guild. As is to be expected, these authors advocated that design of the garden should be the purview of the architect as opposed to the landscape designer. Establishing their right to design gardens was a crucial

37. Walter Crane, "The Old English Garden," *Floral Fantasy in an Old English Garden*, London, 1899. (Source: Dumbarton Oaks, Studies in Landscape Architecture, Photo Archive.)

38. Walter Crane, *The Formal Garden*, c. 1904. (Source: V & A Picture Library.)

issue for these architects and one not easily resolved because a schism had developed between garden designers claiming professional affiliation with architecture and those who considered themselves landscape gardeners (and, therefore, eschewed buildings and focused on gardens). Many landscape gardeners, including William Robinson, viewed architects with suspicion, seeing them as interlopers who threatened their livelihood and who had little intuitive understanding of nature and landscape design. In turn, a number of architects accused landscape gardeners of inadequate formal training and knowledge of design principles.

Part of the conflict lay in the common procedure for building a new house and garden whereby the house was built first and the garden laid out afterward in accordance with points of view established by the house. Landscape designer Henry Ernest Milner, in 1897, spoke out publicly against this practice and recommended that the "landscape gardener be first called in to lay out the site, and when he has concluded his labours the Architect may be allowed to design the house, fitting his building to the design of the garden."[68] It takes little imagination to foresee how either process could give rise to heated exchanges between architect and landscape gardener. Thomas Mawson, in his treatise *The Art and Craft of Garden Making* (first published 1900), attempted to diminish wrangling between landscape gardeners and architects and he sized up the problem this way:

> Having, in the course of an extensive practice, had considerable oppor-
> tunities for studying gardens, more especially garden design in its rela-
> tion to the house and its architectural character, I have realised the fact
> that one must be a complement of the other. I can therefore, sympa-
> thise, on the one hand, with those architects who claim the right to
> design the setting or garden frame to the house they have designed,
> and, on the other, with those landscape gardeners who have felt, more
> especially in the later years of their practice, that to ensure a successful
> garden it is necessary that the designer have some say in the arrange-
> ment and disposal of the house on the site, and also in the selection of
> the site itself. . . . By giving in a handy form some of the experience
> gained in the special department of garden design, I venture to hope
> that some of the difficulties, which now face architects who essay to
> design the gardens, will be considerably lessened. If I fail in this, I still
> hope to show that garden designers are much more in sympathy with
> architectural ideals than recent writers would have us suppose.[69]

The most logical solution to this problem – professionalization of the design of gardens and landscapes (with an accompanying rhetoric that established those practices to be associated with the profession) – did not occur in Great Britain until 1929 with the founding of the British Association of Garden Architects, shortly thereafter renamed the Institute of Landscape Architects, with Thomas Mawson as the first president. (By contrast, the American Society of Landscape Architects was founded in 1899.)

Members of the Art Workers Guild, when writing about landscape design, accordingly devoted most of their discussion to the relationship between house and garden, giving relatively little attention to plant material. Surrendering design of the garden to architects, they realized, might be objected to on the grounds that the architect would simply impose a predrawn plan on the site with little attention to the character of the place. They addressed this point by beginning most of their treatises with a discussion of how the architect should examine the site closely and consider how natural features could be used most wisely. Architect John Belcher instructed his audience that the first duty of the architect as garden designer was to study the *whole site* (not merely the little patch of ground on which the house is to be built). Its aspect, its prospect, the nature of the soil and variations of levels, its important trees or other special features, and then to turn them severally to advantage in giving that special character to the house which is at once recognised as appropriate to its place, and to no other.[70]

The formal garden thus promised to be in keeping with local traditions in true Arts and Crafts fashion.

The contribution of the architect was "to connect his building with the site, to tie it down to earth as it were, to throw out long tendril-like cords, to bind it lovingly to nature."[71] A key way to establish this relationship was through the terrace, which created an architectural transition zone between the house and the landscape. As Sedding explained, "to pitch your house down upon the grass with no architectural accessories about it, to link it to the soil, is to vulgarise it, to rob it of importance, to give it the look of a pastoral farm."[72] Designed in proportion to the house and typically composed of the same materials as the house, the terrace advanced the lines of the house into the landscape. Garden walls, balustrading, walks, and outbuildings also linked the house to its surroundings (Fig. 39).[73]

39. F. Inigo Thomas, "A Terraced Garden: Kingston House: Bradford-on-Avon," from Reginald Blomfield, *The Formal Garden*, London, 1901. (Source: Dumbarton Oaks, Studies in Landscape Architecture, Photo Archive.)

Positioning the garden relative to the house was thus central to design of the formal garden. E. S. Prior offered two options: either the house could be situated in the middle of the garden in a manner that reminded the visitor of a great hall with the house as the central ornament, or the garden could be treated as another room, or series of rooms, extending from the house.[74] The latter tended to prevail in discussions by guild architects; J. D. Sedding, for example, recommended that gardens

> should, if possible, lie towards the best parts of the house or towards the rooms most commonly in use by the family, and endeavour should be made to plant them so that to step from the house on to the terrace, or from the terrace to the various parts of the gardens, should only seem like going from one room to another.[75]

In either case, the house was an integral part of the design, and garden architects attributed the supposedly new recognition accorded the house in garden design to reforms in domestic architecture undertaken at the end of the nineteenth century. The improving spirit had not spread everywhere, they cautioned; and repeatedly they advised erecting high walls or hedges to block out the surrounding suburban landscape that did not accord with their aesthetic. Unlike the grand country-house owners of old, the guild's audience of small country-house owners could not afford to buy up the surrounding property. They were forced, as Prior instructed, to fence their gardens off from the outer world as "everything beyond the close circuit of one's own enclosure is at the mercy of the builder and threatened with the unseemly squalor of spreading suburbs, the vagaries of estate developers, and all the unblushing ambition of our architects."[76]

Here Prior touches on a central paradox of the back-to-the-land movement (as well as suburbia): by luring urbanites from the city with promises of the countryside as a place of relative tranquillity and isolation, back-to-the-landers destroyed what they desired most. Each home owner must create his or her own utopia with walls and hedges, as *Country Life* explained in an article on Shipton Court: "in the old days" the home owner may have wanted a direct view from the house to the nearby road or highway, but modern home owners "must shut out the world, buy up the right-of-way, plant out the railway, in a vain effort to forget that our treasure is in the city, and our hearts turning there also."[77]

Implementation of strict boundaries was essential to the overall layout of the formal garden. Most architects advocated that its internal space should also be strictly divided, with each section fulfilling a special function, like rooms of a house, so that, for example, the space for lawn tennis would not be confused with the area for flowers. The sense of an ordered division of space was to begin with the approach to the house itself. From the approach, one should enter an enclosed forecourt or courtyard, preferably regular in plan. On the garden side of the house, the motif of a square or some other geometric figure, such as an oblong or circle, was typically repeated in the overall design (Figs. 40, 41). This space would then be subdivided with respect to symmetry, simplicity, and balance.[78] Internal subdivisions could be achieved through hedges or straight-edged walks and alleys. The fact that these roomlike spaces situated along strongly marked axes were often juxtaposed with a terrace or elevated viewing platform might suggest the whole garden would be revealed or known at once; but architects fought this tendency and advocated that the layout of features and placement of walks be such that when moving through the garden's sequence of rooms the contents of the next space would be only hinted at, and the full view occluded.[79]

To ornament internal subdivisions, architects turned to water features, statues, sundials, and flowers, the latter arranged in demarcated beds to maintain the desired sense of order. Most architects preferred plain flower beds as compared to elaborate parterres of the sixteenth and seventeenth centuries; Blomfield, for example, drew a lesson from the eighteenth century's repudiation of the formal garden and warned readers away from extravagant knot or broidery patterns formed with inorganic materials, preferring simple arrangements of grass and flowers.[80] The choice of flowers or how they should be displayed within the beds was even more vaguely described, but the architects nearly uniformly recommended old-fashioned or native specimens in contrast to hybrids or exotics used in bedded-out or wild gardens. To frame flower beds, they recommended hedges: when cut low these marked the outline of beds, when taller they also provided shelter for plants and could act as a backdrop of green against which the bright blooms would stand out. Trim hedges and topiary became hallmarks for the formal garden: they signified artfulness and symbolized disdain for the natural beauty of plants associated with the wild or natural garden. To enhance the garden, architects also turned to garden buildings that could house equipment and/or provide shelter. Most of the architects provided surprisingly little discussion of the actual construction of garden buildings, but E. S. Prior instructed readers to "view commercial wares with suspicion," in particular "the show-devices of the horticulture firms," because of their supposedly inherent vulgarity, which did not accord with principles of good design set forth by the guild.

The process of designing a formal garden could be long, elaborate, and expensive (despite architects' protests to the contrary). F. Inigo Thomas, for example, would first assess the site and then prepare a series of oil sketches. Once he had

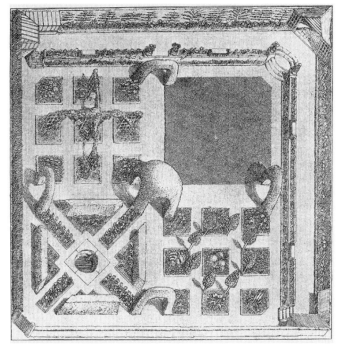

40. "Square Flower Garden," from E. S. Prior, "Gardening-Making II– The Conditions of Practice," *The Studio,* 1900. (Source: This item is reproduced with permission of *The Huntington Library, San Marino, California.*)

the full picture in mind, he prepared a survey of the grounds, followed by a small-scale drawing of the whole. Aware of the ephemerality of garden plans and concerned to ensure his place in history, Thomas would have these drawings mounted and framed "for hanging in the house as a guide to the next generation in carrying on the scheme" (Fig. 42).[81] To derive their plans, architects often resorted to illustrated source material, such as *Country Life,* or put together source collections themselves: Mervyn Macartney published a collection of late-seventeenth- and early-eighteenth-century views of formal gardens, and Harry Inigo Triggs provided measured drawings and brief descriptions of historic formal gardens in *Formal Gardens in England and Scotland* (1902).[82]

New Gardens in the Old Style

Good examples of Thomas's drawings are associated with Athelhampton, near Puddleton, Dorchester, where the architect constructed a "new garden in the old

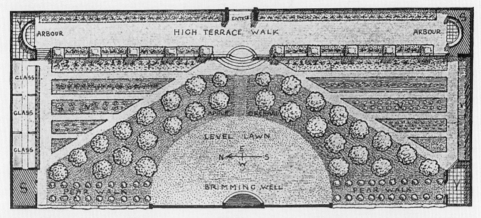

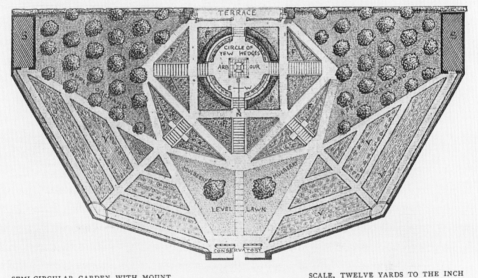

41. "Oblong Garden and Semi-Circular Garden with Mount," from E. S. Prior, "Gardening-Making II– The Conditions of Practice," *The Studio,* 1900. (Source: This item is reproduced with permission of *The Huntington Library, San Marino, California.*)

style."[83] Thomas worked there in the early 1890s for Alfred Cart de Lafontaine, the new owner of the largely sixteenth-century house. Lafontaine came from London and "purchased all of it that money could buy, to enjoy the retirement and old-world charm of the Dorsetshire country," at a time "when all accessible parts of England were being searched for ancient homes for those who find in a newly-built country house something garish and disturbing."[84] He represented the new breed of country-house owners who emerged during the last quarter of the nineteenth century. By this time the influence of landed wealth was declining sharply in favor of incomes earned in the city. In the 1840s and 1850s, squires constituted 38 percent and peers 16 percent of new house construction; after the turn of the century the two groups combined represented only 8 percent, whereas manufacturers ordered 38 percent of total construction, with an additional 19 percent coming from the professional classes; 13 percent was built by bankers, and those earning money through food, drink, and groceries contributed another 13 percent in construction.[85] The pattern of country-house building followed the general shift in income, when "for the first time in history, non-landed incomes and wealth had begun to overtake land alone as the main source of economic power."[86] The new class of country-house owners also availed itself of older properties put on the market initially because of the agricultural depression and, after 1911, because of new taxes on land and the raising of death duties. The "People's Budget" taxes brought about the "greatest permanent transfer of land since the dissolution of the monasteries" when the landed classes liquidated assets that proved no longer profitable or sustainable.[87] Ironically, just when architects and garden designers were seeking to recover local traditions, the sense of localness was disappearing as the traditional rural hierarchy eroded with changes in land ownership.

New country-house owners viewed their relationship to the countryside very differently from their predecessors. They "did not want to establish themselves as full fledged landed proprietors. They regarded the country as a place for rest and repose, where money was spent not made, and they were fully contented with the amenities of rural living – riding, hunting, shooting and entertaining."[88] To this list we should add gardening – not physically back-breaking work, which was typically executed by relatively cheap rural labor – but planning the design of the space, perhaps some light tasks of planting and maintenance, and using the garden for recreation and entertainment. By moving to the countryside, with its manor houses, country houses, and old castles, many of these new country-house owners felt they were participating in what was increasingly regarded as a national heritage.

The appeal of country life, Thomas understood, fueled his career. In an 1896 lecture he explained how the spread of the railways with the attendant erection of "dreary villadom," along with the speed and anonymity of "our huge metropolis," led to the pursuit of rural living and, more importantly, a desire for older houses and gardens that could make the values of the past, such as 'honest sentiment' live again.[89] Acquisition of older country houses became ever more fevered with the accessibility permitted by the introduction of the motor car:

> Within a radius of forty miles of every large town in England every Tudor or Georgian manor house stands to-day at a premium. They are snapped up by those who rush up to town and back in their motor cars from the time of the blossoming of the daffodil to the ripening of the nut. It may indeed be said that whilst the country poor are daily turning their faces townwards, the city man has his set towards the country.[90]

119

When Lafontaine purchased Athelhampton, the grounds were in disrepair, providing Thomas a blank slate. The only significant limitation he faced was the house sat in a hollow that denied construction of the terrace platform around the house that most guild architects recommended. Nevertheless, he was able to link the house to the gardens (Fig. 43) through three long axial lines of symmetry, adopting a strategy he observed in early-eighteenth-century prints of English Renaissance gardens:

> One [line] from the south garden gate in the foreground catches the reflection of the house in the long pool, passes through the doorway in the south front, and out into the court beyond; thence between the piers that are just visible it is continued down the centre of the tennis lawn, and across the pools at the end to a sculptured figure in the yew hedge by the river. Another line, centering with the window in the left wing, passes down the rose garden and through the circular coronet to a niche fountain between the two arches in the foreground. The third is taken from a summer-house in the grove to the right, across the south garden, through the coronet, and up a flight of steps, with a wrought iron gate, to the sunk garden. Here it catches the fountain and continues up another flight of steps to end in a stone seat that projects from the back of the terrace.[91]

The garden was generally executed as Thomas described with the exception of the tennis lawn above the house, statues in the great court, and pyramidal yews in the private garden shown on the perspective view; missing also were the maze and flower beds between the house and "coronet." The grounds today display the roomlike subdivision favored by the guild architects, with a wall circumscribing the entire complex and each clearly demarcated compartment devoted to a different feature or function: (from south to north) an elevated terrace anchored

42. F. Inigo Thomas, Plan of Athelhampton, c. 1891. (Source: Courtesy of R. G. Cooke, Athelhampton House & Gardens.)

by two garden houses, a great court with rose beds and pyramidal yews (that have since overgrown their original shape and forced out the roses) around a fountain (Plate III), the "coronet," and the large rectangular pool garden, called the private garden or green court.

Each feature is set off from its neighbor by enclosures and a gradual descent in level. Thomas's vistas permit views from one space to the next, but narrow openings ensure that the visitor can never see the entire adjacent room; anticipation therefore builds as one moves through the garden. The sequencing of room-like enclosures also endows the site with an additive quality, as though each compartment reflected a different generation of building. As Robert Williams has observed, this imparted authenticity to the site: "various parts of the garden have a cumulative effect on the visitor [so that] the "new garden in the old style" would appear genuinely old, and to have been adjusted, enlarged, altered or refashioned over the centuries."[92]

The garden, however, never threatens to fragment into disparate units as geometrical order pertains throughout. Rectangles, squares, and circles are repeated from one space to the next and even the plants adhere to the straight line.

Flowers are set in rectilinear beds and yews are trimmed into pyramidal shapes akin to those at Brickwall, East Sussex, a seventeenth-century house and garden greatly admired by Blomfield and featured in his articles and books (Fig. 44). The use of local stone throughout also unifies the site. Reportedly 40,000 tons of Ham Hill stone were brought to the site to construct the garden terrace and walls. The orange-tinted stone is indigenous and used conspicuously in houses in this area, most notably Montacute, which provided an important model for Thomas. Roughcast treatment of the stone in some areas, as in pool edging and walls, also created a sense of age, as though time had eroded these surfaces; this sensation is reinforced by introduction of creeping, clinging plants, such as clematis, roses, and honeysuckle, that embrace and further naturalize the stone as a timeless part of the landscape (Fig. 45).

&ʃ 121

  In the design of many of these stone elements, Thomas set up a dialogue between Athelhampton and the formal gardens of the past, especially those cited by Blomfield and himself in *The Formal Garden in England*. Obelisk finials, for example, are found both in the terrace balustrading and the coronet at Athel-

43. F. Inigo Thomas, "Example of Old House as Central Feature of a Garden Design [Athel-hampton]," from E. S. Prior, "Garden Making," *The Studio,* 1900. (Source: This item is repro-duced with permission of *The Huntington Library, San Marino, California.*)

44. Reginald Blomfield and F. Inigo Thomas, "The Old Gardens at Brickwall Near Northiam: Sussex," from Reginald Blomfield, *The Formal Garden,* London, 1901. (Source: Dumbarton Oaks, Studies in Landscape Architecture, Photo Archive.)

45. "A Fountain," "Country Homes, Gardens Old & New, Athelhampton Hall, Dorchester, The Seat of A. C. LaFontaine," *Country Life,* September 2, 1899. (Source: Country Life Picture Library.)

46. East Court, Montacute, 1993. (Source: Author's photograph.)

hampton and the garden wall at Montacute (Fig. 46). The notion of concluding the terrace with two pavilions is also carried out at Montacute as are the centrally placed fountains. Through a vocabulary constituted by materials and designs that signified the past, localness, and Englishness, Thomas arrived at a garden that would be read as the appropriate accompaniment to the house.

Creation of "new old" gardens attracted some critics, largely for the false sense of authenticity the architects created. Calling for a more balanced treatment of past and present, an essay in *The Times* lamented "the construction of gardens with a ready-made atmosphere of antiquity," contending that it had been carried too far. They dismissed "the use of old building materials, the planting of hedges of well-grown yew and purchasable topiary works, the affecting of box edges and sundials and 'old-fashioned' flowers" as clever counterfeits that could not deceive the truly knowledgeable and that would not stand the test of time.[93] In 1909 Thomas Mawson found himself caught in just such a backlash when he ventured what Robert Williams has described as "one of the most ambitious attempts at recovering time past by means of an atmospheric accretion" at Rushton Hall,

47. "The West Front," from T., "Country Homes, Gardens Old & New, Rotherfield Hall, Sussex, The Seat of Sir Lindsay-Hogg, Bt.," *Country Life,* August 14, 1909. (Source: Country Life Picture Library.)

intended to be a new old garden in the manner of Thomas and Blomfield.[94] In his memoir, Mawson described how he worked to create a garden in sympathy with the Jacobean house by erecting terraces, using rough stones to imitate effects of age, leaving chinks in stone walls, and knocking off corners of paving stones to allow gaps for plants. As a result, the garden appeared "mellowed and weather-stained, promising in a year or two to be quite in keeping with the ancient Hall itself."[95] Unfortunately, the client, a wealthy American, was not so pleased and saw Mawson's illusions of great age as defects and attempts to shortchange him and took the case to arbitration, which the architect lost.

Nonetheless, Thomas, Blomfield, and other guild members devoted significant portions of their professional careers to new gardens in the old style. Examples are plentiful. For Thomas, Athelhampton created a pattern he repeated for subsequent sites, such as Barrow Court (Somerset) for H. Martin Gibbs, Chantmarle (Dorset) for F. E. Savile, and Rotherfield Hall (Sussex) for Lindsay-Hogg.[96] With respect to the latter, the house is situated on a terrace with stairs, akin to those at nearby Kingston House, leading to a parterre garden that overlooks the lower lawn (Fig. 47). The layout is on axis to the house, with a strong central line

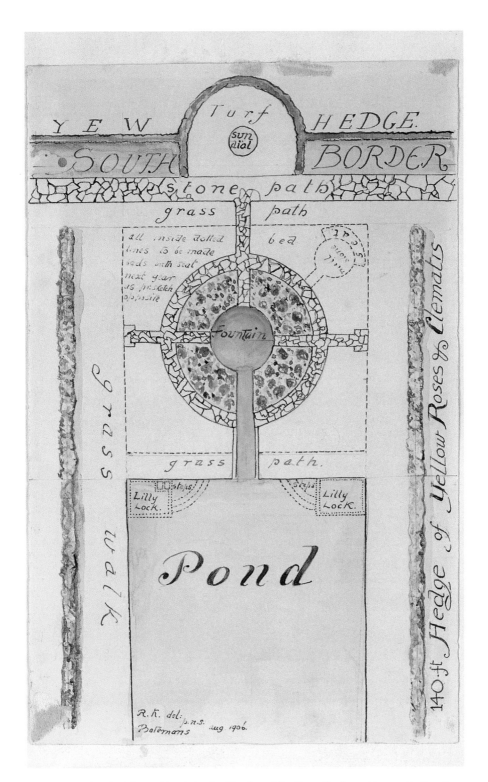

PLATE I. Rudyard Kipling, "Sketch for the Planting of the Rose Garden at Bateman's, East Sussex," 1906. (Source: National Trust; Kipling Collection. National Trust Photographic Library/Angelo Hornak.)

PLATE II. Helen Allingham, *Unstead Farm, Godalming,* n.d. (Source: © Christie's Images New York.)

PLATE III. View from South Terrace, Athelhampton, 1998. (Source: Author's photograph.)

PLATE IV. Munstead Wood from the Heath Garden, 1998. (Source: Author's photograph.)

PLATE V. Herbert Cowley, Center Portion of Hardy Flower Border, Munstead Wood, c. 1910. (Source: Country Life Picture Library.)

PLATE VI. Garden Court, Goddards, 1998. (Source: Author's photograph.)

PLATE VII. Wild Garden, Upton Grey, 1998. (Source: Author's photograph.)

PLATE VIII. Great Plat, Hestercombe, 1994. (Source: Author's photograph.)

of symmetry, and changes in level demarcate different garden spaces. *Country Life* praised the gardens for their simplicity and reserve – those very qualities that Blomfield sought in design and claimed as uniquely English – as well as their evocation, without exacting replication, of features of the English Renaissance.[97]

Some of these same principles can be seen in Blomfield's designs for Caythorpe Court (Fig. 48). Unlike gardens discussed previously, this one was for a new house, built in emulation of seventeenth-century Lincolnshire vernacular practices.[98] The house was erected in 1899 for new wealth seeking old roots: Edgar Lubbock, managing director of Whitbread's brewery, a director of the Bank of England, and master of the Blankney Foxhounds. He chose a site on a hill overlooking the countryside near the Belvoir and Blankney hunting grounds and intended the house to be used as a hunting lodge. A walled forecourt of dry rubble stone with dressed coping, balustrades, and ball finials leads to the house, composed of the same local Ancaster stone, also seen in the nearby fourteenth-century St. Vincent's Church.

125

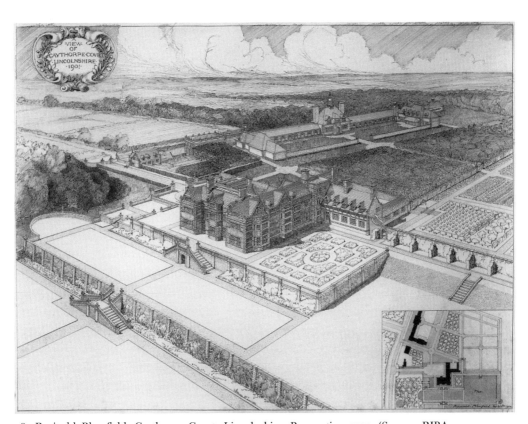

48. Reginald Blomfield, Caythorpe Court, Lincolnshire, Perspective, 1901. (Source: RIBA Library Drawings Collection.)

The garden takes its cues from the house. It is composed of three descending terraces placed around the house like a skirt. These required substantial buttressing at the western end so the second and most substantial terrace juts out into the park landscape. The symmetrical garden facade pivots on a central bay window that provides the main axis for the terraces and the alignment for the terrace stairs. These steps employ the same combination of dry stone with dressed balustrades and ball finials found in the forecourt; dry stone is also used for the terrace platform and the walled flower garden to the east of the house. Each of the three projecting bays of the garden facade features a rectangular window topped by a half circle, a form reused for the layout of the second terrace with the hemisphere located to the west, like the apse of a church, and the rectangle or basilica of lawn (used for tennis) running parallel to the house.

At Godinton (Fig. 49), Blomfield eschewed the strongly marked axes of Caythorpe and the commanding platforms that endowed the site with perhaps more grandeur than expected of a hunting lodge. Instead he employed the concept of a garden as a series of rooms. Property of the Toke family, rural Kent squires, Godinton had been sold to George Ashley Dodd in 1895. The structure dated from the fourteenth century but had been substantially enlarged and renovated in succeeding centuries; extensive improvements had taken place in the 1630s, and the house is now regarded as chiefly seventeenth century. For the garden Blomfield was asked to provide something in keeping with what was imagined to be its original appearance. He therefore supplied a formal garden with extensive topiaries. It lies close to the house and is clearly distinguished from the surrounding parkland by trimmed yew hedges (that are probably much taller today than originally intended). Within the hedged enclosure and just before the main entrance is a regular forecourt. To its left, Blomfield placed what *Country Life* called a "box-edged plat" – a square parterre garden composed of trimmed hedges that echo the repeating pattern of the roof line (again the hedges are probably taller today than intended).[99] Behind this garden is a rectangular level area of grass, perhaps used as a tennis or croquet lawn. A gravel walk separates this space from the next room of the garden, herbaceous borders flanking a perpendicular gravel path. The latter leads to the next feature: a rectangular fish pond edged with stone, bordered with hedges, and ornamented with statuary, just as Blomfield had recommended in *The Formal Garden in England* (Figs. 50, 51). A rose garden punctuated with statuary and bounded by yew hedges lies immediately off the south terrace of the house. Wandering through the changing rooms of the garden is akin to walking through the house where each room is a record of the centuries of ownership and improvement. In the opinion of *Country Life*, the gardens "hardly show[ed] their newness."[100]

49. Topiary Plat, Godinton, 1994. (Source: Author's photograph.)

At Moundsmere, Hampshire, built in 1908 for merchant Wilfred Buckley, Blomfield departed from the vocabulary of Elizabethan age in favor of the "Wrenaissance" in the design of the house, but continued to apply principles he had developed in *The Formal Garden in England* in the grounds. The gardens around the house are disposed in a series of roomlike spaces, the centerpiece of which is the sunken terrace oriented to the main door of the garden facade (Fig. 52). Framed by a raised terrace opposite, the garden features a pool similar in form to that in the private garden at Athelhampton. The raised terrace, reached by a flight of semicircular steps that reverberate with circular windows on the facade, creates a small apse to the basilica of the sunken terrace. Here the terrace wall is made of brick, reflecting the material of the house. This boundary demarcates the garden from the parkland while still permitting views out to the landscape, much like the terraces at Caythorpe Court and Godinton.

The sense of geometry and symmetry achieved by Blomfield carries over to the work of other guild architects. At Ardenrun, built in 1906 for H. H. König, Ernest Newton exploited the H-plan of the house in his garden design (Fig. 53). The axis created by the door of the house runs like a spine through the largely

50. Formal Pool, Godinton, 1994. (Source: Author's photograph.)

51. F. Inigo Thomas, "The Fishpond: Wrest: Bedfordshire," from Reginald Blomfield, *The Formal Garden,* London, 1901. (Source: Dumbarton Oaks, Studies in Landscape Architecture, Photo Archive.)

ৰ্ঞ 129

52. Sunken Terrace and Pool, Moundsmere, 1998. (Source: Author's photograph.)

symmetrical garden that slowly descends from the terrace platform of the house. The subdivisions of the garden take their cue from the house: the pillars and roses decorating the grass parterre below the terrace, for example, are aligned with the outer walls of the two wings of the house as are the flower borders that define the inside boundaries of the tennis courts below the grass parterre. The entire garden is encompassed in a basilicalike shape achieved by joining a half circle with a rectangle, and these forms are repeated in the inner subdivisions of the garden. This play of joined and intersecting squares, rectangles, and half circles was a frequent motif in Newton's garden design. Witness his plan for Redcourt, Haslemere (1894), one of his earliest designs (Fig. 54), and Scotman's Field, Church Stretton (1908) (Fig. 55); it is also found in the designs of his contemporaries, such as The Links, Hythe, Kent (1914) by Gerald Horsley (Figs. 56, 57).[101] E. S. Prior used geometry ingeniously, as at Byron Cross, where the site and the arrangement of the house did not allow for rigid axial treatment of the garden (Fig. 58). Taking his axis from the terrace rather than the main reception rooms of the house, Prior devised a garden plan composed of squares set within squares.

Although the architects' designs reveal an ability to solve problems of spatial division and allocation through recourse to geometry and the vocabulary of buildings (e.g., basilica plans), for the owners these designs were perhaps more significant in their ability to accommodate their leisure activities and to suggest old age, particularly the Elizabethan age prized in the popular imagination.

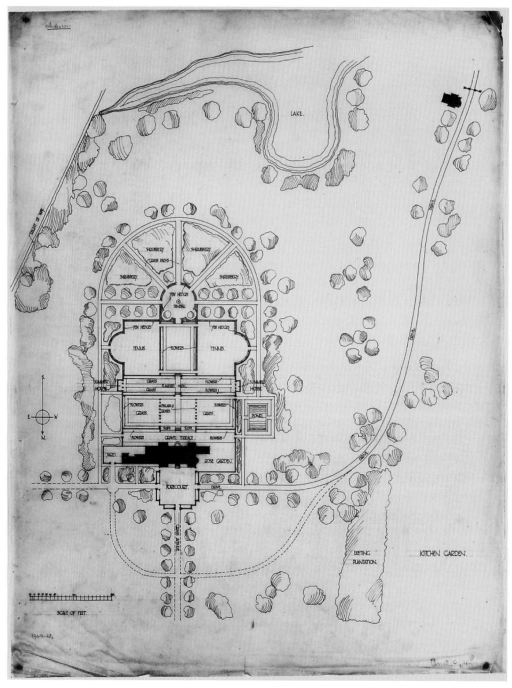

53. Ernest Newton, "General Lay-Out, Ardenrun," 1906, from William Godfrey Newton, *The Work of Ernest Newton, R.A.,* London, 1925. (Source: RIBA Library Photographs Collection.)

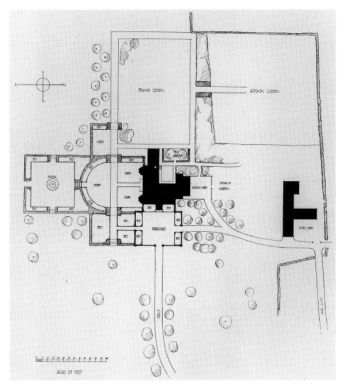

54. Ernest Newton, "The Garden Plan, Redcourt," 1894, from William Godfrey Newton, *The Work of Ernest Newton, R.A.,* London, 1925. (Source: RIBA Library Photographs Collection.)

Rooted in the local (albeit a portable localness), the formal garden wove wealthy newcomers into the fabric of the rural landscape. The appeal of this art form also lay in its supposed resolutely English vocabulary, the meanings of which were secured through the writings of the guild architects.

But how secure were these readings of Englishness? Garden designers such as Harold Peto made recourse to such motifs as terraces and hedged enclosures, as at Wayford Manor. But, in the case of Peto, his work was positioned more within the tradition of the Italian garden and its revival in Edwardian England.[102] Even more pertinent to the fate of the formal garden revival initiated by Blomfield and his colleagues was the challenge to the label *English* mounted by William Robinson, who argued that the natural garden style was the true and authentic manner of English gardening. This conflict erupted in 1892 with publication of inflammatory texts by Robinson and Blomfield. These books propelled the division of the garden design world into two camps and a competition to write, and thereby claim, the history of English garden design. This, concomitantly, led designers and critics to search for means by which to reconcile these factions.

131

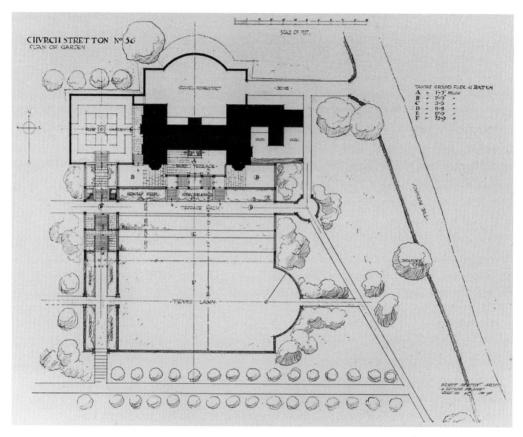

55. Ernest Newton, "The Garden Plan, Scotman's Field," 1908, from William Godfrey Newton, *The Work of Ernest Newton, R.A.,* London, 1925. (Source: RIBA Library Photographs Collection.)

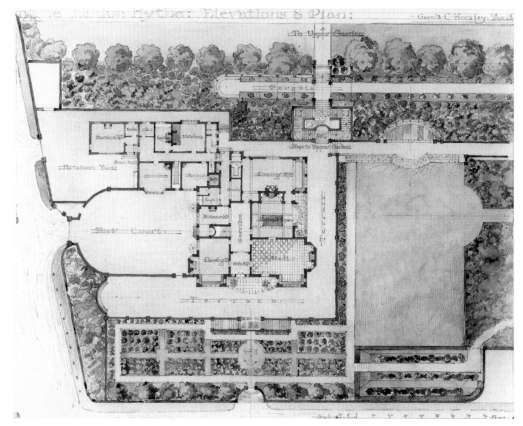

56. Gerald Callcott Horsley, Design for a House and Garden, The Links, Hythe, Kent, 1914.
(Source: RIBA Library Photographs Collection.)

57. Gerald Callcott Horsley, The South Elevation, The Links, Hythe, Kent, 1914. (Source:
RIBA Library Photographs Collection.

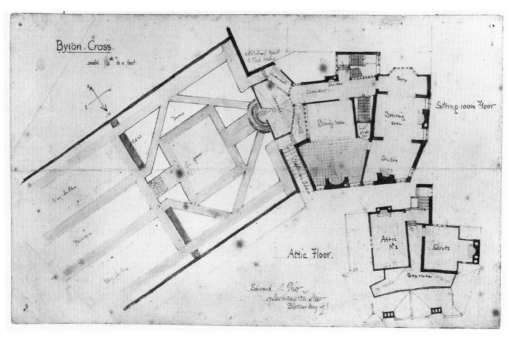

58. E. S. Prior, Byron Cross, Byron Hill, Harrow, n.d. (Source: RIBA Library Photographs Collection.)

Chapter 5

The Battle of the Styles and the Recounting of English Garden History

A fierce debate between proponents of natural or landscape gardening and formal garden design distinguished English garden design at the turn of the century. Played out largely in texts, this war of words centered on questions of professionalism (asking under whose purview the garden fell), aesthetics (what form best suited English houses and grounds), and history (what style did the English past legitimize or, in a kind of Hegelian maneuver, what should be the ideal garden as determined by the patterns and progress of the past). Embedded in discussions of the latter were the broader meanings of each style of garden design and, in particular, what sense of Englishness each disseminated. These debates may seem petty or overly heated today, and indeed a number of commentators outside garden circles suggested as much at the time, but the stakes were high for the gardening community and English culture at large. For if it was universally agreed that the garden symbolized Englishness, it mattered a great deal what sort of garden would be claimed as the leading style, because each form inscribed a different, nearly opposing, appearance and set of meanings on the landscape. This conflict and struggle reveal how highly charged the garden was within English culture at this time.

The notion of a "battle of the styles" was not new; the late eighteenth century was concerned with ancients vs. moderns, for example; the French academy in the early nineteenth century pitched the Romantic Delacroix against the Neoclassical Ingres; and, in 1857, the forces for classicism bested the Gothic revivalists in the commission for a new Foreign Office building in London despite the cunning of Sir Gilbert Scott. Out of these ongoing debates emerged the realization that classicism could no longer claim to be the universal, transcendental medium of expression, and with plurality came dispute.[1] With respect to turn-of-the-century garden design, the terminology of warfare was often used to characterize the stylistic debates: F. Inigo Thomas, reflecting on the 1890s from the vantage point of 1926, remembered "the battle raged in the press for a year or two" and the intensity of the criticisms might have led one to think "the issue might almost have been Free Trade and Protection."[2] The chief combatants were Blomfield, championing the cause of formalism and representing the discipline of architecture, and Robinson, advocating natural gardening and the viewpoint of the landscape gardener.

A lack of clarity in the terms *formal, natural,* and *landscape gardening* helped fuel the debate. The term *landscape* or *natural* gardening was fairly elastic. It referred to the mode of design most commonly associated with the eighteenth century but also, at the end of the nineteenth century, to nearly any garden that did not embody the characteristics of formalism, which came to be almost as equally broadly defined. Henry Ernest Milner, for example, defined landscape gardening "as taking the true cognizance of Nature's means for the expression of beauty, and so disposing those means artistically as to co-operate for our delight in given conditions," a remarkably imprecise definition. The breadth of Milner's sense of landscape gardening is evidenced by his text, in which he devoted a chapter to the terrace and argued that "the treatment of ground next the house shall be artistically formal . . . displaying harmony, so far as may be, with the architectural character of the building."[3]

With respect to *formal gardens,* Robinson claimed that the term should be applied to

> gardens in which both the design and planting were formally and stupidly formal like the upper terrace of the Crystal Palace, Kensington Gore, as laid out by Nesfield[,] . . . and Shrubland, as laid out by Barry, in which, as in others of these architects' gardens, strict orders were given that no plants were to be allowed on the walls. The architect was so proud of his design, that he did not want the gardener at all, except to pound up bricks to take the place of flower colour![4]

Yet Blomfield never argued such a position, and, indeed, both Blomfield and Robinson dismissed the broidery parterre—box and colored gravels or broken bricks set out in elaborate patterns—although they never acknowledged their agreement.

For his part, Blomfield summed up landscape gardening with the succinct claim that the discipline, as explicated by Robinson, involved copying nature as much as possible; the landscape gardener's primary concern, after achieving a reasonable facsimile of nature, was to create the impression that the garden was of great size, with no thought given to the relationship of the garden to the house.[5] This does little justice to the complexities of Robinson's aesthetic or his activities following the publication of *The Wild Garden.* In 1883 he published *The English Flower Garden,* a widely read treatise on the practical aspects of laying out a flower garden and cultivating plants that went into fifteen editions. This text included a discussion of terraced gardens (although Robinson recommended them with caution because they often ruined prospects)—the very feature Blomfield claimed as a distinctive feature of formal gardening.[6] Despite such affinities, or perhaps because of them, the two designers never found a publicly declared point of agreement.

The First Wave

The battle began with treatises issued by members of the Art Workers Guild, who established the legitimacy of their style, in part, by faulting landscape gardening. One of the first volleys was launched by John Belcher, in the Art Workers Guild's 1889 symposium, "The Architectural Treatment of Gardens," when he opened his lecture by pronouncing that "There are few specialists who have more disgraced themselves than the 'landscape gardener.'" According to Belcher, the landscape gardener had a propensity "to lay out a 'prospect' for you which may have little or no relation to the county you are in, or the nature of the site."[7] By thus demeaning the profession of landscape design, Belcher reinforced his and his colleagues' professional niche; and by claiming that only architects possessed the wherewithal to recognize the "genius of the place," he robbed landscape designers of perhaps their most long-standing raison d'être. Moreover, the guild architects denied ties to the local landscape that had informed the development of Robinson's aesthetic. Tales of how landscape gardeners dismantled old sixteenth- and seventeenth-century gardens further lowered this profession in the esteem of the architects.[8] The battle mounted in intensity, and became more personal in nature, with the publication of Sedding's and Blomfield's treatises as they singled out Robinson, and to a lesser degree Henry Ernest Milner, for attack.

Although Sedding professed admiration for wild nature, claiming its healing influence was necessary to counter "the pessimistic distress we moderns are all prone [to]," he maintained a clear distinction between wild nature and nature in the garden. Within the garden, nature should be harmonized through "a frankly decorative arrangement" utilizing symmetry and repeated patterns; outside the garden, nature was free and unfettered. The latter sense of nature, he acknowledged, could be incorporated into a garden, but it would be unsuitable for England. He opined that wild gardens were appropriate only for places like the colonies, which he believed lacked a long history of cultivation, whereas England – "an old land" with a history of building and designing landscapes – required an old-fashioned formal garden. Given this sentiment, it is not surprising that Sedding objected to much of Robinson's theories, although he admitted that Robinson had good advice on the selection of plants. Selectively quoting from Robinson's *The English Flower Garden,* he positioned the gardener as an authoritarian dictator unwilling to recognize points of view other than his own and firmly opposed to formalism – "ever girding" against architectural accessories and geometrical arrangement.[9] Blomfield followed up by accusing landscape gardeners such as Milner and Robinson of scholarly imprecision, confusion, and total absence of design principles. He denigrated landscape gardening further by insisting that it appealed "to the average person who "knows what he likes," whereas cognoscente "with a feeling for design and order" preferred formal gardens.[10]

The Second Wave

Robinson had unconsciously issued preemptive attacks against the formalists in *The English Flower Garden* (1883) when he charged, among other offenses, that whereas landscape gardeners designed grounds through the process of observing the site and then staking a design on the grounds, architects drew the design on paper and then transferred it to the ground so the resulting garden failed to acknowledge the site and gave little attention to displaying the beauty of plants. In 1892, immediately following the publication of Blomfield's *The Formal Garden in England,* Robinson mounted a deliberate assault with an illustrated pamphlet, *Garden Design and Architects' Gardens.* Therein he offered his critique of formal gardening, zeroing in on Sedding and Blomfield. In the opening pages of the preface he set the terms of the battle: it was being fought for the right to define the English garden:

> The one English thing that has touched the heart of the world is the English garden. Proof of this we have in such noble gardens as the English park at Munich, the garden of the Emperor of Austria at Laxenburg, the Petit Trianon at Versailles, the parks formed of recent years round Paris, and many lovely gardens in Europe and America. The good sense of English writers and landscape gardeners refused to accept as right or reasonable the architect's garden, a thing set out as bricks and stones, and the very trees of which were mutilated to meet his views as to "design," or rather to prove his not being able to see the simplest elements of design in landscape beauty or natural form. And some way or other they destroyed nearly all signs of it throughout the land.[11]

In this passage, Robinson did not precisely define his notion of the English garden, but his cited examples, such as the Englischer Garten in Munich, built as a landscape park, indicate he was referring to a manner of garden design that could be traced to the eighteenth-century landscape park or natural garden. Indeed, later in the preface he claimed that England was "the home of landscape gardening."

Dismayed at the prospect of the formal garden replacing the landscape or natural garden, Robinson set out to demonstrate the continued legitimacy of the natural garden through reference to extant examples.[12] Using such sites was an important tactic because much of Blomfield's and Sedding's arguments in favor of the formal garden rested on demonstrating how this manner of garden design had been utilized in significant historic sites that readers could go see for themselves. Robinson needed to provide an equally compelling litany of sites. He also needed to show that the trajectory of English garden history did not point to the resuscitation of the formal garden but to the preservation and continuation of the landscape garden, albeit practiced in a far different manner than in the eighteenth century. History, in other words, would prove the validity of the principles of natural gardening and protect the discipline from the encroachment of the architect.

Robinson began his project of reclaiming history by dismissing the premodern treatises referred to by Blomfield and Sedding as texts "written by men who know books better than gardens," and arguing that they were not appropriate to the modern, "mechanical" age. The rural landscape, not the old formal garden, should be the focus of preservationists and revivalists, he argued. The nation's heritage, he continued, was "our beautiful English real landscapes." Historic sites, such as Elizabethan country houses, should not be destroyed, he was careful to explain, because he admired and wanted to preserve "all that remains" of such sites. Yet they should not be used as models for contemporary design because they were responses to a particular set of historical conditions that no longer applied. What was needed was a garden style that corresponded to the needs of contemporary English society. The most pressing issue facing Englanders, he argued, was the "ever-growing city, pushing its hard face over the once beautiful land," and the duty of every citizen was "to save all we can save of the natural beauty of the earth."[13] Robinson never actually addressed how the latter would be accomplished, but he did advocate that gardens embody ideal representations of rustic nature.

This notion of an ideal is crucial to understanding Robinson's aesthetic. Angered by Blomfield's charge that landscape gardeners simply copied whatever fell before their gaze, he insisted that "the central and essential idea of the landscape art is [the] choice of what is beautiful." Beauty in nature, he argued, was based on "eternal laws," such as those that applied in all the arts: just as the Venus de Milo was the representation of an ideal rather than a real woman, the landscape garden was based on an ideal of beauty. To exemplify ideal beauty, Robinson turned once again to the work of landscape painters such as Corot and Turner and argued that although they studied nature closely, their images were not mimetic representations but judicious selections from, and improvements on, observed nature.[14]

In Robinson's aesthetic, ideal beauty was arrived at not by reviving the arts of the past, as Sedding and Blomfield had argued, but by carefully selecting and arranging plants. Indeed, he held that the true purpose of a garden was to cultivate plants, with special regard for "plants *not* in our woods and mostly from other countries than our own!"[15] With these criteria in mind, he then reclaimed older gardens for his cause by demonstrating how a number of pre-eighteenth-century gardens were compatible with his theories. At twelfth-century Berkeley Castle, for example, terrace walls provided support for "Fig and Vine and Rose"; at Ightham Mote, where the guild had its first country outing, a "delicate veil of beautiful climbers and flowers" colored the courtyard walls.[16]

Robinson also put history on his side by using extant sites to demonstrate the major points of his aesthetic. He defended, for example, the principle of allowing the lawn to come to the door of the house, a practice dismissed by the guild architects, by pointing to such sites as eighteenth-century Goodwood (West Sussex) and Knole (Kent), the latter dating back to the fifteenth century.[17] Pointing to Wakehurst, Kent, an Elizabethan house without a terrace, Robinson held that this feature was not always necessary. He also established that the Elizabethan past sanctioned picturesque planting, with trees left in their natural state, by citing Athelhampton (where Thomas had not yet begun to work) and Longleat (where Capability Brown had designed a parkland garden).[18] Although Robinson had not made as extensive a study of country houses as Blomfield and Thomas – his examples were largely drawn from his home county of West Sussex and neighboring regions – he nonetheless wished to demonstrate that an equally powerful case could be made for natural or landscape gardening based on the surviving past.

Pursuing another tactic, Robinson argued that landscape gardening was capable of addressing the very same issues highlighted by the formal garden. Landscape gardeners, he insisted, were just as interested in the relationship between the house and its surroundings as the formalists; indeed, as the cities expanded and the countryside shrank, the question of how to negotiate this relationship became of increasing importance.[19] In addition, landscape gardeners were not fundamentally opposed to a formally designed flower garden if this better suited the site, as at Haddon Hall, a garden also admired by Blomfield.[20] Indeed, by 1900, Robinson came to praise the upper flower garden at Shrubland Park, a site he had formerly condemned. The new design, most likely by the gardener himself, of island beds of roses set in the lawn and rectangular beds hugging the terrace seems surprisingly like designs featured in Blomfield's or Sedding's treatises. Robinson explained that the new beds were "planned to suit their places" and were an improvement over the previous "complex pattern beds for carpet bedding, sand, [and] coloured brick" (Fig. 59). The plants, he noted, were not to be arranged in "little dots" as the plan might suggest; rather, they were to be planted in "bold groups here and there running together . . . sometimes softened by dwarf plants running below the taller ones."[21] Robinson's aesthetic proved to be remarkably flexible.

Whereas Robinson was willing to entertain certain principles associated with formal gardening if the site warranted it, he was much less willing to cede the design of gardens to the architectural profession. Garden design, as a professional practice, was tenuous at best. Gaining recognition for landscape gardening had been a hard fought battle, one that was not yet over. The early-nineteenth-century landscape gardener Humphry Repton, for example, devoted much of his career to professionalizing and raising the status of his chosen occupation through his treatises and interactions with clients.[22] Among the difficulties faced by landscape gardeners were educating clients as to the needs of their services and distinguishing themselves from gardeners who were in charge of the day-to-day physical activities of the garden. Moreover, because no examinations or other recognized certifications of specialization were needed to construct a garden, it was difficult, if not nearly impossible, for practitioners to police training and practicing. Anyone could do it, as Robinson himself acknowledged: "There is no organized profession to help, any one may call himself a landscape gardener, and others without any training undertake the work, and many nurserymen advertise themselves as landscape gardeners."[23] Those who wanted to pursue garden design as a professional career had, as it were, to invent examinations and certificates; their treatises often functioned in this manner, offering displays of their erudition and technical abilities. Defining garden design as a profession had become especially important at the end of the nineteenth century as this was the period in which the notion of the professional ideal – "based on trained expertise and selection by merit, a selec-

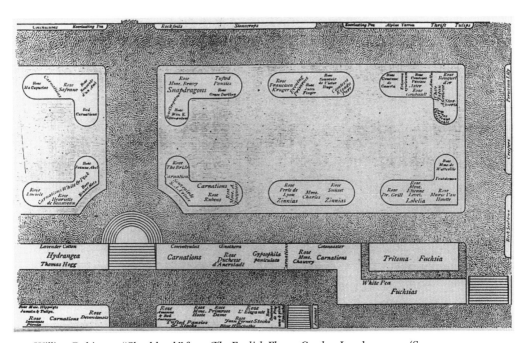

59. William Robinson, "Shrubland," from *The English Flower Garden*, London, 1900. (Source: Dumbarton Oaks, Studies in Landscape Architecture, Photo Archives.)

tion made not by the open market but by the judgment of similarly educated experts" – began to replace the entrepreneurial ideal as an organizing force in English society. As Harold Perkin has observed, "the professional class can only exist by persuading the rest of society to accept a distributive justice which recognizes expert service based on selection by merit and long, arduous training."[24]

In the field of garden design, texts were the key means by which designers attempted to define the terms by which merit would be awarded, as well as the very scope of the discipline. According to Robinson, the architect should be allowed to design only the house and surrounding stonework because the profession lacked the necessary skills to design landscapes. As the purpose of the garden was to grow and to display plants, only persons with related experience should be permitted to create gardens. Allowance was made for landscape painters, "whose tastes and training" suited them to assist the landscape gardener.[25] In *The Garden Beautiful,* the gardener reinforced his case against the architect by arguing that by relying on plans derived from pattern books, architects created gardens that bore little relationship to the unique qualities of the local landscape.[26] As in the case of history, sensitivity to localness was something that both camps wished to claim in their effort to win over potential clients.

The Third Wave

Faced with such a dense, rapid attack, Blomfield could not restrain himself from returning fire. For the second edition of *The Formal Garden in England,* he wrote a new preface to counter Robinson's disparagement of architects as landscape designers. Building up steam, he contended that if home owners wanted gardens that operated as botanical collections, then by all means hire someone like Robinson, who possessed great skill "as a tree-planter, or as a flower-grower." But if one desired "quiet and retirement and [to] be sheltered from the outside world by a yew hedge or a tapestry of roses and jasmine against the garden wall," then a formal garden and an architect were required. Furthermore, he charged that natural or landscape gardeners lacked "any artistic capacity."[27]

The latter was a particularly savage line of attack, because Robinson had consistently used art to legitimize his theories of garden design. In addition, he had wielded art as a weapon against Blomfield by reiterating his claim that artists favored only natural gardens and detested "the common garden with its formality and bedding."[28] The illustrations to Blomfield's treatise, Robinson maintained, proved his point: "they are careful architect's drawings, deficient in light and shade; not engraved, but reproduced by a hard process . . . [and] show the *evil,* not the good, of the system advocated, by their hard lines and the emphasising of ugly forms."[29] Unfortunately for Blomfield, critics apparently agreed. The

British Architect, which theoretically should have been supportive of Blomfield, speculated that the public "would go heart and soul in favor of Mr. Robinson's pretty pictures and desires for informality in preference to Messrs. Blomfield and Thomas's scratchy, thin diagrams of architectural design, with which they support the theories of clipped hedges and formal parterres."[30]

Such criticism struck at the very underpinnings of the guild enterprise, which strove to unite the arts, and Blomfield fought to defend his position. He returned fire carefully, however, because most of Robinson's illustrations were by Alfred Parsons, a fellow guild member. He referred to Parsons as a "skilful artist" and praised Robinson for his astute selection of "admirable drawings of trees and foliage to prove his point." Rather than critique Parsons's illustrations, he went after Robinson's assertion that artists eschewed the formal garden. Blomfield countered that many artists adopted the formal garden as subject; he, for example, wrote essays to accompany two exhibitions of paintings of formal gardens by George Elgood.[31] Belcher had already laid out this line of argument in his 1889 lecture when he referred to John Everett Millais's oil painting *The Old Garden* as legitimizing the aesthetic of formal gardening:

> That the beauty of an architectural treatment of gardens is becoming more appreciated may be gathered from the number of garden pictures in the present exhibitions, commencing with Millais' fine work in the Academy. When the architect has formed the garden, the painter soon finds out what opportunities there are for colour arrangements. He knows how valuable an old red brick wall is; he appreciates the deep shadows of a yew hedge. He sees endless pictures in the quiet corners and retreats – the fountain, the statue, the shaded seat – and they are fine "properties" for him in his work.[32]

Correspondingly, Blomfield challenged the notion that landscape gardening held a unique claim to the title "artistic" because it set forth an idealized representation of nature. The essence of the design process, he countered, was not to select and to reproduce from nature, but to impose the imagination of the designer on nature.[33]

Blomfield left the most charged issue – the question of Englishness – until the conclusion of his new preface. His rebuttal to Robinson, as might be anticipated, was through history. The landscape garden, he charged, could not exclusively claim the label "the English garden" because the formal garden predated the landscape garden. Implicitly acknowledging that Europeans had emulated the English landscape model, he countered that the formal garden derived from "a tradition of design that prevailed throughout the most brilliant period of European art," thus giving the formal garden an equally compelling pedigree. Turning to the question of models, he rejected Robinson's notion of looking to nature and announced his preference for "the men of the Renaissance."[34] In the new

conclusion added to the 1901 edition of his book, he referred to Robinson's position as "hopeless modernism in the worst sense" because it revealed "an insensi-
bility to what has been done in the past."[35]

As these exchanges indicate, throughout the battle the primary antagonists
hunkered deeper and deeper in their trenches so no rapprochement appeared
possible, despite points of shared agreement. It was left to critics and other
designers to advocate a bridge between the formal and natural styles, as in the
case of a reviewer for the *Magazine of Art*, who remarked with surprise on the
acrimoniousness riddling the discipline of garden design:

> Differences between doctors are proverbial; but we were only lately
> made aware of the extent to which gardeners could differ, and say bitter
> things of each other. We have always thought of gardeners as mild,
> sweet-mannered men, whose hearts were so full of love for their work,
> and the delights which spring from it, that there was no space left in
> them for any gall or bitterness: but a short time since Messrs. Macmil-
> lan published a little book by Mr. Reginald Blomfield, illustrated by
> Mr. F. Inigo Thomas, which was something of a surprise as to the bit-
> terness which could exist between the formal gardener and the land-
> scape gardener: and quite recently a reply has appeared in the interests
> of the latter which lacks little of the bitterness of the attack. . . . But why
> should the advocates of the natural and the artificial fight over our
> sweet resting-place? Are there not charms in both forms of gardens?[36]

To arrive at a compromise between the two schools, critics were forced to reex-
amine the history of English garden design and how the natural and formal styles
had gained legitimacy and claims to Englishness.

Writing Garden History

In 1892, the year of Robinson's and Blomfield's polemical treatises, Julia
Cartwright (who went on to publish a history of Italian Renaissance gardens in
1914) weighed in on the debate with an article, "Gardens," published in *The Portfolio*, which had also published Blomfield's early articles on his travels in south-
west England. The article was primarily a review of the books published by Blomfield and Robinson that year. Despite Cartwright's evident appreciation for formal
gardens (in which she detected far more Italian influence than Blomfield and
other members of the guild generally allowed), she attempted to be evenhanded in
discussing the rivalry that had erupted. She acknowledged, for example, that topiary could be "grotesque, and even in some cases slightly ridiculous," but found
merits in trimming plant material. On the equally fraught issue of marking the
boundaries of the garden, she advocated that both points of view – blurring gar-

den and parkland as in the landscape garden or erecting high walls as in the formal garden – were valid, because a garden should provide "a place of shelter and seclusion, a quiet retreat from the outside world" while also possessing "points of connexion with the outer world" in the form of views to distant prospects.

As Cartwright evaluated the merits and defects of both sides, she brought a cautionary tone to the debate. Landscape gardens, she noted, could really only be carried off by large landowners, whereas formal gardens were "within the reach of humbler persons," because they required much less space. She also attempted to sidestep the debate by insisting that home owners need not be troubled by hard and fast rules; the primary goal of a garden was simply to express "an individual idea" and to "realise the owner's individual dream." Here Cartwright touched on a major difficulty facing the battle participants: they were offering stylistic guidelines in an age in which home owners, following the prevailing domestic ideology and a trickle-down Arts and Crafts ethos, had come to believe that the home was an expression of not just one's station in life but also one's individual character.

The idea of expressing individual character was of central concern to many in England's comfortable classes at the turn of the century. Mass manufacturing had made a wide variety of goods available to a broad panoply of England's society. A number of the wealthy had turned to the Arts and Crafts movement, with its emphasis on handcrafted products, in an effort to mark themselves apart from those who bought, as it were, "off the rack." Garden design, Cartwright hints, threatened to become a sort of mass manufactured product through the increasingly rigid guidelines offered by Robinson and Blomfield. Home owners, she implied, should not be bullied into accepting someone else's notion of good taste in place of their own ideas. Although such comments point up the difficulties garden designers faced in attempting to persuade potential clients, the greater importance for the discussion at hand lies in Cartwright's forthright assumption and confirmation of the garden's ability to signal identity.

In addition to addressing the garden as an expression of individuality, Cartwright considered its ability to function as a rallying point for collective identity. She recognized that garden history, by selecting and elevating certain historic sites and new gardens, could shape the growing sense of national heritage. Indeed, many of the estates cited by Blomfield and Robinson, such as Montacute, Penshurst, or Haddon Hall, had been argued throughout the nineteenth century to embody a uniquely national tradition, despite that they were private property. Prints, novels, travel guides, and other accounts established this national heritage and tourists went forth in droves to experience celebrated places firsthand.[37] Most of these historic houses and gardens were in the hands of the aristocracy, but the rise of death duties, the agricultural depression, and other economic changes made it clear that not all landed families would be able to maintain their great country houses and gardens. Preservationists came forward to argue that houses and gardens of historic value should be regarded as the responsibility of the nation in recognition of their contribution to a communal heritage that must, in the words of C. R. Ashbee, "not be local, nor reserved to any particular class."[38]

Cartwright acknowledged this discourse and offered reasons for preserving both formal and natural gardens. The value of the formal garden lay in its ability to connect with or conjure up the past, in particular the Elizabethan past that witnessed the founding of the nation's most important values and characteristics. By contrast, the value of the landscape garden did not lie in history, but in its materials – unfettered plants, streams, rolling hills, and woods. Cartwright was apparently concerned that readers might not realize the value of landscape gardens because they were often attached to country houses less familiar to the public than those associated with formal gardens. Yet these gardens or parks replicated unspoiled nature – "all that is best and fairest in woodland scenery" – in a manner that was impossible in the formal garden. Picking up on Robinson's argument that it was the duty of every citizen to preserve nature from the encroachment of industrialization, she offered a means by which this could be accomplished: "Let the wealthy owners of these our stately parks preserve them carefully, let them watch over them jealously, as part of that beauty of earth which it is our sacred duty to guard for the sake of our children."[39]

In her account Cartwright brought out the two chief axioms of England's national identity attached to the garden at the end of the nineteenth century – the unspoiled countryside and the heroic Elizabethan past. The essence of England in the popular imagination at this moment, as historians have repeatedly noted, was that it was "an *old* country" and "at heart, *country*."[40] Yet the battle of the styles was asking Englanders to choose between these two key elements and to choose over the very thing – the garden – that held the promise of cultural unity. Given that the formal and the landscape garden were regarded as crucial components of the nation's history and identity, the compelling question became how to end the battle of the styles in a satisfactory manner, allowing for both manners of design to coexist as happily as they did in Englanders' conceptions of themselves.

The rewriting of garden history became crucial to establishing a rapprochement between the formalists and the naturalists. Insight into this process can be gained from examining three surveys of garden design and history written around this time: Alicia Amherst's *A History of Gardening in England* (1895), the three-volume series *Gardens Old and New* published by *Country Life* between 1900 and 1908, and the three-volume series on *The Gardens of England* published by *The Studio*, probably in response to the popularity of *Country Life*'s series, between 1907 and 1911.[41]

Amherst's account begins with the claim that gardens exemplify the "national characteristics" of their makers and is thus reminiscent of Blomfield's remarks on this point.[42] What distinguishes her history, set forth in chronological order beginning with the Roman conquest, from that offered by Blomfield was that she was not writing to advocate a particular style. So, although she, like Blomfield, described the Elizabethan garden as a "purely national style" that resulted from a combination of "older fashions in English gardens . . . with the new ideas imported from France, Italy, and Holland," she broke ranks with Blomfield in her discussion of the eighteenth century, giving a far more evenhanded treatment and offering a much closer reading of the major treatises of the period. She concluded that "landscape gardening had by this time become the recognized National style of England, and it was copied on the Continent, in France, Italy and Germany."[43] For the nineteenth century, her account becomes sketchier, restricted largely to changes in horticulture and plant material, including the reaction led by Robinson against tender exotics in favor of hardy perennials. Her historical narrative closed with a brief reference to the revival of the formal garden in the 1890s.

Despite the preponderance of evidence Amherst marshaled on behalf of the Elizabethan garden, she disinclined to support one manner of gardening over another. Echoing Cartwright, she cautioned that "no hard and fast rules of style can be laid down," recommending that home owners select a style in accordance with the house, its siting, and locality. Yet buried in these disclaimers is her proposal for an ideal garden: designed to harmonize with the architecture of the house with a wild garden beyond, separated from the formal garden by "some suitable enclosure."[44] Amherst may not have realized the significance of this suggestion: it reflects a broader pattern or mode of design that became increasingly popular in the early decades of the twentieth century.

The notion of effecting some compromise between the two styles was reiterated by *Country Life* in the first and second volumes of its three-volume series *Gardens Old and New, The Country House and Its Garden Environment,* edited respectively by John Leyland and H. Avray Tipping.[45] The series proved extremely popular as indicated by a biscuit tin of the time that mimics a stack of books including *Gardens Old and New.* Each volume of the series began with an introduction that discusses contemporary and historic garden aesthetics. In volume 1 the ideal garden is spelled out (in rich prose) as a formally defined space that allows flowers, such as lilies, hollyhock, foxgloves, and larkspurs, to take center stage. In addition, the

> sentinel yews, the hedges, and box edgings, are there to give order and distinction, with the right degree of formality that belongs to the structure that is adorned. The moral sundial, the splashing fountain, the sheltered arbour, and the fragrant pergola, all have their places in such a garden. Nor need the landscape, and the woodland with the lake be contemned. [sic] These lie outside the enclosed gardens, and all are

beautiful and entrancing in their degree and place. The final fact is simple after all, and the garden designer must make it his own. It is that the house and the garden are the two parts of a single whole, and happy is he who can best interpret their sweet relationship.[46]

In the third volume, editor H. Avray Tipping argued for an even more balanced design. He insisted that true moderns possessed a "catholicity of taste" that permitted terraces and wildernesses, cut yews and unclipped thickets, square lily ponds and meandering brooklets to coexist happily. With a sense of relief, the author reported that "the hot controversy of a few years ago between the protagonists of the formal and those of the natural school has cooled down with the mellowing of the fanatical spirit that can tolerate only its own narrow opinions."[47] His text included gardens by formalists, such as Athelhampton, and he also called attention to the work of Edwin Lutyens and Gertrude Jekyll, as at Deanery Garden, where Jekyll introduced a note of "organic luxuriance" to the architectural framework supplied by Lutyens.[48]

In 1907 *The Studio* introduced its own three-volume series on the state of garden design in England. Founded in 1892 by Charles Holme, who had an active interest in the Arts and Crafts movement as well as Asian artifacts, the magazine, like *Country Life,* was targeted to the educated middle classes. Yet it participated more actively in the design reform movement by supporting the work of such progressive designers and architects as Charles Rennie Mackintosh, C. R. Ashbee, and C. F. A. Voysey.[49] In the first volume of the series, art critic A. L. Baldry offered his version of English garden history, which was remarkably similar to its predecessors. A canon was forming.

Addressing the present day, Baldry explained that although the revival of formal gardening had proved popular, it had not displaced the landscape garden, which had become increasingly interested in capturing the "spontaneity and charming irregularity" of nature. In contemporary gardens, he stated, the "two types of work flourish . . . side by side," citing as an example Ammerdown, designed by Lutyens, in which "the formality of the design, carefully contrived as it is, does not in any way exceed legitimate bounds" so that "nature has been allowed to riot pleasantly and to hide by a free growth of foliage many of the terrace walls."[50]

This balance between formal and landscape was important, it was explained in volume 3, for maintaining the collective health of the nation and shaping the nation's identity. "Without such a link to nature," Baldry intoned, "we should be in very real danger of sinking into hopeless materialism and of losing what remains to us of healthy sentiment and quiet romance; the artificialities of civilisation would overwhelm us and we should degenerate from sensitive, thinking beings into mere parts of a complicated social machine."[51] Concomitantly, the nation needed to maintain links to the past through historic gardens, "which the nation ought to treasure as evidence of its artistic progress and of its understanding of the value of civilisation."[52]

Within this frame, it becomes clear why, in the end, most observers of the battle wanted neither side to be able to declare a definitive victory, as Jekyll observed in her review of gardening literature written in 1896:

> Both are right and both are wrong. The formal army are architects to a man; they are undoubtedly right in upholding the simple dignity and sweetness and quiet beauty of the old formal garden but they parade its limitations as if they were the end of all art; they ignore the immense resources that are the precious possession of modern gardeners, and therefore offer no sort of encouragement to their utilisation. If for a moment they leave the safe harbourage of encircling yew hedge, or let go of the handrail of the balustrade, and venture for an excursion into the unknown country of horticulture, they exhibit the weakness of an army that is campaigning at too great a distance from its "base" and certainly do expose themselves to the assaults of the enemy.[53]

149

Compromise emerged as the best solution, and in this context the work of Jekyll and Lutyens was promoted. In an 1899 *Country Life* article, ostensibly on Athelhampton, the author remarked on the battle of the styles and insisted that "there is much to be said on both sides. That is to say, the architect, in designing his house, must think of the work which the gardener has to do afterwards; and the gardener, in his turn, must think of the opportunities which the architect has given to him." The ideal solution, the author proposed, was a gardener who could work with an architect, namely Gertrude Jekyll, who together with architect Edwin Lutyens, produced the "House Beautiful and the Environment Beautiful."[54]

A number of other designers, including Mervyn Macartney, Thomas Mawson, and C. E. Mallows, easily combined formalism and naturalism. Macartney was active in the formal garden revival, but at his home Rosebank (Fig. 60) he combined a sunken bowling green and basin garden, both near the house, with fields of heather and walks to the distant woodland so the effect was of a "garden beautiful and cultivated in itself, while yet in keeping with its framing of the wild, like a gem in a rough but rich setting.[55] Mawson was also associated with the formalists and had joined the guild in 1905. Yet his training was in horticulture rather than architecture and he had entered the profession of garden design through his family's nursery business. His popular book, *The Art and Craft of Garden Making* (first published 1900), may recall Sedding's book of several years earlier, but the text preached versatility.[56] The house, he explained, should be the centerpiece of any design and its architecture should dictate the layout of the grounds immediately adjacent; but, then, if possible, the garden should gradually "lead to the freer and more natural landscape."[57] Addressed to both landscape gardeners and gar-

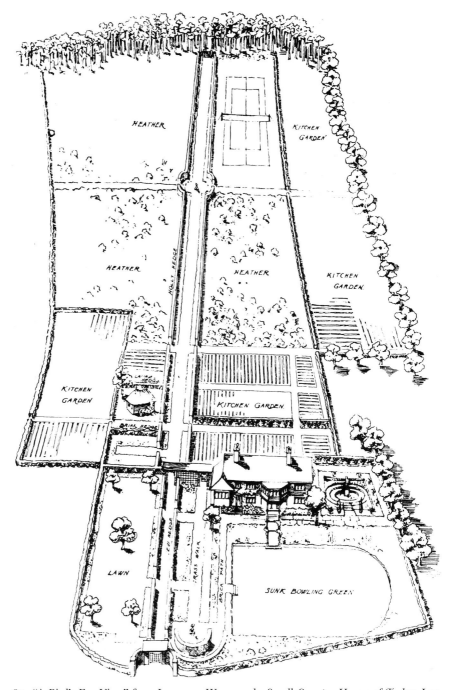

60. "A Bird's-Eye View," from Lawrence Weaver, ed., *Small Country Houses of To-day*, London, 1910. (Source: Harry Ransom Humanities Research Center, The University of Texas at Austin.)

61. House and Flower Border, Tirley Garth, 1998. (Source: Author's photograph.)

den architects, his text included many principles favored by members of the guild as well as advice on planting for landscape effects in the manner of Robinson. C. E. Mallows, who had trained with Frank Mercer and worked closely with Mawson, struck a similar position. Although he advocated that "to obtain anything like success in garden design, the house plan must be extended beyond the walls, and include the entire garden scheme," he also praised landscape gardening for its "softening effect on garden work in general."[58]

The site of Tirley Garth, executed between 1906 and 1912, exemplifies well the rhetoric of the two designers. The small country house, by Mallows, was begun for industrialist Bryan Leesmith, but in 1908 he sold the property, house unfinished, and eventually it was purchased by his employer, Brunner Mond, which leased it in 1911 to R. H. Prestwich, a mill owner and textile manufacturer who eventually became chairman of Burberrys. The house (Fig. 61), of local Cheshire stone, takes its cues from earlier country and manor houses with its projecting window bays, leaded glass windows, and broken roof line. Mallows did much of the initial planning of the gardens, which take advantage of the house's situation atop a hill, and then entered into collaboration with Mawson, who advised about the plantings.[59]

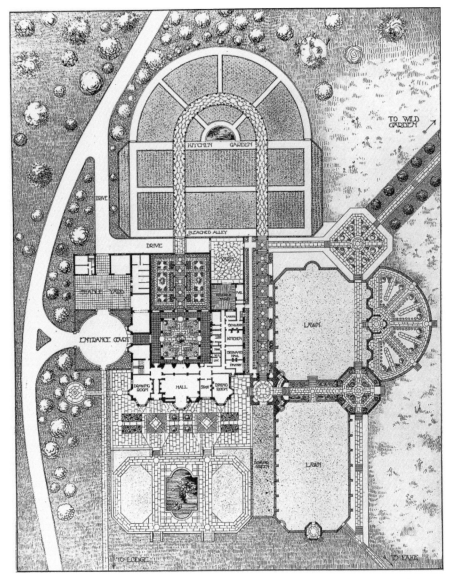

62. C. E. Mallows, "Plan of Tirley Garth Court and Gardens," from *The Studio*, 1908. (Source: This item is reproduced by permission of *The Huntington Library, San Marino, California.*)

The first garden plan (Fig. 62) hints at an intention to use the vocabularies of both formal and natural gardening: the garden immediately around the house is disposed in geometric units with a stone terrace, paths, and a pergola extending the architecture of the house into the landscape; an avenue in the upper right corner of the plan leads to a wild garden. In the final plan, this combination is made much clearer (Fig. 63). The terrace along the western side of the house has been retained, although simplified, with a sundial instead of a pool of water beneath the central window bay and beds of roses bounded by patterned stone walls and grass. Just below the house and terrace, softening their transition into the landscape, is a deep flower border.

The terrace looks over a broad expanse of lawn that gives way to a stream that courses alongside the southern flank of the house at the bottom of the hill. Beside the stream, broadened at several points to create pools, a wild garden was built with the importation of plants, shrubs, and trees, including irises, daffodils, and rhododendrons. Access to the wild garden, or dell, is gained by paths and steps of rough-hewn rock emanating from the lawn along the southern garden front. Along this side of the house, the garden is composed of a terrace, a sequence of low walled tennis/croquet lawns, and, to the east, a hemispherical rose garden that descends the hill (Fig. 64). Tall hedges separate the roses from the seemingly more natural garden along the stream. The rose garden, in effect, hinges together the two aspects of the garden, giving egress to the wild garden and anchoring the axis that runs alongside the tennis lawns and concludes at the circular kitchen garden. The latter is located at the easternmost point of the garden and also per-

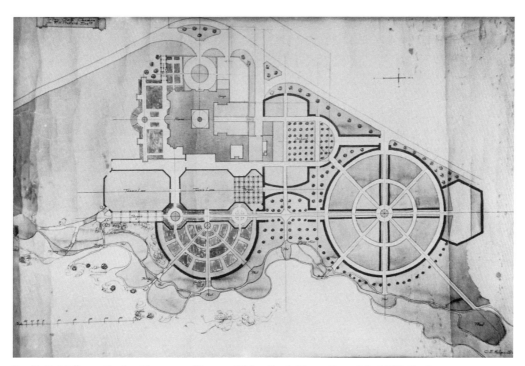

63. C. E. Mallows, Garden Plan, 1912. (Source: Tirley Garth Trust; Copyright MRA Productions, London.)

64. Rose Garden, Tirley Garth, 1998. (Source: Author's photograph.)

mits access to the dell. Shifts in stone treatment, more dressed and laid in more intricate patterns the closer one approaches the house, also register the transition from natural to formal. The garden merges imperceptibly with the existing landscape along its edges and, closer to the house, increasingly reveals a sense of imposed order and art, just as Mawson and Mallows had insisted an ideal garden should. The possibility of compromise between the feuding styles had been demonstrated, and in this context the careers of Gertrude Jekyll and Edwin Lutyens flourished.

Chapter 6

Gertrude Jekyll

Transforming the Local into the National

The quarrel between Robinson and Blomfield failed to settle the question of what should be the modern manner of designing gardens; moreover, other garden writers clearly chafed at the overly polemical positions staked out by these two authors. The anonymous author of an article that appeared in the *Spectator* in 1903 argued that the past had proven both the benefits and detractions of formal and natural gardening. The best garden design, according to this author, utilized an ordered plan linking the garden to the house and combined this with an "eclectic" selection from nature. Readers in need of models could turn to the Surrey gardens of Orchards and Munstead Wood, both by Gertrude Jekyll and Edwin Lutyens, which exemplified modern garden design at its best.[1] Standard-bearers for the cause of unifying the formal and the natural had been anointed.

Although other garden designers, most notably C. E. Mallows and Thomas Mawson, had also hit on a similar solution, much of the literature on Edwardian garden design, both at the time and today, focused on the work of Jekyll and Lutyens. Perhaps we should not be surprised, because both had provided garden designs for two of the leading publishers in home design and decoration: Charles Holme, founder of *The Studio,* and Edward Hudson, founder of *Country Life.* The latter journal, in particular, did much to further the careers of Jekyll and Lutyens, publishing Jekyll's writings, issuing surveys of their work, and featuring their projects. In the pages of *Country Life,* the work of Jekyll and Lutyens appeared cheek to jowl with articles on Elizabethan manors, aged cottages, country pursuits, and gardening advice. This context ensured that their work was understood as authentically rural and in keeping with traditions the journal emphatically insisted were purely English. Moreover, *Country Life,* a general-interest magazine rather than a professional horticultural journal, was aimed precisely at the well-educated, financially comfortable reader who might commission work from Jekyll and Lutyens. But Jekyll's and Lutyens's significance for the Edwardian period cannot be attributed solely to clever marketing; their work also gained recognition because of the ways in which it deployed existing garden tropes that signified Englishness, such as the natural garden, the cottage garden, and the formal garden.

Old West Surrey (1904)

Through her writings, Jekyll linked herself inextricably with the Surrey landscape, positioning herself as someone thoroughly versed in the local environment and practices of "our working folk."[2] This was an act of willful education on her part because she came from a well-to-do family and had been born in the fashionable Mayfair district of London. At the age of five her family moved to Surrey, to the village of Bramley near Guildford, where they adopted the lifestyle of the minor landed gentry; in the 1860s they moved to Wargrave Hill in Berkshire and then returned to Surrey in the 1870s. In her writings, Jekyll oscillates between speaking from the point of view of a longtime inhabitant familiar with "the ways and lives and habitations of the older people of the country" and from the point of view of the educated, detached observer, who saw Surrey as an "undiscovered" land, a turn of phrase that suggests it awaited someone bringing knowledge and appreciation acquired elsewhere to identify and to categorize its hidden riches.[3]

In reality, Jekyll's southwest corner of Surrey was no longer "undiscovered" at the time of the publication of her book *Old West Surrey, Some Notes and Memories* (1904). A veritable invasion was taking place as urbanites colonized the countryside, bringing with them "the strain and throng and unceasing restlessness that have been induced by all kinds of competition" and thus robbing the countryside "of its older charms of peace and retirement," as Jekyll herself recognized.[4] The garden writer realized that she could not stop the tides of change, but she hoped to draw readers' attention to hitherto ignored aspects of rural culture, particularly those demonstrating quality craftsmanship and design in keeping with her training and interest in the Arts and Crafts movement. (She enrolled around 1860 in the South Kensington School of Art, an institution devoted in large measure to preparing students for careers in the decorative arts, and schooled herself in the writings of John Ruskin and William Morris – she met the latter in 1869.) To assist in this task, Jekyll turned to photography, and her books featured images she had accumulated since learning the medium in 1885. Indeed, Jekyll was one of the first garden writers working in England to take full advantage of the new possibility to illustrate a text primarily with photographs as opposed to wood engravings.

Jekyll was not alone in surveying photographically a landscape threatened by change. By the end of the century, photography had become a popular pastime among wealthy amateurs who could afford the necessary materials and time to master the craft. Although many of these images emulated the subjects and styles of painting, more common was "topographical photography" as the *Art Journal* labeled it: documentary images intended as "a record of the buildings of historical and other interest which sooner or later will be swept away by the follies of modern municipal growth."[5] This practice of surveying, although largely an amateur pastime, was nonetheless institutionalized in such activities as the Warwickshire Photographic Survey, established in the mid-1880s. The intent of the organization was to "make a total and unbiased record illustrating the archaeology, architecture, landscape and scenery, ethnology, botany, geology and town life of the county."[6] Because the project hinged on the premise that such objects were rapidly disappearing or being changed beyond recognition and that photographs were the best means to fix and thus preserve a record of appearances, the resulting images were, despite their claim of objectivity, tinged with sentimentality and a profound sense of loss (Fig. 65).[7]

Photographic surveys were indexes of not only the dislocation produced by modernity, but also of the intense struggle over who would possess the countryside: longtime inhabitants – often described by surveyors as "natives" in a rhetorical move that inscribed distance between the more urbanite, upper-class recorder and the object of his or her gaze – or tourists. "Class consciousness, competition for space and the right to define the appearance of the country" marked this contention.[8] Jekyll's photographs participated in this conflict, and the accompanying text reveals the complicated position she established with respect to her subject matter. She sympathized with and, indeed, admired the rural working-class people she studied. Nevertheless she repeatedly underscored the social gulf between them and herself by commenting pejoratively on cottagers' seeming lack of interest in their own traditions and preference for modern goods. She recorded with disdain how cottage owners parted willingly with "solid furniture of pure material and excellent design" for "cheap pretentious articles, got up with veneer and varnish and shoddy material."[9] She was dismayed by how often cottagers were seduced by the new goods of modernism, how they were "tempted by the shops that present their wares in a convenient and superficially attractive way," and how "every sort of folly or absurdity is com-

65. Compton Wynyates, Warwickshire Photographic Survey, 1891 (Source: Reproduced by permission of Birmingham Library Services.)

mitted by these poor people in this insane striving to be what they think is 'fashionable.'"[10] Jekyll, from her class and educational vantage point, perceived the goods of the countryside not as signs of a past that needed to be cast off, as did rural cottagers, but as aesthetic signifiers of honest labor and unadulterated, high-quality craftsmanship.

The photographs accompanying her book further fetishized and commodified the possessions of the working classes (Fig. 66). Carefully centered compositions with very little background information ensured that nothing would detract from the featured object. Lifted out of their normal context and usage, these objects – furniture, tools, clothing, and so on – were invited to circulate within the arenas constituted by the educated middle- to upper-class readers of Jekyll's book. While documenting the objects described in Jekyll's text, the photographs also became souvenirs, allowing readers to savor symbolically a talisman of rural life made even more poignant by its threatened disappearance. Thus an ordinary object, such as a candlestick, as described and photographed by Jekyll, became a signifier for a whole set of ideas about how the educated urban classes viewed

66. Gertrude Jekyll, "Iron Spiral Candlesticks," from *Old West Surrey,* London, 1904. (Source: Dumbarton Oaks, Studies in Landscape Architecture, Photo Archive.)

the countryside through a narrowed, nostalgic lens that obscured the tensions marking late-nineteenth-century agricultural communities. Jekyll's texts reflect a metaphorical collapsing of time and space as wealthy urbanites turned to rural objects, and the countryside itself, in order to reconnect with traditions of the past. Working-class country dwellers used the money received for these goods to purchase new, desirable fashions associated with the city. Such trafficking paradoxically eroded away the sense of rural localness at the same time it was being elevated to a national ideal.[11]

Likewise, Jekyll's photographs of broader landscapes transformed common rural sites and activities into pictorial views and thus endowed the landscape with new values for her intended audience. Her published books, as well as her notebooks in which she stored her photographic studies, are filled with images of seemingly ordinary places, such as country lanes, which she perceived as potentially artistic subjects. This mode of perception owes much to the writings of John Ruskin and the circle of artists associated with the critic. He instructed artists to study nature closely – a principle clearly adhered to in Jekyll's photographs, which, like her images of rural goods, used carefully constructed compositions to draw attention to those aspects of the landscape she found most notable, as in her photograph *Beech, Unstead Lane* (Fig. 67). Here Jekyll has cropped the tree trunks to focus the image on the tree roots, which stretch in a broad diagonal from the lower right corner to the upper left. Her attempt to hold the image in a general, overall field of focus so the grasses in the foreground are as clearly delineated as the ivy creeping over the cracked tree bark in the middle ground is reminiscent of the painting practices associated with the Pre-Raphaelites, known for their detailed depiction of nature as well as their veneration of the ordinary landscape as opposed to the older categories of the sublime or the picturesque.

Whereas Jekyll's photographs were informed by painting practices, they were also embedded in contemporary developments in photography. In these decades English photography was, in part, shaped by a dispute between H. P. Robinson, whose combination photographs (made by printing a single image from multiple joined negatives) were intended to rival genre paintings, and P. H. Emerson, who argued that photography should be regarded as an independent art form able to reproduce how the human eye saw the world. Emerson urged photographers to move out of the studio and into the landscape to photograph their subjects in their accustomed settings. In 1886 Emerson exemplified this advice with the publication of a series of photographs of the people, activities, and landscape of the Norfolk Broads, a collection of images of rural laborers that suggests the influence of seventeenth-century Dutch landscape painting and nineteenth-century French realism. Emerson refused to idealize in conventional terms; yet his images of the daily activities of workers in their soggy landscape exemplify his belief that "the poetry is all in nature, all pathos and tragedy is in nature, and only wants finding and tearing forth."[12] Both Emerson and Jekyll were concerned with recording rural pursuits, crafts, and occupations, and a number of similarities can be found between such images as Emerson's *Furze-Cutting on a Suffolk Common* (Fig. 68) and Jekyll's *Cutting Heath-Turf* (Fig. 69), which both show male laborers wresting resources from the land in practices that dated from medieval times. Such potential naturalistic subjects simply awaited the artist to recognize them and position them into the photographic frame.

But Jekyll should not be considered a direct follower of Emerson's aesthetic. She, for example, eschewed the slightly out-of-focus approach of the photographer. Moreover, many of her photographs have a staged quality suggestive of Robinson's work.[13] In addition, her photographs of broader landscapes embody guidelines set forth by Robinson. He urged photographers to overcome photography's inability to make "material alterations in landscapes and views embracing wide expanses" by adopting compositional rules evolved by painters.[14] Photography would thus rise above its status as a mere mechanical recorder. In Jekyll's photo albums, we can see her experimenting with compositional structures in successive prints of the same scene. For example, in a set of landscape views, she adjusts the frame so the focus of the composition shifts from the expanse of road leading to the distance (Fig. 70) to the small pond and ridge backed by trees closer to the foreground (Fig. 71). In the latter image, the road is now a dynamic

163 161

67. Getrude Jekyll, *Beech, Unstead Lane,* #291, Album II, 1885/86. (Source: Gertrude Jekyll Collection (1955-1) Environmental Design Archives, University of California, Berkeley.)

diagonal in the lower right corner. As is common in photographic survey work executed in this period, Jekyll's works thus slip between the modes of documentation and art.[15]

In sum, through her photographic oeuvre, Jekyll took what was essentially the flotsam and jettison of the working classes – old battered household goods, or the tangled vegetation of a roadside – and transformed them into valuable commodities and pleasing pictures, inscribing these objects and sites with values appropriate to her class. A further paradox marks *Old West Surrey:* although Jekyll's ostensible aim was to arrest the passage of time and the incursion of modernity into the countryside, her enticing account of the countryside encouraged further change by drawing would-be back-to-the-landers to Surrey, and she, herself, fit this paradigm.

The gardener advanced her locale into the national limelight by charging

68. P. H. Emerson, *Furze-Cutting on a Suffolk Common*, 1886. (Source: Courtesy George Eastman House.)

that the preservation of the Surrey countryside was not just a local but also a national concern. In discussing the nearby town of Godalming, for example, Jekyll argued that destroying "beautiful old houses" to make way for new commercial structures undermined the town's unique architectural heritage (which she recognized helped attract "people of the better sort" to the neighborhood) and should be regarded as an instructive case study for the entire nation. Appealing to patriotic sentiments, she insisted that everyone in England should be concerned by the threat posed by modern capitalism to older cultural forms and that it was every citizen's responsibility to preserve the past as a form of national patrimony.[16] Her text thus not only made the local accessible to a national audience but also instructed readers to equate the local and the national as well as the past and the nation. Borrowing Benedict Anderson's terms, *Old West Surrey* formed an imagined community, creating synchronic and diachronic bonds.

The dynamic that informs Jekyll's photography also shaped her landscape designs. Working from her local context – learning from surrounding cottage gar-

69. Gertrude Jekyll, "Cutting Heath-Turf," from *Old West Surrey,* London, 1904. (Source: Dumbarton Oaks, Studies in Landscape Architecture, Photo Archive.)

dens and the heath landscape at her own home at Munstead Wood – Jekyll offered lessons to the educated middle and upper classes in her published garden writings, creating the possibility of a national aesthetic. In borrowing from the gardening practices of her rural working-class neighbors, Jekyll performed the same maneuver she had with rural goods: seeing the artistic possibilities in long-standing rural crafts. And just as she could transform an ordinary country road into an artistic picture, Jekyll reworked landscapes traditionally conceived as wastelands – heaths, scrubby woodlands – into well-arranged compositions, thus recasting the detritus of agricultural production into desirable places appro-

70. Gertrude Jekyll, Landscape Study, #96, Album I, 1885. (Source: Gertrude Jekyll Collection (1955-1) Environmental Design Archives, University of California, Berkeley.)

priate for middle-class home owners. She was also willing to restage the landscape artistically, just as she did in her photographs, introducing notes of artificialness and exoticism in her flower borders.

The Gardens at Munstead Wood, 1883–c. 1892

The first Surrey garden Jekyll designed was for her mother, Julia Jekyll, at Munstead House, located at Munstead Heath; there Gertrude would also locate her own house, Munstead Wood, just across the road from her mother's property.[17] Julia Jekyll moved from Wargrave Hill, Berkshire, to Munstead House, Surrey, in 1878; and by 1883 her daughter had transformed the "wild heath land, diversified with picturesque clusters of Hollies, Scotch Firs, wild Junipers, and a variety of other spontaneous growth" into a landscape garden along the lines of those suggested by William Robinson. Gertrude kept much of the grounds intact and added rock, auricula, and alpine gardens (the latter being another specialty of Robinson), and a rhododendron bank as well as an orchard, reserve garden, and a kitchen garden framed by a hardy flower border on one side and seedbeds on the other.[18]

The heath, gorse, bracken, Scotch firs, and birch that Jekyll retained at her mother's home were considered characteristic of southeast England, particularly the region of the High Weald, and were the product of both local sandy soil and weather conditions and centuries of human occupation. Through the late twelfth and early fourteenth centuries, much of the timber of this region was cleared for

71. Gertrude Jekyll, Landscape Study, #96a, Album I, 1885. (Source: Gertrude Jekyll Collection (1955-1) Environmental Design Archives, University of California, Berkeley.)

settlement purposes.[19] Large-scale trees were not permitted to retake the land as settlers hacked back the woodlands to keep open areas for grazing and planting, although in periods of economic depression scrubby woodland reclaimed some portions of the land.[20] The growth of the iron industry in the sixteenth, seventeenth, and early eighteenth centuries put further pressure on the timber supply. In these conditions, quick-growing trees such as Scotch pines (introduced in the late eighteenth century) and birches fared best; and beneath this relatively open canopy, heath, gorse, and bracken thrived.[21] The agricultural writer William Cobbett on occasion described the Wealden landscape disparagingly for its lack of agricultural productivity. At the estate of Lord Erskine near Horsham, Surrey, for example, he found "a *bare heath* with here and there, in the better parts of it, some scrubby *birch*. It has been, in part, planted with fir-trees, which are as ugly as the heath was; and, in short, it is a most villainous tract."[22]

Jekyll viewed this supposed wasteland through an artistic eye, trained by the writings of her friend William Robinson, whom she had known since 1875; she contributed frequently to his journal *The Garden*. Jekyll and Robinson had learned to capitalize on the landscape in the High Weald of Kent and Sussex. Conceiving neglected fields and scrubby woodlands as potential models for garden design was a crucial maneuver. It shifted the vocabulary of landscape design away from clearly distinguishing between what was aesthetic or landscaped and what was not, that is, worked or waste (as in the work of Nesfield) to blurring these categories (as in the eighteenth-century landscape garden).

The pressure of suburban expansion contributed to the realignment of the designed landscape aesthetic when the High Weald, because of its limited agricultural value, came to be settled by members of the middle classes seeking a rural escape within striking distance of London.[23] Jekyll and her family took advantage of the available open space. By the early 1880s the family purchased an additional 15 acres; and the parcel of Munstead Wood was given to Gertrude in accordance with her mother's wish that she build a home there because Gertrude's brother Herbert would inherit Munstead House. The house was eventually sited in the approximate center of the triangular plot. The construction of the gardenscape was relatively unusual in that large portions of it predated the erection of the house. Work on the site began in 1883, when a survey marking existing trees and paths was executed, but not until nearly ten years later, in 1892, did Jekyll's architect, Edwin Lutyens, produce the first plan for the house. By the time Lutyens was brought to the project, much of the woodland garden was in place, as well as many of the built features, such as walls, the pergola, and utilitarian buildings (Fig. 72).

Attention was first directed to the woodland garden, a roughly 10-acre area composed from an existing copse:

> A small wood of ten acres adjoins my garden. Formerly it was a wood of Scotch Pine of some seventy year's growth. Under the close-growing trees the ground was bare but for a scant sprinkling of Whortleberry, Heath and Bracken at the lighter edges. Thirty-five years ago [c. 1880] the Pines were cut and the ground left bare. Soon it became covered with Heath, Ling and short Bracken, and, on one side especially, a stronger growth of Whortleberry. Then, year by year, tree seedlings of many kinds came up in considerable quantity so that there is not a yard of ground without one or more. This went on for some nine or ten years before the land came into my hands, and by then the seedlings were in many places so thick that it was impossible to get between them. From that time onwards the problem was how best to thin them, and to cut out a few paths on the easiest lines to serve the future laying out of the ground where house and garden were to be.[24]

Jekyll's goal was to create naturalistic, artistic compositions akin to those prescribed by Robinson.[25] By 1899 portions of the copse were underplanted with daffodils, again echoing Robinson's designs, and naturalizable exotics such as the American trillium and Solomon's seal (plants specifically mentioned by Robinson) were intermixed with the existing bracken (Fig. 73).[26] A fern walk – a path framed by 9-foot-wide banks of ferns, Solomon's seal, and wood rush – was also constructed.[27] A visitor to the site in 1900 praised the woodland area,

> because it has been so admirably managed, and because the marks of interference with Nature have been so artistically concealed. Nature has been compelled, so to speak, to group the trees. . . . In fact, that wood is

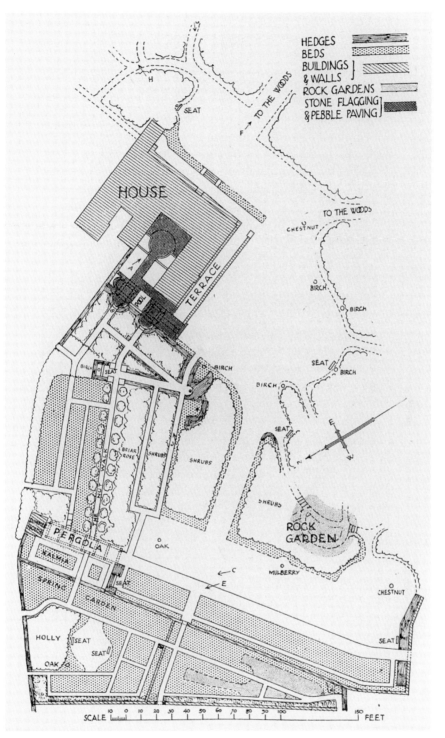

72. "A Garden in West Surrey: General Plan [Munstead Wood]." (Source: Gertrude Jekyll and Lawrence Weaver, *Gardens for Small Country Houses,* London, 1920.)

a perfect example of how much may be done to improve a thoroughly
wild spot without depriving it of its essential wildness.[28]

Jekyll's approach to landscaping was exactly the opposite of what was advocated at midcentury when Shirley Hibberd insisted that

> it should be borne in mind by every cultivator of taste in gardening,
> that a garden is an *artificial* contrivance, it is not a piece scooped out of
> a wood, but in some sense a continuation of the house. Since it is a cre-
> ation of art, not a patch of wild nature . . . so it should everywhere show
> the evidence of artistic taste.[29]

168

Jekyll, also an ardent believer that artistic taste was necessary for a good garden, nonetheless also took her cues from nature, like Robinson, his mentor
Robert Marnock, and other designers of the 1860s and 1870s, as well as her fellow gardeners G. F. Wilson and S. Reynolds Hole, who advocated a return to
aspects of picturesque or gardenesque planting methods of the late eighteenth
and early nineteenth centuries while retaining the horticultural improvements of
their own age. The goal was to rid gardening of references to architectural and
revivalist styles, such as the Italianate manner of Nesfield.[30] Canon S. Reynolds
Hole, who had the Deanery at Rochester, for example, acclaimed the eighteenth-
century gardeners Alexander Pope and William Kent for instituting what he considered to be the ideal garden, one based on natural systems and resulting in

> a collection of the most beautiful trees, shrubs, and flowers which you
> can procure for the space at your disposal, so arranged and tended that
> they may seem indigenous, and happy in their homes, each to be
> admired for its individual merits, and mutually enhancing the charms
> of its neighbour by contrast or by combination.[31]

The architect, he admonished, should be confined to the precinct immediately
adjoining the house.[32]

Woodland gardens represented a well-established tradition in English garden design, and particularly significant examples, such as the eighteenth-century estates of Painshill and Woburn Farm, were located in Jekyll's home district of Surrey and principles exemplified by these sites were discussed amply
in gardening literature.[33] Going back to the eighteenth century, examples can
be found of landowners thinning and selectively planting woodlands to create a
garden, as in the case of Dr. John Fothergill's American garden in which he
introduced kalmias, azaleas, magnolias, and other flowering shrubs into a "little wilderness," referring to the eighteenth-century garden feature composed of
trees set in a planned arrangement and, often, with an understory of flower-

ing shrubs.[34] This feature gradually evolved into the shrubbery, an ornamental planting feature that could include flowers and trees, in addition to its obvious emphasis on shrubs.[35] Although Jekyll's garden, with its exotics set off by indigenous vegetation and walks winding through planned environments, is reminiscent of its eighteenth-century predecessors, the gardener maintained that her garden was not a true "shrub-wilderness."[36]

Jekyll's woodland garden is closer in form to one of the earliest incarnations of wildernesses and shrubberies: wood walks. In the mid–eighteenth century, the estate owner Norborne Berkeley, with the assistance of Thomas Wright, instituted meandering paths bordered by decorative shrubs through his "wood garden" at Stoke Park. Clearings were constructed and bordered with exotic trees, shrubs, and flowers.[37] In addition, flowers were planted alongside paths and at the edges of clearings, as well as "scattered on the margins of thickets" or arranged in island beds in the midst of lawns.[38] The effect is not unlike what Jekyll achieved by introducing the wild garden to a woodland setting, as had Robinson and G. F. Wilson, whose garden at Wisley Jekyll admired.

73. Gertrude Jekyll, "Daffodils among Junipers Where Garden Joins Copse," from *Wood and Garden,* London, 1899. (Source: Dumbarton Oaks, Studies in Landscape Architecture, Photo Archive.)

Yet when describing possible influences on her work, Jekyll eschewed historical references and antecedents and typically cited either her contemporaries, such as Robinson and Wilson, or the landscapes she witnessed around her. Such rhetoric reinforced her position, touted with much modesty, as a working amateur and underscores further the importance of the local for her gardening aesthetic. Nonetheless, her style of gardening was highly dependent on the wide range of exotic horticultural material introduced into England over the previous decades and the gardening practices developed to accommodate this material. Jekyll pushed even further the notion of working after nature while also assisting nature.

In preparation for siting the house, Jekyll began converting the area north of the woodland garden to lawn in the 1880s. Although lawns, as garden features,

have clear references to meadow clearings, they are nonetheless manifestly artificial, requiring frequent seeding and extensive maintenance in order to keep clear
of weeds and volunteer plantings. Jekyll worked against this characteristic by
turning to materials available in her nearby woodland. The lawn area was initially
covered with rough heath and fine-leaved wild grasses; she used the latter,
blended with local species such as "Sheep's Fescue" or "Crested Dog's tail," to
establish the lawn in the belief that they went "better with the Heath and Fir and
Bracken that belong to the place."[39] Here we see an early manifestation of Jekyll's
oft-repeated tenet that the garden should seem to emerge imperceptibly and logically from the site and its surrounding landscape.[40]

Within the first few years of owning the land Jekyll also constructed a rock
garden, to support more fragile and exotic vegetation, in a small space adjoining
the woodland garden and lawn. By 1900 this rock garden, "made with a few simple parallel ridges of stone," housed "small shrubs, such as Gaultheria and
Alpine Rhodendron, with hardy Ferns, and groups of two or three plants of conspicuously handsome foliage, such as *Saxifraga peltata* and *Rodgersia
podophylla*."[41] Thus the rock garden both managed the physical transition from
lawn to copse and registered a shift from "natural" to "artificial," for although it
was meant to imitate natural outcroppings, the vegetation was clearly nonindigenous. The house would eventually be sited in relatively close proximity to this
rock garden in keeping with Jekyll's precept that the most frankly manipulated
features should be located near the house and, as the landscape moved outward,
increasingly naturalistic features should be developed, thus blurring the distinction between the improved and unimproved landscape at the edges of the
grounds. (This aesthetic presumed a relatively isolated plot of land and was ill
suited to dense suburban developments.)

In 1887 Jekyll added a nut-walk in the northern portion of her grounds, adjacent to the house plot.[42] This historic garden feature utilized woodland trees
arranged in a quincunx pattern that frankly indicated the intervening hand of the
gardener. Within a few years, along the outer edge of the upper copse, Jekyll
added a rhododendron plantation, an even more frankly artificial, nonindigenous
note, in her effort to "make pleasant ways from lawn to copse" (Fig. 74).[43] Here
Jekyll partakes of the tradition of the wood walk/wilderness/shrubbery in both
the selection of rhododendrons, popularly associated with this tradition, and the
placement of her rhododendron plantation, which invokes the use of the shrubbery as a transition from the area around the house to the more woodland or
parklike features beyond.

She balanced the exotic artificiality of the rhododendrons by intermingling
the bushes with ferns that enabled the flowering shrubs to blend more convinc-
ingly with the surrounding landscape.[44] She followed a similar plan with the aza-

74. Gertrude Jekyll, "Rhododendrons Where the Copse and Garden Meet," from *Wood and Garden,* London, 1899. (Source: Dumbarton Oaks, Studies in Landscape Architecture, Photo Archive.)

lea garden, located in the midst of the copse. Again, the notion of a plantation of exotics had been anticipated at such sites as Stoke Park, although an entire garden devoted to azaleas was not conceivable until the introduction of the plant in the late nineteenth century.[45] The azaleas, arranged in a long band over about half an acre, were intermixed with

> a natural growth of the wild Ling *(Calluna)* and Whortleberry, and the small, white-flowered Bed-straw, with the fine-bladed Sheep's-fescue grass, the kind most abundant in heath-land. The surrounding ground is copse, of a wild, forest-like character, of birch and small oak. A wood-path of wild heath cut short winds through the planted group.[46]

Jekyll later modified the woodland along its northern perimeter by planting "groups of Juniper, Holly, Mountain Ash, and Ilex," materials indigenous to the area, as well as introducing Cistuses, one of Robinson's favorite naturalizable flowering shrubs. By the time work began on her house, Jekyll had already established the main theme of her garden: the indigenous landscape, artistically managed, as a frame to carefully selected exotics.

Writing from Munstead Wood

Jekyll's experience in transforming Munstead Wood was crucial to her subsequent garden writing, which was the chief means by which most Englanders became familiar with her work. She began writing on a regular basis around the turn of the century when she was hired by Edward Hudson to be co-editor for *The Garden,* a publication began by Robinson but then owned by Hudson. She accepted this task for one year, 1901, but soon became more involved in writing for another Hudson venture, *Country Life.* In 1900 she had begun to contribute to the "Garden Notes" column of that magazine and eventually published several volumes on garden design and advice with *Country Life.* Her writings dealt relatively little with garden design or layout when compared with texts by members of the Art Workers Guild; instead, she focused on plants and their arrangement, much like her mentor Robinson. Like Robinson, she too believed gardening was essential to the English character. Her first book, *Wood and Garden* (1899), opened with the statement, typical in its iron-willed conviction wrapped in an self-effacing demeanor: "There are already many and excellent books about gardening; but the love of a garden, already so deeply implanted in the English heart, is so rapidly growing, that no excuse is needed for putting forth another."[47]

With this book, tellingly subtitled "Notes and Thoughts, Practical and Critical of a Working Amateur," Jekyll established a speaking position of modesty that she retained throughout her career. In the introduction she stated,

> I lay no claim either to literary ability, or to botanical knowledge, or even to knowing the best practical methods of cultivation; but I have lived among outdoor flowers for many years, and have not spared myself in the way of actual labour, and have come to be on closely intimate and friendly terms with a great many growing things, and have acquired certain instincts which, though not clearly defined, are of the nature of useful knowledge.[48]

A reviewer writing for *Country Life* picked up on this discourse, pointing out that Jekyll "disclaims literary ability and botanical knowledge" and was "no doctrinaire."[49]

By focusing attention on her experience tending a garden, Jekyll established her authenticity as a garden expert while obscuring her evident scholarship. This contrasted with Blomfield's bombastic polemic, which rested on his study of older treatises and sites with little discussion of actual garden work. The differences between the two voices owe much to their respective agendas and positions relative to the profession, but also to notions of decorum associated with contemporaneous gender roles.

Although professional women garden writers were certainly not an anomaly by the 1890s – Jane Loudon, for example, had written extensively at midcentury – many garden writers nonetheless maintained that women did not belong in the garden because they lacked sufficient rational intellect to order and to control the space. Walter Wright, for example, in his 1908 book, argued that

> women have the capacity for getting greater enjoyment out of gardens than men, but not a greater power of forming them. They love flowers, and, forgetting that affection does not always suffice, sometimes crowd their gardens with far too many kinds. . . . Every garden has it limits, and a small one quickly becomes so overcrowded that the plants suffer. This does not make for perfect gardens.[50]

173

Other supposed limitations of women included physical frailty and an inability to command sufficient respect requisite for giving orders to hired labor.

Inroads were gradually made, however. An article that appeared in *Country Life* in November 1899 claimed that "in gardening, curiously enough, it is not the woman of theory but of practice that succeeds."[51] Jekyll was thus taking advantage of an avenue open to her for expression through recourse to practical experience. By denying any knowledge other than that gleaned from daily experience in her garden, Jekyll also endeared herself to readers who could readily identify with her. This rhetorical maneuver was shared by numerous other female garden writers of the period, according to Dianne Harris, who has conducted a study of American and British gardening handbooks written by women from 1870 to 1920. Female authors repeatedly took "a subservient, overly modest, and self-deprecating tone that is used as a defense against their predominantly male professional critics, [and] as an ingratiating technique to appeal to their female audience by making themselves appear to be 'average women' (another frequently used phrase)."[52] Parallels can also be found in botanical tracts by female authors. Ann Shtier, in her study of eighteenth- and nineteenth-century female botanical writers, has detected a shift in tone by the 1830s so that "in contrast to much writing by women about botany during the Linnean years, 1760–1830, the voices of women botanical writers in early Victorian England were muted and more tentative, less intellectual in range and aspiration," and evoked such descriptors as "sweet, even-tempered, unpretentious," and "modest."[53]

Yet Harris cautions us against a one-sided reading of female garden writing. She situates this material within the formation of "women's culture," meaning a network of cultural practices that "sought to empower women through increased self-esteem, independence, and the advocation of assumed proprietary rights over real property."[54] Indeed, implicit in Jekyll's writings is her ownership of Munstead Wood, where she completely controlled the grounds and directed her laborers. She was a moderately successful businesswoman, supplementing her inheritance with a steady stream of garden writing and a nursery business, which directly benefited from her design commissions because she often directed clients to buy her plants (albeit at prices that were often below those of other nurseries).

Although Jekyll claimed amateur status, she was, in reality, a professional and traveled in a circle of like-minded women, such as Emily Davies, promoter of women's education, and Octavia Hill, philanthropist and social reformer.[55] Her close friend Barbara Leigh Smith Bodichon was active in art, philanthropy, politics, feminism, and education, founding Girton College for women. Bodichon was known for supporting and encouraging younger women, as did Jekyll, if only in the form of prose. In 1916, in the midst of the Great War, Jekyll wrote an article on "Women as Gardeners" that began with the bold claim "The profession of gardening for women has now for some years passed beyond the stage of experiment and has now become a familiar and established fact." Jekyll acknowledged that the absence of men on the home front increased the need for female gardeners, but nonetheless insisted that historical circumstances notwithstanding, women were well suited to the tasks given their ability for "infinite detail . . . [and] unceasing watchfulness and sympathy." She even proposed that women gardeners band together to run a market garden of a few acres. "The life would be laborious," she cautioned, but added, in the feminist spirit described by Harris, that "there would be joy of possession and of freedom."[56]

Jekyll's first book, in addition to establishing her rhetorical voice, which communicated calm competence couched in the nonthreatening language of amateurism, set in place a general formula she would follow in subsequent writings. Organized in the manner of old gardening treatises as a month-by-month guide to tasks to be undertaken in the garden, *Wood and Garden* championed the local landscape as a firsthand source. For example, after reporting on a walk through a "little wild valley" adjoining a neighboring farm, Jekyll recommended to her readers that

> such a bit of wild forest as this small valley and the hilly land beyond are precious lessons in the best kind of tree and shrub planting. No artificial planting can ever equal that of Nature, but one may learn from it the great lesson of the importance of moderation and reserve, of simplicity of intention, and directness of purpose, and the inestimable value of the quality called "breadth" in painting.[57]

This repeated reference to the local landscape continues the project of developing specifically English sources for English garden design begun by Robinson. In *Home and Garden* (1900), Jekyll chided home owners for beginning their gardens by buying quantities of flowers and shrubs rather than working from the existing

canvas. The local should be the guide – a late-nineteenth-century twist on the eighteenth-century precept to "consult the genius of the place." Jekyll thus taught her
audiences what she had already learned at Munstead Wood: to appreciate the landscapes around them. Bracken, gorse, and heath no longer signified "waste" or
"rough" uncultivable land that needed to be cleared in order to introduce the requisite gardening materials; rather they represented the core of a garden:

> Many places that would be beautiful if almost left alone are spoiled by
> doing away with some simple natural feature in order to put in its place
> some hackneyed form of gardening. . . . Houses great and small are
> being built on tracts of natural heath-land. A perfect undergrowth of
> wild Heaths is there already. If it is old and overgrown, it can be easily
> renewed by clearing it off and lightly digging the ground over, when the
> Heaths will quickly spring up again. Often there are already thriving
> young Scotch Firs and Birches. Where such conditions exist, a beauti-
> ful garden can be easily made at the least possible cost, jealously saving
> all that there is already, and then using in some simple way such plants
> as I have recommended.[58]

Jekyll's phrase "if almost left alone," however, is very much a deception. As
garden historians have noted for several decades, Jekyll's gardens required extensive effort to create and to maintain. More importantly, she was not suggesting
that any landscape could be "almost left alone" and yet be a garden. The landscape had to contain artistic possibilities recognized and brought to the fore by
the gardener/artist. The task was akin to that of the late-nineteenth-century photographer bent on proving the artistic merits of the medium: to take the real –
nature – and present it in such a manner that the viewer recognizes it as art and
not just the detritus of everyday life that happened to fall before the activated
lens. To rise above the literal, H. P. Robinson instructed photographers to
"refine," "transfigure," and "glorify" as they sought out beauty. To accomplish
this required an "educated eye," in other words, "subsequent study, and a higher
knowledge of the resources of art."[59] Such training enabled the photographer "to
seize the salient features, to determine the most suitable view, and to arrange the
light so as to bring out the effect of character; at the same time giving force and
prominence to natural advantages, and concealing or subduing natural
defects."[60] Jekyll, in her own writing, repeatedly insisted that artistic knowledge
was required to fully appreciate the beauty of nature. For example, in *Home and
Garden,* she insisted that "the much more numerous and delicate of Nature's
pictorial moods or incidents can only be enjoyed or understood when presented
in the form of a painted picture by the artist who understands Nature's speech
and can act as her interpreter."[61]

Jekyll not only transformed what was regarded as waste into art, she elevated neglected landscapes into national icons. Like novelists of her age, such as Thomas Hardy, she found beauty in "tree and bush, fern and flower, rampant tangle and garland of wild Rose and Honeysuckle, Hop and Briony" found in hedgerows, roadside banks, and other liminal zones. She then asked her readers, "Is it only an instance of patriotic prejudice, or is it really, as I believe, a fact, that no country roads and lanes in the temperate world are so full of sweet and homely pictorial incident as those of our dear England?"[62]

Building Munstead Wood

Ensuring that her home was in keeping with the local context she prized was a primary concern for Jekyll. In May 1889, through the rhododendron collector Harry Mangles, she met architect Edwin Lutyens, who had recently struck out on his own after training at the South Kensington School of Art and then apprenticing in the office of Ernest George and Peto. Like many architects of his generation, Lutyens was greatly influenced by the work of Philip Webb and Richard Norman Shaw and so was sympathetic to Jekyll's interest in the Arts and Crafts. Nonetheless, Jekyll proceeded cautiously, traveling the local area with the architect, a Surrey native, examining exemplary vernacular domestic architecture. Not until 1892 did Lutyens submit his first plan for the house, which was summarily rejected for inappropriateness: Jekyll's nickname "Plazzaoh" suggests that the architectural vocabulary was deemed too Italianate. Jekyll also dismissed a small cottage structure, later called The Hut, but a year later reversed her position. The Hut was completed by 1895, when Jekyll moved into it upon the death of her mother. Although Jekyll adopted The Hut as her residence while awaiting the completion of the main house, it was intended for servants or workers and partook of local designs for rural working-class residences.[63]

Lutyens took up the project for the main house again in 1896. At this stage, work advanced relatively rapidly, although evidence suggests he had to submit every step of the design process to his patron and respond to her comments and suggestions.[64] In designing the house, following the success of The Hut, Lutyens looked to the Surrey environment for inspiration so the final house (Plate IV) was, in Jekyll's words, "built in the thorough and honest spirit of the good work of old days, and the body of it, so fashioned and reared, has, as it were, taken to itself the soul of a more ancient dwelling-place."[65] Local stone and brick were used as well as half-timbering, constructed of locally grown, hand-hewn English oak, common to cottages and manor houses in the area.[66] Later Jekyll wrote with conspicuous pride regarding Lutyens's ability to construct a "new-old" house that easily assimilated to the site. She believed strongly that architects should adopt well-tried and proven building materials and techniques of the locale in which they worked:

> I always think it a pity to use in any one place the distinctive methods of another. Every part of the country has its own traditional ways, and if these have in the course of many centuries become "crystallised" into any particular form we may be sure that there is some good reason for it, and it follows that the attempt to use the ways and methods of some distant place is sure to give an impression as of something uncomfortably exotic, or geographical confusion, of perhaps right thing in the wrong place.[67]

~§ 177

By adapting from local building traditions, Lutyens produced a design that, according to Jekyll, straddled the past and present, and thus participated in the old and new paradigm that coursed through this period. And, like many designs of the Art Workers Guild, the house borrowed from the past without copying any one site wholesale so that rather than representing a moment frozen in time, like historic house museums today, it made the past live again as an organic entity.[68] Ironically, however, although Jekyll constantly appealed to local tradition in her writings and designs, her texts invited readers to take up her Surrey-based motifs in distant places, and in her own garden, she welcomed exotic introductions, although she expended considerable effort to ensure these non-natives would always appear appropriate to their settings.

Siting the house was a particular challenge, given that much of the garden structure was already in place when Lutyens arrived. Stephen King, who supervised the recent restoration of the gardens at Munstead Wood, has observed that Lutyens positioned the house "in such a way as to place it a full 30° off the main axis of the original garden" (Fig. 72).[69] The effect of this decision can be observed in such features as the nut-walk, which takes a decisive bend to meet up with the projecting wing of the house, or the Pergola, which bears no obvious orientation to the house. To mask the awkward relation between features, triangular plots were devised, and much of the grounds reflect triangular motifs.[70]

Whereas Lutyens's siting created challenges for the subsequent design of the southern portion of the grounds, it allowed him take advantage of the northern copse so the doorway along that side of the house looks to the wide Green Wood Walk. Thus although Jekyll's garden eschewed the rigid formal geometry adopted by designers such as Reginald Blomfield, paths and views are nonetheless oriented to the architecture. The chief walks through the copse on the southern side of the house all converge on the South Terrace, either at its far corners or at the center doorway. On the western side of the house, the distinctive chimney housing that projects out from the house establishes the terminus of the paths leading to The Hut and Rock Garden. Along the northern U-shaped side of the house, key pathways emerge from the North Court, located in the courtyard created by the two wings, so the North Court establishes a strong axis continued into the northern border garden.

In turn, Jekyll fixed focal points in the garden. Particularly strong are those established at the terminations of the main axial paths, which draw the visitor from the house into the landscape, as was done in eighteenth-century sites such as Chiswick House. But unlike Chiswick, which used architectural or sculptural objects to punctuate the conclusions or key junctures of paths, Jekyll's eye-catchers were plantings, in keeping with her naturalistic aesthetic (Fig. 75).[71] At the terminus of the Green Wood Walk, for example, was a forked Scots pine, which also served as the anchor point for "Second Avenue," which ran parallel to the southern perimeter of the property. Between these two angled avenues were placed a myriad of secondary paths, some straight and some serpentine, in the manner of eighteenth-century groves and woods.

The Gardens at Munstead Wood, c. 1892–1914

In the early 1890s, Jekyll continued to develop her gardens, instituting a number of specialized gardens, including the Spring Garden situated against the northern perimeter of the ornamental grounds. The Spring Garden answered the need of where to plant spring bulbs, which provided color for only a brief period of the year, and should therefore be, according to Jekyll, placed in their own space, rather than, as was the custom, in the mixed border, which Jekyll described as "the worst place of all, for when in flower they only show as forlorn little patches of bloom rather far apart, and when their leaves die down, leaving their places looking empty, the ruthless spade or trowel stabs into them when it is desired to fill the space with some other plant."[72] In the southern copse, she had added, by 1899, a Rose Thicket near the rhododendron area as well as a Shrub Garden in which masses of flowering shrubs, such as sweetbriar, water-elder, and medlar, were arranged in graduated heights to create a subtle transition from the obviously cultivated gardenscape to the less obviously improved woodscape.[73] A shrub clump in the form of a "long, low bank, five or six paces wide, highest in the middle" was also planted across from the nut-walk.[74] Again, these features – clump, shrubbery, and thicket – were discussed frequently in mid-eighteenth-century and nineteenth-century gardening texts as a means by which to display exotic plants (although Jekyll modestly described those at Munstead Wood simply as places to house "things I like best, whether new friends or old").[75] Jekyll's subsequent creation of gardens devoted to particular species, such as her Prim-

75. Gertrude Jekyll, "A Grass Path in the Copse," from *Wood and Garden,* London, 1899. (Source: Dumbarton Oaks, Studies in Landscape Architecture, Photo Archive.)

rose, Auricula, and Peony gardens, also has important precedents in late-eigh-teenth-century and nineteenth-century gardening practices, but the notion of placing specialized gardens in naturalistic settings, as she did with the Primrose Garden, was new. The Primrose Garden was placed in a woodland clearing, where it was "half shaded by Oak, Chestnut, and Hazel."[76]

Also in the 1890s, Jekyll developed the design feature that came to be a defin-ing feature of late Victorian and Edwardian gardens: the hardy flower border (Plate V). Located to the west of the Spring Garden, the border was backed by an 11-foot sandstone wall that divided it from a triangular plot of land designated as the Summer or Cutting Garden. The border, 200 feet long and 14 feet wide, housed summer flowers and exemplified Jekyll's color theories, often recognized as her major contribution to gardening theory. She arrived at this garden form through adroitly synthesizing references drawn, once more, from her local environment, previous garden practices, and contemporary design debates.

Jekyll referred to her large flower border, or south border, in most of her writings, but perhaps the best description can be found in *Colour Schemes for the Flower Garden* (1908):

> The planting of the border is designed to show a distinct scheme of colour arrangement. At the two ends there is a groundwork of grey and glaucous foliage. . . . With this, at the near or western end, there are flowers of pure blue, grey-blue, white, palest yellow and palest pink; each colour partly in distinct masses and partly intergrouped. The colouring then passes through stronger yellows to orange and red. By the time the middle space of the border is reached the colour is strong and gorgeous, but, as it is in good harmonies, it is never garish. Then the colour strength recedes in an inverse sequence through orange and deep yellow to pale yellow, white and palest pink; again with blue-grey foliage. But at this, the eastern end, instead of the pure blues we have purples and lilacs.
>
> Looked at from a little way forward, for a wide space of grass allows this point of view, the whole border can be seen as one picture, the cool colouring at the ends enhancing the brilliant warmth of the middle. Then, passing along the wide path next to the border, the value of the colour arrangement is still more strongly felt. Each portion now becomes a picture in itself, and every one is of such a colouring that it best prepares the eye, in accordance with natural law, for what is to follow. Standing for a few moments before the endmost region of grey and blue, and saturating the eye to its utmost capacity with these colours, it passes with extraordinary avidity to the succeeding yellows. These intermingle in a pleasant harmony with the reds and scarlets, blood-reds and clarets, and then lead again to yellows. Now the eye has again become saturated, this time with the rich colouring, and has therefore, by the law of complementary colour, acquired a strong appetite for the greys and purples. These therefore assume an appearance of brilliancy that they would not have had without the preparation provided by their recently received complementary colour.[77]

Implicit in this discussion was Jekyll's manner of planting in "drifts," that is, in long irregular shapes rather than "block-shaped patches." With drift plantings, according to Jekyll, dead foliage was less noticeable and a better pictorial effect was achieved.[78] Drift planting came out of the earlier tradition of massed planting that had developed over the course of the late eighteenth and nineteenth centuries in contrast to the "mingled" style.

By the early nineteenth century, several methods for planting flower borders existed, according to John Claudius Loudon. The most popular was the mingled flower garden, the goal of which was to "plant an equal number of every color, and such a variety in regard to time of flowering as may afford some of very color in flower from February to October."[79] According to this manner of gardening, the *"Flowers in borders should always be planted in rows,* or in some regular form. . . . Every approach to irregularity, and a wild, confused, crowded, or natural-like appearance, must be avoided in gardens avowedly artificial."[80] Within each row a rhythmic patterning of color and blooming cycles was established, very much like the Baroque *plate-bande* and its checkerboard effect.[81] Jane Loudon allowed that plants need not be placed in rows if a border "is to be composed of a great variety of flowers," but nonetheless demanded that "a space must be apportioned to each plant according to its width; keeping in view the necessity of leaving a clear space round each plant, whether large or small." She took little note of color relationships but rather was guided by principles of equal distribution: "The object ought to be to have an equal number of plants in flower in each of the floral months; and among the plants of each month to have as nearly as possible an equal number of each of the principal colours."[82]

Although Jekyll also espoused rhythmic patterns, she largely eschewed grid patterns, symmetry, and bare spaces around plants in favor of bold masses or drifts that connoted a naturalistic irregularity as opposed to an artificial order. The difference between the mingled style and Jekyll's planting methods is clearly borne out in their plans. Jekyll indicated her undulating drifts with biomorphic forms (Fig. 76), whereas, in his *Encyclopedia,* J. C. Loudon had provided a highly regularized and ordered plan for a mingled flower border organized around the colors red, white, blue, and yellow (indicated by r, w, b, y on the plan with the numbers indicating the blooming seasons: 1 = February and March, 2 = March and April, 3 = May and June, 4 = July, 5 = August, 6 = September and October) (Fig. 77).

But elsewhere in his text, J. C. Loudon had suggested a manner of planting that related directly to the effect that Jekyll wished to achieve in her garden. With respect to the shrubbery, he proposed, as an alternative to the mingled style, the "grouped" manner of planting, which referred to massing by genus, species, or variety with gradual blending from one type to the next.[83] This second approach was gradually adopted in herbaceous borders, as indicated by Frances Jane Hope's *Notes and Thoughts on Gardens and Woodlands* (1881), in which she states, "we have our borders arranged in rows for convenience of hoeing, and to know exactly where each plant is; but I know some prefer to plant their borders in groups, and the effect is, perhaps, less formal than it otherwise would be."[84] Jekyll capitalized on these developments, and, as Brent Elliott has argued, although she was not the originator of informal drift planting, she clearly helped to disseminate and popularize this method.[85]

But rather than point to textual precedents in explaining how she arrived at the manner of planting in drifts, Jekyll claimed that much of her inspiration came from studying and photographing cottage gardens, which she admired for their seeming disregard of rules.[86] Her constant textual references to cottage gardens reinforced the impression that the foundations of her gardening theory rested in the local environment, a space that also simultaneously registered as emblematic of all of England. These references also reinscribed Jekyll as an amateur, who simply adapted from what she observed around her.

Yet Jekyll's theories were part and parcel of ongoing changes in professional gardening circles. To organize her border with respect to color graduation and contrast, Jekyll turned to the latest developments in color theory, which had their roots in the eighteenth century. The late-eighteenth-century designer William Chambers, for example, claimed to have learned from the Chinese that gardens should be governed by gradual transitions in height and color.[87] Writing over a hundred years later, Jekyll's use of color sequencing seems like a necessary conclusion to Chambers's remarks. In the intervening period, a number of writers had systematized color further, building on Sir Isaac Newton's color scale or wheel and his initial investigations into the complementary properties of color.[88] Perhaps the most crucial contribution to nineteenth-century color theory came from the French chemist Michel-Eugène Chevreul, who observed that the perceived dullness of the Gobelins' tapestries he was hired to improve was "due not to the quality of the dyestuffs but to the subjective effect of optical mixture: adjacent threads of complementary or near-complementary hues were mixing in the eye to a neutral grey." He concluded, "In the case where the eye sees at the same time two contiguous colours, they will appear as dissimilar as possible, both in

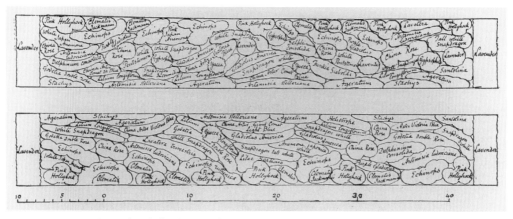

76. Gertrude Jekyll, "A Special Border of Grey, White, Pink and Purple." (Source: Gertrude Jekyll and Lawrence Weaver, *Gardens for Small Country Houses*, London, 1920.)

their optical composition and in the height of their tone," as well as that "in the Harmony of Contrast the complementary assortment is superior to every other."[89] Gardeners and garden writers, such as John Lindley and W. P. Ayres, adapted these theories in the 1850s.[90] Jekyll likewise drew on Chevreul's theories in her notion that strong colors, when observed from a distance, would activate vision, driving the viewer from the grays and purples at the end of her border to the strong oranges and reds at the center in search of complementary contrast. Her application of Chevreul's theories to garden design was justified further by the scientist himself who discussed gardening in his treatise (which was translated into English).[91] Moreover, Chevreul's theories were widely adopted by nineteenth-century painters. Jekyll herself received early training in painting and always claimed to have "had great delight in the study of color, as the word is understood by artists . . . [as dealing with] relation and proportion."[92] She sought out friendships with artists, such as the amateur watercolorist Hercules Brabazon Brabazon, who had emerged from relative obscurity in the 1890s with critics' enthusiastic reception of his sensitive landscapes rendered as veils of mingled and contrasting colors. Like her painting colleagues, Jekyll studied closely the effects of color, even to the point of analyzing how colors behaved in relationship to sunlight. For example, with respect to her rhododendron garden, Jekyll placed the purple flowering bushes in the shade and the reddish bushes in the sun with the understanding that darkness would deepen the purple shades and brightness would enhance the brilliance of the reds.[93]

Jekyll's arrangement of color in the flower border was innovative in another respect, as Brent Elliott has explained. Although her account of her border may suggest a "progression of hues" by virtue of such phrases as "passes through,"

77. Anon., "The Manner of Planting a Bed or Border in the Mingled Style," from J. C. Loudon, *Encyclopedia of Gardening,* London, 1824. (Source: Dumbarton Oaks, Studies in Landscape Architecture, Photo Archive.)

she, in fact, advocated "an interrupted sequence," or put more simply, mixing within the larger context of drifts of color: for example, "a paler yellow followed by white would instantly connect the warm colors with the lilacs and purples, and a colder white would combine them pleasantly with low-growing plants with cool-coloured leaves."[94] This careful use of contrasts and juxtapositions is illustrated by an account of Jekyll's south border, c. 1900, provided in *Happy England.* Describing the far end of the garden, where an arched wooden door in the brick wall gives egress to the Spring Garden and Cutting Garden, the author explained why cool colors were selectively introduced to this portion of the border in order to contrast with the predominant yellows, reds, and oranges:

> The orange red flowers hanging over the wall are those of *Bignonia grandiflora;* the bushes on either side of the archway with white flowers are choisyas, and the adjoining ones are red and yellow dahlias, flanked by tritonias (red-hot pokers); the oranges in front are African marigolds . . . , with white marguerites; the grey-leaved plant to the left is the *Cineraria maritima.* Miss Jekyll does not entirely keep to her arrangement of masses of colour; whilst, as an artist, she affects rich masses of colour, she is not above experimenting by breaking in varieties.[95]

This notion of "breaking in varieties" also applied to Jekyll's choice of plants throughout her garden. As already discussed, in her woodland or wild garden, Jekyll relied heavily on existing vegetation to set the foundation into which she introduced her local favorites found along country lanes, such as mullein and foxglove, as well as non-native plants, including trillium and dog-tooth violet.[96] Like her mentor William Robinson, Jekyll turned to cottage gardeners for assistance in locating plant material. She privileged, for example, older varieties of roses found in cottage gardens, recording her encounters with particularly spectacular examples in both textual anecdotes and photographs (Fig. 78).[97] Cottage gardens were also an excellent source for what she referred to as "old garden flowers," such as wallflowers, double daisies, white rosebushes, pink, thrift, and London pride, which she often featured in her hardy flower border.[98] She condemned hybridization and the "improvement" of flowers with regard to size and color as distorted deformities that appealed to the "vulgar and uneducated eye" and instead argued that the enlightened gardener, one uncorrupted by the seductive inducements of the commercial plant trade, should prefer "old favourites."[99]

Yet Jekyll never completely rejected the tender exotics that had previously been the hallmark of well-to-do gardens. Although she typically selected naturalized plants, many plants in her garden were nonetheless imports, as in the case of the rhododendrons from Asia Minor and the United States that managed the transition from garden to woodland, and the North American trillium introduced into the woodland.[100] Jekyll was also willing to use non-naturalizable plants, par-

78. Gertrude Jekyll, "A Roadside Cottage Garden," from *Wood and Garden,* London, 1899. (Source: Dumbarton Oaks, Studies in Landscape Architecture, Photo Archive.)

ticularly those associated with the Italian revival parterre. She used, for example, geraniums and cannas to line a stone-edged flower bed near her tank garden (Fig. 79) and relied on geraniums, salvias, calceolarias, and begonias as well as gladioli and dahlias to fill in bare spaces in her flower border in June.[101] Dahlias are native to Mexico as are the choisyas used in her flower border, which were planted next to bignonias, native to South America, and tritonias and marigolds, native to Africa. As Judith Tankard has explained, Jekyll defended her inclusion of tender exotics, annuals, and biennials in her supposedly hardy flower border by stating that she did not possess "dogmatic views about having in the so-called hardy flower-border none but hardy flowers. All flowers are welcome that are right in colours, and that make a brave show where a brave show is wanted."[102] Nonetheless, she claimed to want to limit her use of such plants, arguing that their associations ill suited the "cottage character of my house."[103]

Jekyll's frequent appeal to localness and hence rusticity as a guide to design often obscured not only her use of imported plants, as already noted, but also the ways in which her design theories intersected with the growth of capitalism and consumerism. Arguably, gardens are always necessarily embedded in consumer practices given their ties to economies of circulation between sources of plants and markets, as well as notions of collecting, display, and usefulness.[104] Yet these associations seem particularly intensified at the end of the nineteenth century. The American Thorstein Veblen, in his incisive analysis of the "leisure class," first published in 1899, pointed out that by the late nineteenth century a peculiar phenomenon had taken place in garden design: wealth could now be signified both by an extravagant "demonstration of expensiveness," as in topiary and flower beds, and also, to his surprise, by the "appearance of thrift," as in rustic or natural arrangements. The latter, although perhaps not intuitively associated with the excessive expenditure of funds, in fact often required great sums and was intended to register the owner's taste and "instinct of workmanship."[105] In Great Britain the notion of investing a family fortune into a natural garden was nothing new – in the eighteenth century Charles Hamilton drove himself into bankruptcy in pursuit of his plans at Painshill – but what was perhaps remarkable at the close of the nineteenth century was the degree to which this practice was being adopted by the comfortable middle classes.

In the nineteenth century, despite, or perhaps because of, the increased number of imported plants available to the public and the higher rates of successful maturation as compared to the eighteenth century, plants continued to register as signs of affluence. Collecting was a veritable Victorian passion. The growth of industry and the expansion of the economy, aided by imperial resources and markets, fueled such displays so that numerous observers of English society, including Karl Marx, remarked on the "'mania for possessions.'"[106] Plants fit eas-

79. Gertrude Jekyll, "Space in Step and Tank-Garden for Lilies, Cannas, and Geraniums," from *Wood and Garden*, London, 1899. (Source: Dumbarton Oaks, Studies in Landscape Architecture, Photo Archive.)

80. "A Border of Flowers, from Sutton's Seeds, in the Garden of Mrs. Dominic Watson," from *Sutton's Amateur Guide,* 1908. (Source: Rural History Centre, University of Reading.)

ily with this mania. Seed companies at the time, such as Sutton's, for example, often sold plants in collections so gardeners were encouraged to buy mass quantities. In its catalogs of this period, Sutton's featured photographs of massed flower borders as illustrations to and inducements for their advertised seed collections (Fig. 80). Jekyll also wrote with considerable pride about and repeatedly photographed her plants, such as *Lilium giganteum,* a native to the Himalayan mountains, which she had introduced in large groupings along the edge of her woodland copse.[107] This plant also reflects how imports from overseas added to the vast quantities of brightly hued goods available to the Victorian consumer. Turkish carpets and textiles from India were just a few of the items that became fixtures in a well-appointed middle-class home. Behind Jekyll's prose of artful amateurism and the effects of rusticity and "repose, and refreshment, and purest enjoyment of beauty"[108] she promised her readers lay the world of goods – the circuits of exchange and inducements to consume that drove the economy of late Victorian and Edwardian Britain and linked it to an increasingly global network.

Chapter 7

Jekyll and Lutyens

Resolving the Debate

In addition to her activities as a writer, gardener, and nursery owner, Jekyll designed gardens for clients, working both independently and with architects, most frequently with Edwin Lutyens. By the close of her career, Jekyll had designed over three hundred gardens; of these, roughly one hundred were done with Lutyens.[1] Lutyens had begun his career as an independent architect in the early 1890s in west Surrey, and his early client base resulted from a dense network of friends and patrons in the area.[2] Jekyll played an important role in these early years, helping Lutyens secure clients and collaborating with the architect on garden designs, particularly in the decades around the turn of the century.[3] At first Jekyll visited sites with Lutyens, but by the early 1900s she traveled rarely and relied on the architect and clients to send her site plans, topographical information, and soil samples. With regard to the division of work, putting it in the simplest terms, Lutyens would provide the architectural structure of the garden while Jekyll clothed and softened the framework with plantings and color.

Although much is known of Jekyll's theories on garden design thanks to her myriad publications, less is known of Lutyens's views. Scholarly attention has focused on a brief talk he delivered on April 8, 1908, following a paper on garden design by Thomas Mawson. In this talk, like Mawson and Mallows, Lutyens strove to rise above the Robinson-Blomfield controversy. He hinted at the fallacies of handcuffing designers to particular styles by pointing out that Robinson used a relatively formal layout in his terrace at Gravetye and that Blomfield employed a more naturalistic design in his cliffside garden at his home, Point Hill, Rye.[4] Lutyens's own designs reveal that his architectural vocabulary ranged from Surrey vernacular to Georgian and classical. The architect was also more forthright than Blomfield about his adoption of styles and motifs adopted from sources outside

England. In an early 1890s design scheme for Munstead Corner, owned by C. D. Heatley, Lutyens created a simple formal garden, based on a sequence of squares and semicircles, that he labeled "Dutch Garden" (Fig. 81); at Ammerdown he designed an "Italian" garden for Lady Alice Hylton, who "loved all things Italian."[5] Nonetheless, aspects of Lutyens's design aesthetic, as expressed in his 1908 paper, dovetail with Blomfield's, most notably the notion that "a garden scheme should have a backbone, a central idea beautifully phrased. Every wall, path, stone, and flower should have its relationship to the central idea."

That central idea, although unstated, was the house, and its relationship to the garden: the view from the house to the garden and the view from the garden to the house. Like many of the architects of the Art Workers Guild (which he joined in 1903), Lutyens conceived of the "vertical face of the house," particularly the orientation of the staircase window, as dictating the layout (and presumably the main axis) of the garden.[6] That main axis, usually placed to take advantage of the best view possible, would become the backbone of the garden, organized in a series of geometric spaces. Views were attended to, but the garden nonetheless generated the impression of enclosure, which was the key aspect of the formal garden manner described by guild architects.[7]

One could argue that Lutyens took these precepts even further than his colleagues, more strongly underscoring the architectural frame of the garden and treating the internal subdivisions of the garden with greater plasticity. The leitmotifs of a Lutyens garden emerged in an early design: "The Little White House" (1896), his fantasy of an ideal home sketched in a letter to his wife-to-be, Emily Lytton.[8] The garden extends off the public rooms – the hall and dining and drawing rooms – and in plan takes the form of a square superimposed on a larger cruciform with arms of equal lengths. Yew hedges define the staggered outline of the garden and internal paths reinforce the square and cruciform. The rectilinear character of the garden is modified by the introduction of a fountain, based on circular forms, in the center of the garden. Four diagonal paths, adding a note of dynamism to the garden, connect the fountain to the paths marking the internal cruciform. The garden evokes a calculated, measured rhythm in keeping with Lutyens's own edict that "all architecture must have rhythms, that affect the eye as music does the ear, producing vibrations in the brain."[9] A strong sense of proportion relative to the house and site – as the architecture marches in measured steps into the landscape – undergirds this and most of Lutyens's garden designs. This quality endowed his small country houses with an expansiveness more often associated with larger country houses and differentiated his work from suburban counterparts, as the architect was well aware. At Fulbrook, a Surrey house begun shortly before Orchards, Lutyens forcefully wrote to the client, Mrs. Gerard

81. Edwin Lutyens, Perspective View, Munstead Corner, Surrey, 1891. (Source: V & A Picture Library.)

Streatfeild, that her notion of "A border 2 foot wide & path 3 feet wide against a South wall would look miserable & wretched – quite impossible & would make Fulbrook Villarish!! *please, listen*" and advocated instead a path eight feet wide to ensure "a really pretty thing in proportion & scale to the house."[10]

For the purposes of this study, which seeks to understand the relationship between Jekyll's and Lutyens's work and the discourse of Englishness, a handful of better known sites – Orchards, Goddards, Deanery Garden, Upton Grey, Marsh Court, Little Thakeham, Folly Farm, Abbotswood, and Hestercombe – have been selected for analysis.[11] Using the categories of Lutyens's career established by Daniel O'Neill, these examples represent Lutyens's work in the established vernacular, 1897–1906 (i.e., Orchards, Deanery Garden, Goddards, and Marsh Court); and classical beginnings, 1898–1906 (i.e., Folly Farm).[12] The sites remain generally in good condition, and, more importantly, were touted in their own day, frequently by *Country Life,* as good examples of garden design. They reveal that Jekyll and Lutyens not only bridged the formal vs. natural debate but also participated in the dialogue between old and new as well as urban and rural, and English and foreign, that characterized much of English garden design in this period.

Orchards (1898)

The partnership began in Surrey and, in accordance with Jekyll's writings, much of their work took its cues from the local environment. Orchards, the next Lutyens house after Munstead Wood to be featured in *Country Life* (in an article authored by Jekyll), was built for Sir William and Lady Chance in 1897. It followed closely on the heels of Munstead Wood in terms of architectural vocabulary. Lady Chance was a sculptor interested in the Arts and Crafts movement, and her husband's family money, which came from a lens manufactory, allowed them to build a house in the latest style situated near Munstead and the train station at Godalming, giving Sir William easy access to London where he was a barrister-at-law (Inner Temple).[13] Chance was also honorary secretary of the Central Poor Law Conference and wrote several tracts on the wretched conditions of London's underprivileged, including *The Housing of the Working Classes* (1889), *The Better Administration of the Poor Law* (1895), *Children of the Poor Law* (1897), and *Our Treatment of the Poor* (1899) that suggest he fit neatly with the profile of the back-to-the-lander who, sympathy for London's underclasses notwithstanding, desired a rural retreat. After seeing Munstead Wood, the Chances dismissed their original architect, Halsey Ricardo, and hired Lutyens, who produced a building loosely based on the Surrey vernacular.

 The relationship of the house to its environs alternates between enclosure and expansiveness (Fig. 82). One approaches the house through a courtyard established by the arms of the house and stables. At the southeast corner of the house, the feeling of enclosure is continued via a loggia adjacent to the dining room that descends to the "Dutch garden" (Fig. 83). (This enclosed garden, with its interplay of rectangular and circular forms, bears a strong resemblance to the Dutch garden Lutyens designed for Munstead Corner, Surrey.) In an early sketch of the Dutch garden, Lutyens proposed a gate framed by topiary yews shaped into peacocks, a motif he conceivably borrowed from cottage gardens, although he seems to refer to it with some chagrin. He appended the note "apologies for yews!" to the drawing, as though he was uncomfortable with such a clichéd reference to the vernacular.

On the southern side, adjacent to the dining room and hall, an open terrace overlooks "wild nature," a wild garden in which lawn, nearest the house, gives way to shrubs and trees such as "crabs and amelanchier, with plantings of double-flowered bramble and double gorse, and some of the wilder of the rambling roses," as well as clumps of rhododendrons, azaleas, berberis, and shrubby spiraea (Fig. 84).[14] Jekyll, whom garden historian Jane Brown believes helped a great deal in the design and building of the garden, insisted the house seemed "to grow out of the ground" and assimilated well with the surrounding woodland, thus reflecting the designer's "intimate knowledge of the best traditions of the country."[15]

Perhaps it was Jekyll's desire to insist on the localness of Orchards, and its evident ties to the surrounding 26 acres of open forest with clumps of oak and bracken that had been "carefully preserved" on three sides of the house, that led the writer to downplay the significance of the Dutch garden, which she described simply as a rose garden in her *Country Life* article.[16] This space is governed by a strong sense of geometry akin to that found in the work of Thomas, Blomfield, or Newton. The rectangular garden is bisected along its long axis by a

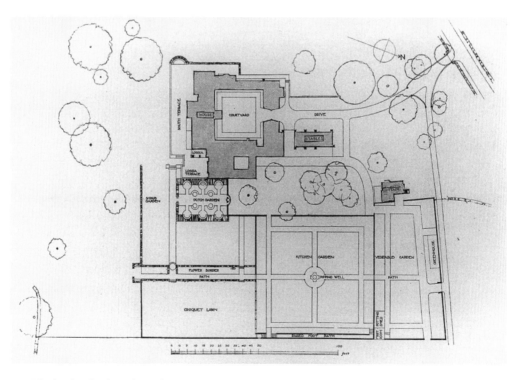

82. "Orchards: Garden Plan." (Source: Lawrence Weaver, *Houses and Gardens by E. L. Lutyens,* London, 1913.)

83. Edwin Lutyens, Garden Plan – Extends from the East Terrace. (Source: RIBA Library Drawings Collection.)

broad stone-paved path leading to an apselike hemisphere with a fountain. This semicircular motif is repeated along each side of the path in the form of six hemispherical recesses housing seats; between each seat is a circular bed of roses. These forms continually direct the visitor inward and outward, the seats pushing

against the boundaries of the garden defined by the background planting of yew

84. "Orchards from the East," from Lawrence Weaver, *Houses and Gardens by E. L. Lutyens,* London, 1913. (Source: Country Life Picture Library.)

hedges and the circular planting beds redirecting attention to the backbone of the central walkway. Here are signs of the geometrical complexity that will increasingly characterize Lutyens's garden designs.

The Dutch garden, as well as other portions of the architectural framework of the garden, reveals another recurring motif in Lutyens's garden designs, that is, the reinforcement of the connection between house and garden through repetition of forms and materials. The arches of the seats, for example, echo the arches of the loggia that rises up behind the garden. The red roof tiles are repeated in the coping of the wall abutting the kitchen garden and the piers at either end of the Dutch garden. The house chimney stacks are brick, which is used again in a herringbone pattern to edge the central stone path of the Dutch garden. This level of detailing reflects Lutyens's working manner, which required in-depth conceptional work, close supervision of the building process (through hand-picked clerks of works, builders, and contractors), and extensive correspondence with clients.

In many respects, the key features of the Dutch garden – its roomlike enclosure, strong sense of geometrical order, and material links to the house – were shared by gardens designed by Blomfield and others, who had insisted on the

Englishness of this vocabulary. The label *Dutch* is further complicated by its initial use in 1908 by H. Avray Tipping in a *Country Life* article. In explaining the feature, he attached the caveat that it is "very unlike anything that ever was in Holland, and, is, indeed, essentially a creation of today, and this particular example belongs to the very original variety which issues from Mr. Lutyens's ingenious and tasteful brain."[17] Then why the choice of the term *Dutch?* Does this simply underscore the imprecision of garden terminology, especially with regard to national styles? Was it because Lutyens, unlike Blomfield, never polemically situated his work in a discourse of Englishness? Was it because, although Lutyens looked to historical examples, he allowed himself to adapt and to invent more freely? That subsequent critics have read various architectural features in Lutyens's gardens as Dutch, or Italian, or Moorish suggests that the association of Englishness attached to them by the discourses of the Art Workers Guild did not remain affixed. If this is true, then why? Perhaps something in the way Lutyens deployed these motifs endowed them with a quality of worldliness that increased the further he moved metaphorically away from his vernacular roots. Robert Williams has argued that, in general, "Lutyens's gardens were never really traditional." With respect to Orchards, if Lutyens had turned to the local neighborhood for extant examples of pre-eighteenth-century gardens, as Blomfield advised, he would have found little; in short, there was not a "usable local tradition" in terms of form, although Lutyens could draw on it for materials.[18]

Nonetheless, Orchards, and much of Lutyens's work in general, maintains a constant dialogue with the English past even if it was not the past specific to the locale in which he was working. The kitchen garden at Orchards, for example, was clearly revivalist, according to Jekyll. The walled squared space featured a raised footpath along the east side that reminded Jekyll of mounts in old Tudor gardens. References to the past were underscored by the plant material, which included hollyhocks, phlox, and sunflowers.[19] The brick and stone materials he used also endowed a sense of agedness to the site because they were common to older homes of the area, and indeed were specifically discussed and photographed by Jekyll in *Old West Surrey*. Orchards thus avoided the "staring newness" that Jekyll objected to in recent building.[20]

If Jekyll could find the English past in what Lutyens labeled Dutch, it suggests that the encoding of Englishness in garden forms and the construction of national identity built on this practice lay in the eye of the beholder. Or, as Blomfield had implied when he described how historical gardening practices of other nations were "grafted" onto an English tradition, Englishness lay not in its difference from other modes, but in its assimilation of the foreign. Jekyll and Robinson had exemplified this by their insertion of exotic plants within a framework of indigenous material. Indeed, the success of the garden as a symbol of national identity seemingly lay in its ability to accommodate the multiplicity of positions then permissible in turn-of-the-century England, from xenophobia to polyglot expansiveness.

Goddards (1898)

In July 1898 Jekyll brought Lutyens another Surrey commission when she introduced the architect to Margaret and Frederick James Mirrielees. Mirrielees came from a mercantile background – his family owned the substantial Muir & Mirrielees department store in Moscow – and was currently employed by his wife's father, who owned the Castle Steamship Company.[21] The couple had purchased property at Abinger Common in order to build a "Home of Rest for Ladies of Small Means" – a philanthropic rural retreat for proper young women, such as nurses, whose limited income would not otherwise permit a holiday. Enclosure and expanse again dictate the grounds at the house, Goddards (Fig. 85). Hedges demarcate the outer boundary of the house precinct on the approach side and entrance is gained by gated gaps in the hedge marked by a U-shaped flagstone path. This entrance borrows heavily from those of local cottages and is markedly different from the long drives used for the residences of the well-to-do. Subtle hints prepare the visitor for the garden court opposite, believed to be designed by Jekyll. A round flat stone placed where the U-shaped path meets the main axis

197

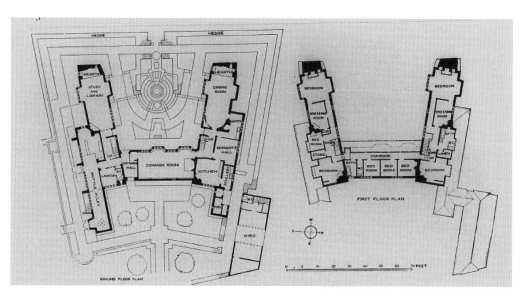

85. "Plans of Goddards." (Source: Lawrence Weaver, *Houses and Gardens by E. L. Lutyens*, London, 1913.)

of the garden hints at the millstones (references to rural agriculture) and other round configurations of stone punctuating doorways and the garden court.

The garden court itself is organized around a sequence of circular motifs originating with the central dipping well, which sends out radiating circles defined by stone, brickwork, and plantings (Plate VI). The diagonals established by the bedroom wings that reach out from the common room at the center of the house finally hem in these circles. The repeating circles are enlivened by the contrasting textures that play across the paving surface of the garden court: irregularly shaped flagstones are juxtaposed with herringbone patterned bricks, bricks laid end to end repeat the radiating spokes of a millstone, and another millstone is encased in bricks running counter to the radiating spokes. Further animation is created by the plants, which creep in between the flagstones as well as populate the encircling beds. From this tightly worked space the garden extends outward along the footprint of the house in a series of terraces that create a platform for the house (Fig. 86). A hedge runs along the inside edge of the upper terrace, creating a vegetative wall that both protects the house and establishes a relationship with the green lawns beyond.

Shared materials, such as brick, used for window casements, door frames, and chimneys, underscore connections between house and garden. Horsham stone slates for the roof sheltering the windows overlooking the garden court form an aesthetic link with the drystone walls of Horsham slate used for the walls supporting the terrace.[22] Again, the use of such materials, found in cottages and other structures of the area, rooted the building in the local environment, an aspect aided by the use of local contractors.[23] Design motifs throughout the house, including the decorative ironwork on the doors and stained glass windows, as well as the sundial placed above the dipping well in the garden court, referred to medieval times, belying the recent date of the house. Indeed, *Country Life* found the house in total sympathy with the Middle Ages.[24] In this instance, Jekyll and Lutyens produced a design firmly rooted in the indigenous environment.

Deanery Garden (1901)

Although Jekyll and Lutyens's roots were in Surrey, they worked in other counties; indeed, for Lutyens this was necessitated by his professional ambitions. In 1899 Lutyens received an opportune commission from Edward Hudson, publisher of *Country Life*, who had begun a working relationship with Jekyll in 1898. Hudson had acquired property containing an old orchard in the town of Sonning in Berkshire. Hudson wanted to keep as much of the orchard intact as possible. Lutyens therefore situated the house, Deanery Garden, nearly abutting the

86. Terrace, Goddards, 1996. (Source: Author's photograph.)

public road, so the garden, carved into the old orchard, gained sufficient room (Fig. 87). Privacy was ensured by a preexisting high red-brick wall that Lutyens retained, thus carrying forward his theme of enclosure and fulfilling contemporaneous desires for privacy. The entrance gate sets up a main axis that extends through the house, to the bridge over the tank garden, and concludes at the circular stairs leading to the grass goosefoot paths (hints of the Baroque) mown in the orchard grass, which is underplanted with daffodils in the Robinson manner. This axis, however, is downplayed by its asymmetrical placement with respect to the house and the sequencing of multilevel terraces on the garden side.

The recessed garden door, the bay window of the hall, and the projecting chimney stack all compete as the originating point for the lines of the garden. The bay window, for example, serves as the anchor to the tank garden, which intersects with the rill running perpendicular to the central axis (Fig. 88). The bay window is balanced across the entrance by the chimney stack, which anchors the upper terrace, the far side of which is defined by a pergola situated parallel to the central axis. The three distinct axes of the garden and intersecting cross paths are relieved and unified by repeating circles and semicircles made obvious in one of Lutyens's working drawings (Fig. 89).

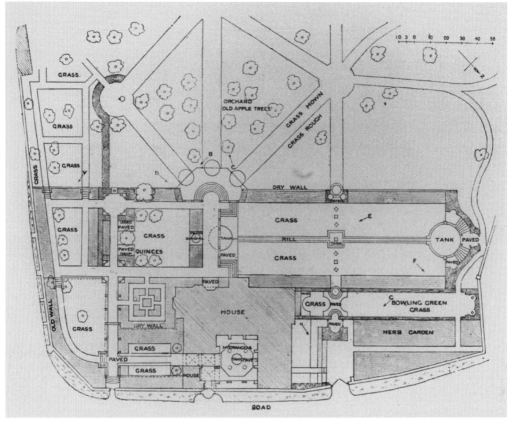

87. "Deanery Garden: Site Plan." (Source: Lawrence Weaver, *Houses and Gardens by E. L. Lutyens,* London, 1913.)

The Tudor-style bay window, the use of red Berkshire brick, and the gray stone throughout the house and grounds again evoke Lutyens's early interest in indigenous building traditions. A mixture of the past and present was also evoked by the borders Jekyll designed for the tank garden in which old-fashioned species such as lavender, hollyhocks, and pinks were mixed with plants readily identifiable as exotics, such as gladioli, yuccas, and irises. The two circular pools of water at either end of the tank garden are reminiscent of wells, another feature deemed characteristic of English cottage life by Jekyll.[25] A narrow stone-lined channel of water that recalls both medieval moats and drains joins these. Yet these rills, according to contemporary Lutyens scholars, also carry suggestions of the irrigation channels employed in Mogul gardens.[26] Lutyens would go on to use these motifs, on a far grander scale, in the Mogul garden he designed for the viceroy's house in New Dehli, c. 1911–31. Is this another instance of the multivalency of garden features that could register both localness and Empire? It is difficult to answer this question because none of the pre-1914

88. "Deanery Garden: The Canal and Terminal Pool," from Lawrence Weaver, *Houses and Gardens by E. L. Lutyens,* London, 1913. (Source: Country Life Picture Library.)

89. Edwin Lutyens, Perspective View of Garden Front, Bird's-Eye Elevation, c. 1899. (Source: RIBA Library Drawings Collection.)

source material consulted for this study linked Lutyens's designs to those of the Mogul Empire. If Lutyens was attempting to reference deliberately the grand gardens of India, this seems to have been lost on his audience. His use of a pergola, however, may have more readily conjured up Italy because Blomfield had designated the feature "of course, Italian."[27]

If the water features connoted foreign territories, this was balanced by references made to southwest England. The pierced parapet of curved tiles along the bridge, for example, is akin in form to the garden walls lining the moat at the Elizabethan mansion Loseley Park, Surrey (a site familiar to *Country Life* readers, having been featured in the journal in 1897 and 1899, as well as to Lutyens, who used this motif for the garden wall at Fulbrook, and Jekyll, who lived relatively close by and later designed borders for the garden in 1902) (Fig. 90).[28] That Lutyens and Jekyll deemed this wall, lifted from a Surrey garden, appropriate in Berkshire suggests that features could be pried from their local context and become part of a nationally available aesthetic. Jekyll's photographs had done this for the Surrey landscape, and Hudson's decision to publish articles of his own home ensured further dissemination.

Lutyens's design apparently pleased his patron, who subsequently offered the architect commissions for Lindisfarne Castle (1903) and Plumpton Place (1928). More importantly, the two cemented a friendship that resulted in over twenty of Lutyens's country houses being featured in Hudson's magazine between 1900 and 1914.[29] *Country Life*'s support of Lutyens's domestic work is even more marked when compared to his relative neglect by professional architectural magazines, such as *The Architectural Review* (whose editors included Lutyens's competitors Blomfield, Macartney, and Newton) or more progressive journals, such as *The Studio*.[30]

Upton Grey (1908)

Nonetheless, when Charles Holme, founder of *The Studio*, needed a garden for his home in Upton Grey, Hampshire, he turned to Jekyll. The renovations to the manor house at Upton Grey had been overseen by guild architect Ernest Newton, who expanded the house by adding a wing and reorienting the front door to make the house more symmetrical without altering its original character, leaving intact and continuing the hung tiles, brick walls, and half-timbering that characterized vernacular manor houses of the region. In 1908 Jekyll began work on the grounds and created an approximately 5-acre garden that encircles the house.[31] North of the house and alongside the drive that Newton had introduced, Jekyll designed a wild garden in the manner of William Robinson (Plate VII). Clumps of naturalized roses and bamboo dot the area, and in the spring the long grass is

90. "The Creeper Clad House." (Source: "Country Homes, Gardens Old & New, Loseley Park, Surrey, The Seat of Mr. W. More-Molyneux," *Country Life*, March 4, 1899.

mingled with daffodils, snowdrops, scilla, and other blooms. Walnut and chestnut trees and a copper beech frame the edges of the space and create an overstory to the shrubs and plants. The wild garden is situated on a slight rise so visitors arriving to the house would have felt as if they were driving into a rural dell. The descent continues on the other side of the house but is managed here as a series of rectangular platforms within a formal garden framed by yew hedges. Enclosed and ordered geometry prevail on this side of the house, whereas seemingly unbounded and unplanned profusion characterizes the approach side. The formal garden is generally symmetrical, framed around a central axis that extends from the bay window jutting from the garden facade (Fig. 91). On the terrace level a pergola, situated perpendicular to the house, anchors the axis to the window bay.

Plans collected by the present owners of Upton Grey reveal that Charles Holme had provided Jekyll with the general outlines of the wild and formal gardens, but Jekyll was responsible for organizing the internal spaces of these gardens. Within the relatively small space of the formal garden, Jekyll utilized an incredible range of features, including a terrace extending to a lawn, a rose garden set in a lawn, a bowling green, and tennis lawns. Each of these motifs is situated on a descending level of the garden so each one is demarcated from its neighbor by drystone walls, which replaced the grass banks that Ernest Newton and Charles Holme had originally planned. The walls, which function as low horizontal barriers within the garden, are clothed with plantings, and the outer boundaries of the garden are likewise organic, being formed largely by yew hedges that shelter deep flower borders on the upper lawn and rose garden levels.

Through restoring the garden, Rosamund Wallinger has observed that Jekyll's designs often simplified and gave more order to the early plans conceived by Newton and Holme.[32] To those unschooled in the gardening debates at the turn of the century these features might seem a heterogeneous jumble, but there is a consistent theme of Englishness – attached by various writers to nearly every feature of the garden – threaded throughout. Moreover, the house reaches out to the garden, through the outward curving brick steps set in the grass at the entrance to the wild garden and the gray stones coursing through every level of the formal garden, which appears as a series of roomlike extensions of the house. The house becomes the linchpin bringing together the wild and formal garden.

The small enclosed space of the manor house's formal garden and its fairly simple geometry – a series of rectangles occasionally broken up with semicircles or implied diagonals – contrasts with the increasingly intricate and elaborated use of these features in contemporaneous gardens Jekyll planned in collaboration with Lutyens, such as Marsh Court and Hestercombe.

Marsh Court (1901)

Marsh Court, located near Stockbridge, Hampshire, was built for Herbert Johnson, a stockbroker who exemplified the new upper-middle-class clientele for small country houses. Jane Brown reports that the commission was the direct result of the publication of Lutyens's work in *Country Life;* perusing the magazine, the client saw Crooksbury, an early Lutyens house built for Arthur and Agnes Chapman, and contacted the architect. Marsh Court, dressed largely in white Hampshire chalk with random dotting of red brick, tile, and black flint, has been called the most Tudor of Lutyens's buildings. It holds notable period details, such as the timber and woodwork used in the first-floor corridor, and the massive oak staircase. But, in some rooms, he also introduced the notion of change over time by adding panel work and ceiling plasterwork suggestive of later centuries.

The house takes the form of an E, and entrance is gained through a rectangular walled forecourt, paved in brick with a quatrefoil inset (Fig. 92). The axis suggested by this entrance, which leads to an arched opening in the porch, is not carried over to the garden side, however. Instead the axis shifts slightly to the east in the form of a paved walkway leading to the square of the south lawn and its centrally located sundial, which "always held an honoured place in the formal garden," according to Blomfield.[33] This axis runs parallel to, and overlooks, two additional axes. One originates in the concavity between the symmetrically pro-

91. Drystone Walls, Rose Garden, and Tennis Lawn, Upton Grey, 1998. (Source: Author's photograph.)

jecting bays of the hall and extends through the sunken pool garden to the west of the south lawn. The second, much longer, echoes the western flank of the house and is accessed from the forecourt by a series of curving steps that permit admittance to the garden without gaining entrance to the house, thus diluting Lutyens's typically fortified entrance (Fig. 93). A path composed of squares and rectangles executed in red brick framed with stone emanates from the steps and is edged on the eastern side by a deep herbaceous border backed by a balustraded wall and a yew hedge on the western side. Enclosure may be broached, but not abandoned. The terminus of this feature is determined by a perpendicular axis, emphasized with a pergola that bounds the south lawn, sunken pool garden, and herbaceous border garden. The play of patterned paving is picked up in the pergola, which is composed of red tile with a sequence of pools marked out with stone and herringbone brick.

The sunken pool garden constitutes the heart of the garden with links to the south lawn, herbaceous border, and pergola (Fig. 94). When viewed from the pergola platform, the garden is framed by gate piers that echo the projecting bays of the garden facade of the house. The pool itself underscores this strong sense of order: it is constructed of a series of inscribed rectangles, each lower than the previous one, that evoke the rectangular forms of the windows. Jane Brown attributes the use of steps leading to the water to Jekyll, who may have brought the motif back from Italy or Spain.[34] The sides of the pool are lined with four evenly spaced square planters that play off the squares inscribed in the paving of the terrace, pergola platform, and herbaceous border. Here Lutyens has brought together a panoply of those features that Blomfield considered indicative of the English formal garden – sundials, terraces, long flower borders framed by balustraded walls, and rectangular sheets of water – and linked them persuasively to his new old house.

But it must be recognized how easily this site could have signified Italy, despite the Tudor associations of the house. The sunken pool garden, as already men-

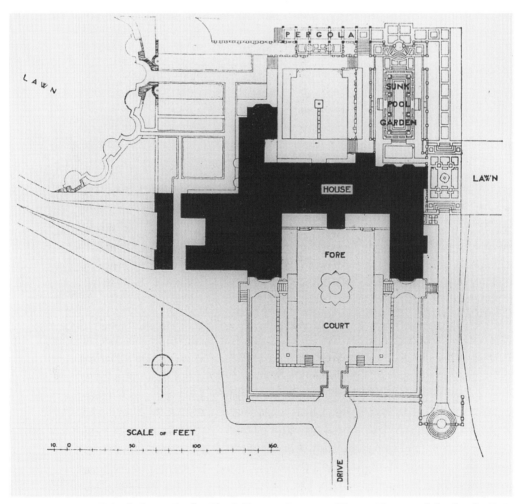

92. "Marsh Court: Garden Plan." (Source: Lawrence Weaver, *Houses and Gardens by E. L. Lutyens,* London, 1913.)

93. "Marsh Court: Entrance Front from North-West," from Lawrence Weaver, *Houses and Gardens by E. L. Lutyens,* London, 1913. (Source: Country Life Picture Library.)

tioned, was a feature that Jekyll attributed to her memories of Italian gardens. The concave-convex stairs at the entrance to the garden (adjacent to the forecourt) recall Bramante's courtyard for the Belvedere, Rome, c. 1505. Circular stairs and sunken pools had been used in other English gardens of this period, such as Blomfield's Moundsmere, and they register these architects' increasing interest in a classical, as opposed to Elizabethan, vocabulary. Bramante's work, as well as that of his intellectual follower Palladio, was greatly admired by the British architect Inigo Jones, who, in turn, became an increasing influence on Lutyens's aesthetic. Lutyens clearly envisioned his work at Marsh Court as taking up the motifs and rules of Palladio, Jones, and Christopher Wren. In a 1903 letter to fellow architect Herbert Baker, Lutyens proclaimed his allegiance to these masters and concluded his letter with sketch plans of Marsh Court and Little Thakeham.[35] Moving forward in time, Lutyens's designs became steadily infused with strong doses of classicism, which gradually diluted the earlier indigenous, Tudor, or Elizabethan associations of his work, although these were never totally suppressed. Thus, although Weaver hailed Marsh Court as "the best example of his [Lutyens's] skill in the vernacular manner," it also demonstrates, as Weaver admitted, Lutyens's eclecticism and willingness, more so than many of his contemporaries, to work within a broad historical range of borrowed and adapted motifs. The garden partakes of the prevailing leitmotifs of garden design established by the guild architects, and thus could signify the vernacular or Englishness, but it also testified to Lutyens's professional allegiances and ambitions through recourse to classical references.

The garden itself, with its geometric order, carries forth the principles of formalism, but the natural is nonetheless incorporated. The pergola frames views of the neighboring countryside, and although no plans for the planting of the flower borders have been found, contemporaneous photographs reveal a profusion of vegetation, seemingly overspilling the bounds of the built features. Roughly eleven years after the house was completed in 1904, Jekyll was invited to plan the garden situated between the entrance drive, east croquet lawn, and the new tennis court. The result was an informal landscape, as at Upton Grey, dotted with naturalizable exotics, including bay and bamboo. Along the drive more "old-fashioned" flowers, such as rock pinks and valerian, arranged in drifts, were introduced.[36]

Little Thakeham (1902)

Many of the elements found at Marsh Court reappear in other country houses of this period. Little Thakeham, according to Daniel O'Neill, is a simplified version of Marsh Court, with the "vernacular style reduced to its essentials."[37] The garden is clearly less elaborate, probably in deference to the client Ernest Blackburn, who was an amateur gardener and desired extensive areas for planting, but shares the devices of a forecourt entrance and, on the garden side, of orienting much of the garden layout to the bay window, as well as fitting a water garden snugly to the building. The axial orientation is much simpler at Little Thakeham. The line established by the symmetrical forecourt is carried through the house to the garden on the other side, where it courses through the terrace and rose gardens and becomes the backbone of the terminating pergola (Fig. 95). A secondary parallel axis is initiated by the path through the paved court in the servants' wing and, on the garden side, bisects the lily pool and water garden. The squares and rectangles of the forecourt and paved court are repeated in the forms of the rose, water, and formal gardens as well as the lily pool. Despite the seemingly basic layout, the underlying geometric order has gained in complexity in comparison with Orchards, and the dense network in which features are situated makes them less recognizable as historical quotes and more a part of an overall rhythmic, patterned fabric that Lutyens has woven.

Although many aspects of this garden seem like reminders of previous designs – the paving includes millstones and red roof tiles, for example, the lily pool is connected to the house by a series of descending steps as at Marsh Court, and the stone-lined rill emanating from the pool is reminiscent of Deanery Garden – the massive pergola, which extends out into the landscape, is particular to the site (Fig. 96). The pergola physically and aesthetically links the house to the

209

94. "Marsh Court: The Sunk Pool Garden," from Lawrence Weaver, *Houses and Gardens by E. L. Lutyens*, London, 1913. (Source: Country Life Picture Library.)

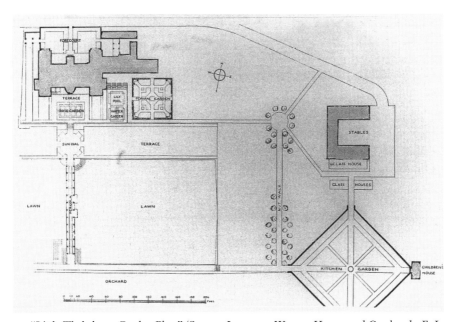

95. "Little Thakeham: Garden Plan." (Source: Lawrence Weaver, *Houses and Gardens by E. L. Lutyens*, London, 1913.)

96. Pergola, Little Thakeham, 1998. (Source: Author's photograph.)

broader landscape. The pillars, made of the same local stone used for the house, echo the more dressed material of the house, whereas the sloping platform on which the pergola sits is made of rubblestone, which carries more associations of rusticity. The drywalling used throughout the garden, as well as the oak beams of the pergola, provides excellent support for plants, which, as they creep upward, root the pergola and help it become the meeting point of formal and natural. The material composing and clothing the pergola also strengthens its ties to the indigenous environment and lessens its ability to signify Italianness.

Folly Farm (1906, 1912)

O'Neill also describes Folly Farm, near Reading, as a descendant of Marsh Court. The house was the result of several building campaigns (Fig. 97). Originally an old farmhouse, it was bought by H. H. Cochrane, who commissioned Lutyens in 1906 to expand the structure greatly. The building changed hands in 1912; the new owner, industrialist Zackary Merton, had Lutyens add a west wing and connecting roof in 1912. The facade of the house reflects Lutyens's growing interest in Georgian designs, but vernacular touches are still apparent.

When Lutyens added the new wing on the southeastern side of the house in 1906, he created a series of walled courts between the house and the old barn and at the entrance to the house, and had them planted with flowers associated with cot-

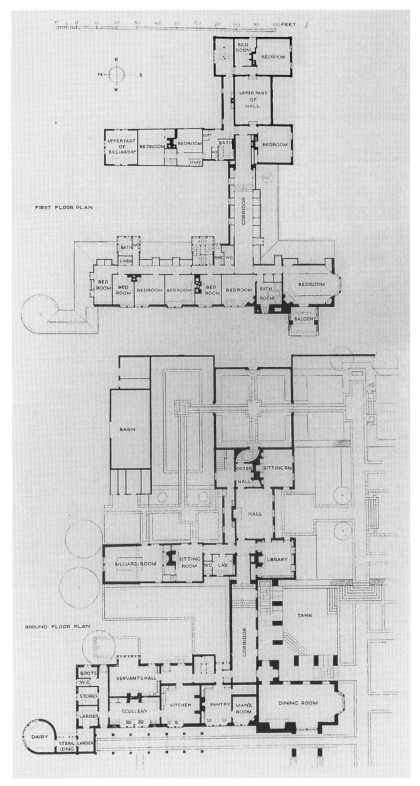

97. "Ground and First-Floor Plans." (Source: Lawrence Weaver, *Houses and Gardens by E. L. Lutyens,* London, 1913.)

tages, such as lavender, pinks, and roses.[38] The later garden, c. 1912, takes its cue from Marsh Court with its series of differently sized, enclosed garden spaces situated on multiple levels and linked together by orthogonal paths of herringbone brick framed with stone.[39] As at Marsh Court, water features (three by 1912) become orienting points of the garden. To the west, a sunken pool garden was built, a tank garden was situated within the L-shape created by the new west wing, and a long canal, on the surface of which could be seen reflections of the house, was built adjacent to the 1906 addition (Fig. 98). The latter was a feature that crossed national boundaries, according to histories of the period, being often associated with the French garden of Le Nôtre and the Dutch garden, but also discussed by Blomfield as a derivation of the English fish pond and utilized in his design at Godinton, Kent.[40] Whereas the canal garden frequently appeared in the design vocabulary of the period, the sunken pool garden is atypical and yet partakes of many key building blocks, such as the concept of enclosure and geometry, common to architects' gardens. This nearly discrete feature, framed with high yew hedges, presents a highly inventive octagonal pool containing a planting bed in the form of a rough cruciform, with semicircles for each arm, in the center (Fig. 99). Not common to the repertoire established by Blomfield and others, it introduces a note of foreignness tempered by the intent to plant heaths, a material indigenous to the area, in the central bed.[41]

Abbotswood (1901)

Water is also a dominant feature in the garden of Abbotswood, Stow-on-the-Wold, Gloucestershire, designed in 1901–2 as part of renovations Lutyens made to the Victorian house. The owner Mark Fenwick, whose family money came from coal, mineral, and banking interests, was an avid amateur gardener and responsible for the planting.[42] The garden, nevertheless, reflected the blending of formal and natural associated with Jekyll and Lutyens. Lawrence Weaver praised how Fenwick had "clad the architectural bones" and argued that the "outlying parts show natural treatment at its best, and in pleasant contrast with the formal lines of paved rose garden and the like which frame the house."[43]

On either side of the drive leading to the forecourt, Fenwick planted a natural or wild garden that gives way to a more formal arrangement on the western and southern faces of the house. The western side of the house, when Lutyens arrived, featured a conservatory and a projecting bay window, which he sheared off. He then added a second gable to create a sense of symmetry and inserted a pedimented window approximately in the center of the facade; the effect is a mixture of references to old manor houses and classical sources. The garden level drops on this front and is divided from the forecourt by a drystone retaining wall, again referencing old Elizabethan country houses. Within the resulting enclosed space,

98. Canal Garden, Folly Farm, 1994. (Source: Author's photograph.)

99. Octagonal Pool, Folly Farm, 1994. (Source: Author's photograph.)

100. Tank Garden, Abbotswood, 1998. (Source: Author's photograph.)

Lutyens placed a rectangular lily pool, oriented perpendicular to the wall space between the two gables, a siting that recalls Marsh Court. The rectangular pool emerges from the house via a circular pool, half of which is covered by a recessed dome secreted in the western flank of the house, an elaboration on the circular pool covered by the arched bridge at Deanery Garden (Fig. 100). By virtue of its arched form and placement below the pedimented window, this water feature reads as classically inspired in contrast to the indigenous associations called up by the adjacent stone walls. The myriad of associations suggested by this space meant that it resisted clear and easy stylistic definition. Lawrence Weaver wrote that it reminded him of the gardens of the Generalife at Granada.[44] This inclusion of motifs suggestive of foreign locales invites an analogy with the work of Robinson in the introduction of notes of exoticism within a framework of the indigenous.

On the southern side of the house, the upper portion of the garden is organized into a series of rectangular spaces situated side by side (Fig. 101). This level of garden, slightly lower than the terrace immediately adjacent to the southern front, is concluded on the eastern side by a stone and timber pergola framed by the rising hillside beyond. Moving farther away from the house, the garden descends yet another level to the tennis lawn and pool garden (Fig. 102). A low stone wall supporting a raised walk, another quote from the history of Elizabethan gardens, surrounds this large grass plat. Overlooking the garden, at the southwestern corner, is a garden house, its doorway set at an angle to the garden in accordance with the advice of seventeenth-century agricultural writer John Worlidge, whom Blomfield cited in his discussion of garden houses.[45]

To construct the platform of the pool garden and tennis lawn, the buttress wall used to shore up the forecourt is picked up again south of the lily pool and wraps around the tennis lawn and pool garden, first increasing and then decreasing in height in correspondence with the gradually sloping hillside. Along the foot of the wall, between the shelter of its buttresses, are deep herbaceous bor-

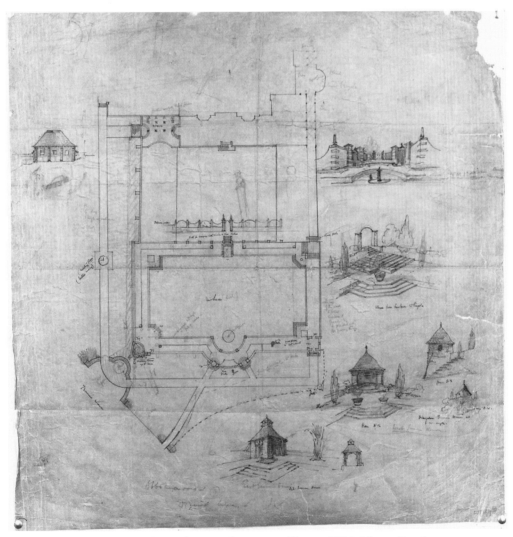

101. Edwin Lutyens, Garden Plan and Perspective, c. 1901. (Source: RIBA Library Drawings Collection.)

102. Pool Garden, Abbotswood, 1998. (Source: Author's photograph.)

ders, which are repeated along the raised walk. From the tennis lawn and pool
garden, access to the countryside beyond was gained by a gate and series of
steps, now moved from their original location in the southeastern corner. The
changes in level from the house to the outer garden or parkland, according to
Weaver, allowed the garden to combine successfully the formal and the natural as
one slowly gave way to the other:

> All levels and flights of levels, planned with skill and purpose, descend
> in quiet progression from the upper terrace to the flower garden, to the
> herbaceous border, to the sunken tennis court, and beyond into the
> surrounding park land of oaks and elms, leading the eye, still descend-
> ing, through Burton Vale, then up to the sky-line where the ridge of
> Eyford Hill frames the picture.[46]

Hestercombe (1906)

Through the Hyltons, for whom Lutyens designed a garden at Ammerdown in
1902, the architect met the Honorable and Mrs. E. W. Portman, who commissioned a garden to accompany their existing country house, a combination of late

eighteenth century and late Victorian. Portman, eldest son of the second viscount William Henry Berkeley Portman, was educated at Eton and Christ Church, Oxford, and served as justice of the peace for Dorset and Somerset, deputy lieutenant for Somerset, and high sheriff of Somerset, 1898. In a letter to his wife, Lutyens described the Portmans' lifestyle as typical of the rural gentry:

> He spends his money on eating, hospitals and cattle breeding and is, to boot, a real good sort (not mine a bit)! She, Lady Bountiful and bazaar opener to the county and surrounded with refractory puppies that never behave or are let behave.[47]

The garden, built around the original terrace on the southern face of the house, is in the form of a rough U-shape, with an eastern extending arm encompassing the Orangery (Fig. 103). The latter, classically inspired, may have been influenced by James Wyatt's Orangery at Ammerdown or by the Orangery that Ernest George and Alfred Yeates were designing for the British Pavilion at the St. Louis Purchase Exposition of 1904. A sequence of squares, circles, and rectangles provides the structure and ornamentation of the garden. A large square – the great plat – is located below the terrace, set off by a narrow intermediary terrace – the Grey Walk, so called because of the color palette of Jekyll's planting scheme. In plan, the Hestercombe plat appears as a descendant of designs for quarters published in Gervase Markham's *The Country Farm* (1615) and reproduced in Blomfield's text; but the scale of Hestercombe is far greater than that intended by Markham, and the planting scheme, with its Jekyllesque massing, would have been entirely different from the carefully trimmed manner of Markham's day (Fig. 104; Plate VIII). The plat is also a descendant of the geometry of the Little White House Garden, seen in the use of inscribed squares, marked by stone paths, to divide the planting areas of the great plat.[48]

The great plat is bordered on the southern end by the long rectangle of a pergola running parallel to the garden front of the house. As at many of Lutyens's other gardens, such as Little Thakeham or Abbotswood, this pergola permits views to the landscape beyond, thus linking this otherwise largely enclosed garden to its local environment. The great plat is flanked on east and west by two rectangular spaces housing water gardens, with a circular pool at the northern end, reminiscent of Abbotswood, hinged to a rectangular tank at the southern end via stone-lined rills, recalling Deanery Garden and Little Thakeham (Fig. 105). Moving closer to the house, the slightly raised rectangular spaces become, to the west, a rose garden, and to the east, a rotunda, which serves as the pivot point for the eastern arm of the garden.

Shifts in level help delineate the different garden spaces, which descend sequentially from the original terrace through four levels before rising again at the pergola terminus. This was a solution that had worked effectively at

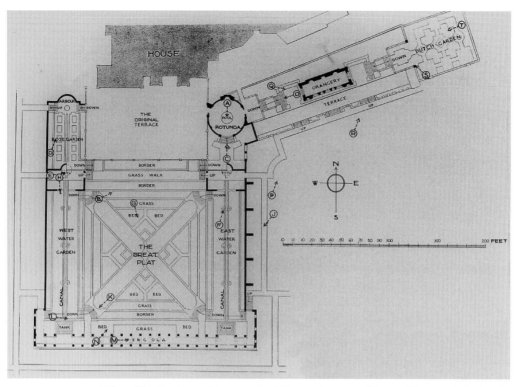

103. "Plan of the Gardens at Hestercombe." (Source: Lawrence Weaver, *Houses and Gardens by E. L. Lutyens*, London, 1913.)

104. "Knots from Markham's Country Farm," from Reginald Blomfield, *The Formal Garden*, London, 1901. (Source: Dumbarton Oaks, Studies in Landscape Architecture, Photo Archive.)

Abbotswood and one discussed and illustrated by Blomfield, who argued with respect to seventeenth-century English garden design that almost invariably "besides the terrace next the house, a terrace was often formed parallel to it at the opposite end of the garden."[49] With respect to managing an extensive drop in elevation in the area of the terrace, as Lutyens faced at Hestercombe, Blomfield recommended dividing the terrace into two levels, citing the example of Kingston House, Bradford-on-Avon (Fig. 39).[50] Lutyens was quite familiar with this house, because he had used it as his template for his design of the British pavilion at the 1900 World's Fair in Paris. For Hester-

105. West Water Garden and Canal, Hestercombe, 1994. (Source: Author's photograph.)

combe he created a second, narrow terrace, to manage the transition from the house platform to the plat below, just as at Kingston House.

At Hestercombe, stairs connect each garden space so the visitor often shifts levels and is constantly surprised by new surroundings. Strong internal visual dividers enhance this experience – most often drystone walls cloaked with plants or fronted by deep flower borders. The garden is sheltered from the surrounding parkland by a stone wall that, along the southern edge, becomes the platform for the pergola. As at Abbotswood, this wall increases in height as the garden platform extends outward in order to adjust to the sloping hillside.

This sequencing of rooms also endows the site with the sense of change over time, as if the garden was slowly added to by generations of owners, a quality enhanced by the variety of materials and stylistic references contained within its walls. Interior split-stone walls are topped with dressed stone, perhaps hinting that an older feature had been adapted to new purposes. The pedimented niche in the rotunda or the concave niches set in the walls add a classical note as do the statues, vases, and other decorative objects carved out of local Somerset Ham stone (Fig. 106). The doorways from the Grass Walk to the water gardens quote from Inigo Jones in the use of alternating bosses and also build a connection to the rusticated quoins of the house (Fig. 107). This motif is used again at the corners of the Orangery, which owes a great debt to the work of Wren and Nicholas Hawksmoor in its overall design and decorative detailing. The "high"-art associ-

106. Rotunda, Hestercombe, 1994. (Source: Author's photograph.)

ations of these references contrast with the rubblestone base of the Orangery as well as the occasional millstones or patterned brickwork set in the flagstone paving of the garden; like the split-stone walls surrounding the garden, these elements are more evocative of indigenous rural traditions (Fig. 108).

The commingling of different traditions might suggest a lack of cohesion. As Lawrence Weaver observed, however, they give the impression of transition from nature to artifice, which neatly parallels the desired effect of bringing together nature and art through combining the natural and formal styles.[51] The arrangement of plants helps realize this project; every architectural feature is accompanied by plants, whether in the form of borders, beds, espaliers, or climbers. By arranging her border plants in graduated heights and long drifts, Jekyll eased the transition from wall to ground, creating a colorful vegetative slope. Likewise, the bed plantings soften the architectural gridwork by spilling over the paving. In addition, plants barely contained by the stonework, clinging to walls, or draping over the pergola give an instant impression of age, as if nature had slowly taken

107. Doorway to Grass Walk, Hestercombe, 1994. (Source: Author's photograph.)

108. Stone Walk, Hestercombe, 1994. (Source: Author's photograph.)

over. The accumulation of varied architectural motifs also suggests the passage of time. When Lutyens returned to the site twenty-seven years later, he remarked that he must have been "190 years old at least to have planned so hoary and old a place."[52]

The notion that a successful small country-house garden could combine a myriad of features was a strong underlying message in many of the publications on garden design issued by *Country Life* before the war. Under the editorship of Lawrence Weaver, the magazine turned its archive of articles and photographs of new country houses to material advantage by using them as the basis for such texts as *Small Country Houses of Today* (1910), *The House and Its Equipment* (1912), *Gardens for Small Country Houses* (1912) (co-written with Jekyll), and *Small Country Houses, Their Repair and Enlargement* (1914). Hudson's multi-pronged publishing campaign ensured the journal's reputation as "the keeper of the architectural conscience of the nation," according to Walter (later Lord) Runciman, president of the Board of Trade.[53] Weaver and his contributing writers clearly saw themselves as arbiters of taste and good design: advising good craftsmanship based on a study of the past and preaching that the house – its structure, design, contents, and grounds – was a total work of art.[54] In *Gardens for Small Country Houses,* they offered readers a panoply of ideas – small sites, hillside gardens, steps, stairways, balustrades, walls, hedges, water, paving, pergolas, gates, garden houses, statues and vases, sundials, seats, and rock gardens are among the topics.

In the straightforward tone of the how-to-do manual sugarcoated with poetic descriptions, these publications made the gardens they portrayed seem realizable and desirable. They were offering, in short, a potentially national aesthetic. It was an aesthetic gradually evolved by Lutyens and Jekyll in their collaborative work that selected and amalgamated key features of the vying styles of their generation as well as the architectural record of the past. With the elasticity and catholicity of his designs, Lutyens stretched the paradigm of Englishness, but never to the point at which it became unrecognizable. In time, his and Jekyll's work would define "the English garden," as demonstrated by gardening and tourist literature today.

Conclusion

A garden may, on the surface, appear the result of a relatively simple trans-action between patron and designer. The patron describes to the designer his or her needs ("a tennis court is wanted for weekend par-ties"), desires ("I am partial to rhododendrons"), and constraints ("my budget for garden maintenance is £50 per annum), and the designer solves the problem presented by the site and the patron's needs, desires, and constraints as success-fully as possible. Of course, the situation is never this straightforward. Moreover, which has been the main thrust of this study, the design process never takes place in a vacuum.

A preference for tennis and rhododendrons and the decision to designate a significant portion of one's annual income to a garden may seem to be highly indi-vidual tastes, but, in fact, are shaped by one's historical moment. I do not mean to suggest that context acts in an oppressive manner, limiting free choice; rather, I mean to point to how making choices constantly connects patron and designer to a larger framework. The patron, for example, may have become convinced of the need for a new garden while visiting the estate of a friend or reading a column about garden parties in a literary journal. In seeking ideas for his or her garden, the patron might peruse the pages of *Country Life* and hit on a design that he or she wishes to emulate. Looking for solutions to the design problem, the designer leafs through treatises, journals, and other materials at hand for inspiration and models. Looking to, borrowing from, and contributing to these sources situates designer and patron within a network of other patrons and professionals con-cerned with gardens. Even those disciplines that did not necessarily see the gar-den as central to their enterprise, such as science, painting, or literary writing, contributed to discourses about gardens and garden design. Sometimes the link was direct, as in the case of Rudyard Kipling's poem "The Glory of the Garden," or sometimes the link was more indirect, as in the case of William Robinson gleaning ideas of plant adaptability from Darwinism and vitalism.

The various strands that contributed to what emerged as a garden discourse and, implicitly, became the stuff from which decisions were made, were made available to the patron and designer (and to the historian today) primarily through text and image. Garden writers took considerable advantage of the advances in print technology at the turn of the century. Treatises appeared in multiple editions: William Robinson's *The English Flower Garden,* for example, appeared in numerous editions, and Mrs. C. R. W. Earle issued successive installments of *Pot-Pourri from a Surrey Garden.* Images were invaluable in the exchange of ideas, whether they appeared as illustrations to accompany magazine articles or books, or on the walls of art galleries and fine arts exhibitions. Reprints of early-eighteenth-century estate views and reproductions of watercolors of old gardens by artists such as George Elgood, Beatrice Parsons, Alfred Parsons, and E. A. Rowe, for example, made the vocabulary of these depicted sites readily available. Journals such as *Country Life* and *The Studio* created a veritable photographic archive of gardens; although, as we have learned, this catalog was often highly selective because editors favored particular designers, as Edward Hudson did Edwin Lutyens, or a designer might even own his own journal, as in the case of William Robinson. Perhaps if we conceptualize the garden not just as a private piece of land belonging to an individual, but also something that was part of public discourse, we come closer to how the garden was understood in the period of 1870 to 1914 and why its style was so fiercely contested.

The notion that a garden is always, and necessarily, embedded in its historical moment does not mean, however, that its appearance was solely determined by events and ideas of that moment. The patron and designer (and perhaps the latter more than the former), in addition to working synchronically, also operate diachronically, responding to the work of previous generations. The choices Robinson made as a designer, and as an author, for example, cannot be understood without a firm grasp of the Italianate parterre and bedded-out manner of gardening that he rejected as well as the seminatural and picturesque modes of gardening he embraced.

Many of the gardens of the period 1870–1914 are best characterized as "old new." Many of the architects and landscape gardeners studied here looked for inspiration in an ideal English past made available through, and indeed even invented, in word and image while also making use of new materials and technologies available to them, namely the products of Empire. Never before had gardeners had access to such a wide variety of plants. The trick became how to integrate these exotics, with their remarkable foliage and colors, into settings that were also supposed to express resolute Englishness.

In considering why gardens appeared the way they did in the period of 1870–1914, this study has emphasized national identity and how differing notions of national identity led to competing styles of garden design. But this is not to say that each designer or patron set out first and foremost to communicate Englishness. What I mean here is that one must acknowledge how the design process and the choices made were filtered through other agendas that sometimes coincided with the project of national identity and sometimes did not. For example, the battle of the styles fought between Robinson and Blomfield was, at many points, about defining their professions – under whose purview, architect or landscape gardener, would landscape design fall? But these debates about professions intersected with debates about national identity when Robinson and Blomfield chose garden history and, more precisely, the definition of the English garden, as their major battlefield.

The various texts and images discussed here not only shaped garden design, they also shaped their audiences. Firstly, for those conscious of class status, many writings about gardens helped articulate a notion of class identity, particularly for those in the upper middle class, who used a newfound appreciation of and interest in the land as a marker of belonging. Secondly, and perhaps more importantly for the arguments regarding national identity presented here, writings and texts about gardens helped bind together individuals into a group by virtue of having participated in a shared cultural practice. And as texts on gardens proclaimed again and again, this group was the nation. *Country Life* made just this point when in 1900 it addressed an article on G. W. Wilson's natural gardens at Heatherbank and Oakwood to

> all who are devoted to gardening, that love of flowers which seems ingrained in our national character, and which, in these days of unrest, or wars and rumours of wars, of fierce competition and striving for the mastery, has a soothing, refining influence, permeating to the nation's advantage its home life. We are transforming ourselves into a nation of gardeners, and pleasant it is to see those in possession of many broad acres seeking horticulture as a pastime, and endeavouring to gain an intimate knowledge of that great world of flowers whose beauties are hidden to so many, a sealed book, which, when opened, reveals something of the great mysteries of Nature.[1]

The ways in which the garden could easily and comfortably fit with the aspirations of the nation's identity can be seen in the 1904 World's Fair, discussed briefly here as a bookend to the Great Exhibition of 1851. The 1904 World's Fair, held in St. Louis, featured pavilions built by each of the participating nations in a manner considered reflective of their national practices and traditions, as was the common practice for world's fairs, particularly after the expositions of 1889 and 1900 held in Paris. In keeping with these models, most of the pavilions at the 1904 fair were revivalist in nature and based on historical models. The British modeled their pavilion after the Orangery at Kensington Palace, London, then attributed to Christopher Wren and now believed to be the work of Nicholas Hawksmoor.[2] The French, who had been among the first to submit their plans to the fair commission, also based their pavilion on an historic garden building, turning to Versailles for their inspiration.

According to the official history of the exposition, the British pavilion was "an embodiment of the dignity, fine proportion, pleasant homeliness and simplicity that characterized English domestic building at one of its happiest periods, when the Gothic and Tudor styles had been superseded by an English development of the Italian Renaissance."[3] Inside, the historicist theme carried over with rooms decorated in the Elizabethan, Queen Anne, and Georgian manners. The escape to the past was completed by the garden, "designed on the lines of those that were usually attached to the mansion residences in England during the reigns of William and Mary, about the latter part of the seventeenth century, and at the time of Queen Anne in the early part of the eighteenth century" (Fig. 109). The latter was a "pleasing combination of Tudor, Jacobean and Dutch styles," as seen in the use of terraces, pleached alleys, parterres with divisions marked with hedges, and topiary, which had been introduced by William, Prince of Orange and signified the Dutch influence.[4] With respect to the history of the formal garden established by Blomfield, the historical moment represented by the pavilion was the last great gasp of the style, before topiary became a "positive mania" and invited ridicule, thus giving rise to the natural or landscape gardens.[5] In his account of the garden, American journalist Murat Halstead claimed that topiaries were reminiscent of "old country places of the English shires," where evergreen statues amazed the tourist. For Halstead, "perhaps the most English of any of the features of this old garden is the pleached alley," which he praised for its secluded shade. He stipulated further that "an English garden without some such adjunct would be vitally incomplete, and when the World's Fair visitor strolls through the embowered alley of the Orangery he may hum with eminent fitness the old song, "For it's English, quite English, you know."[6]

In plan, the garden, developed by Mr. W. Goldring of Kew in consultation with the pavilion architects Ernest George and Alfred Yeates, followed many of the formulas established by seventeenth-century treatises noted in Blomfield's text and revived by contemporaneous architects (Fig. 110). The pavilion, redesigned as a quadrangle to accommodate offices, with an open court and colonnade on the fourth side, faced a bowling green on the court side, and on the opposite side, a terrace descending to a parterre garden backed by a pleached or shade alley. The proportions of the garden took their cue from the pavilion. The bowling green, minus its apselike niches at either end, was exactly the same width as the pavilion, as was the terrace, minus the steps; the parterre and shade alley were slightly wider than the building but still utilize axes established by the building. The central lily pond established the backbone for the symmetrical parterre garden, which was governed by a strong sense of order achieved through the repeated geometry of rectangles and squares. At the center of the rectangular beds stood sundials surrounded by urns; topiary placed at the intersection of paths and along the terrace further decorated the plat.

▾§ 227

Most of the beds were planted with old-fashioned flowers, such as phlox, lilies, and hollyhocks, framing small areas of lawn. An official guide to the fair described the flower border as "a distinctly English motif," citing old-fashioned roses, sweet william, heartsease, phlox, periwinkle, thyme, primrose, gilly flower, and hollyhocks.[7] Such plant material reinforced the sense of contrast between

109. "The Orangery Without," from *Forest City*, St. Louis, 1904. (Source: This item is reproduced by permission of *The Huntington Library, San Marino, California.*)

the English pavilion and those of other countries, such as Cuba, with its tropical garden, or China, with its display of Chinese lilies and peonies. The British contractor responsible for installing the garden noted that the pavilion garden was different from most American gardens with their beds of geraniums surrounded by paling fences.[8]

Notions of simplicity and honesty associated with old-fashioned flowers car-

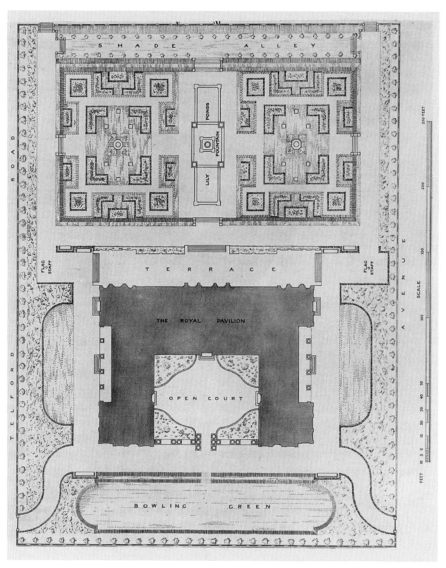

110. "Garden of the Royal Pavilion," Royal Commission, International Exhibition, St. Louis, 1904, *Official Catalogue of the British Section*, St. Louis, 1904. (Source: This item is reproduced by permission of *The Huntington Library, San Marino, California.*)

Conclusion

111. "Sunken Garden between the Mines and Metallurgy Building," from *The Greatest Exposi-tions, Completely Illustrated, Official Views of the Louisiana Purchase Exposition,* St. Louis, 1904. (Source: This item is reproduced by permission of *The Huntington Library, San Marino, California.*)

ried over to their overall arrangement. When explaining the design of the garden, the pavilion organizers stated that "long borders of old-fashioned flowers appeal to everyone in England, and the large beds of simple outline are more in vogue than the embroidered parterres in the Italian style, that do not accord with the present prevalent practice of massing harmonising groups of colour."[9] This state-ment suggests that the flowers were displayed with respect to height in a gradu-ated manner and organized around informal drifts of color in the mode popular-ized by Gertrude Jekyll, rather than in the bedded-out manner.[10] These designs contrasted with other gardens on the grounds. The sunken garden between the Mines and Metallurgy building and the Liberal Arts building, for example, was planted in a far more elaborated parterre style and used exotics, such as cannas, that required constant replanting with the change of seasons over the course of the fair (Fig. 111). The French pavilion used embroidery parterres derived from the seventeenth-century gardens at Versailles.[11] Such displays reinforced the British argument, set forth in their official catalog, that "a pleasant homeliness and simplicity" characterized their nation.[12]

Within the pavilion, all references to imperialism (such as tropical plants)

229

were eschewed in favor of a discourse of Englishness. The British pavilion's ability to evoke Englishness was enhanced because the organizers were not forced to accommodate other cultural groups of Britain. The Irish, for example, petitioned for a separate pavilion. According to the rules of the fair, Ireland could not have its own pavilion because it was not "an independent country or an autonomous State or colony within the British Empire, like Canada."[13] So a group of Irish and Irish-American citizens formed the private Irish Exhibit Company and exhibited as a separate entity in order to promote Ireland's "industrial interests," which hitherto often had been ignored.[14]

British references to Empire were reserved for other locations within the fairgrounds, such as the display of the collection of "famous Jubilee presents sent to Queen Victoria by the subject princes of her Indian Empire, and by her loving subjects in every part of Britain's world-surrounding colonial empire."[15] The objects featured rare and expensive metals and jewels, as well as elaborate craftsmanship, and thus demonstrated the material riches that were at Britain's disposal by virtue of its colonial network. Britain's military investment in Empire was also revealed by "The Anglo-Boer War," a staged entertainment produced by South African showman Frank E. Fillis, which gave no real sense of the complexities of this conflict, which Thomas Pakenham has labeled the "longest (two and three-quarter years), the costliest (over £200 million), the bloodiest (at least twenty-two thousand British, twenty-five thousand Boer and twelve thousand African lives) and the most humiliating war for Britain between 1815 and 1914."[16] As Paul Greenhalgh has argued, at the point at which Britain began to worry over and debate about the future of Empire, British displays at world's fairs increasingly supported the imperial agenda, "attempting to reinforce the unity of empire and to imbue the British public with an imperial pride," and, one could add, to stave off competitors by reference to British military prowess as well as economic wealth.[17]

The range of British displays at the 1904 World's Fair, from the national pavilion to the Boer War reenactment and the chemical, pharmaceutical, and other British technical products shown in the Palace of Varied Industries, underscores the complex multivalency of Britain's character at this particular historical moment: on the one hand, it was the repository of traditions identified with England and that were best encapsulated, according to many, by the garden, with its emphasis on rural life (both that of the cottage and country-house class) and domesticity; on the other hand, it was a leader of industry and one of the last remaining defenders of the principles of free trade, as well as the center of an imperial network of resources, trade, and markets. And each one of these characteristics depended on the other to sustain it. Recall Ruskin's Slade lecture of 1870 in which he argued that England needed to revive and recover her landscapes, threatened by industrialization – "she must yet again become the England she was once . . . under the green avenues of her enchanted garden" – to ensure the continuance of a strong nation to which its citizenry would feel bound by patriotic pride. To accomplish this goal, Ruskin reasoned, England must expand its Empire and found colonies whose attachment to home would be sustained by the image of a pure and beautiful English countryside.

Empire had created a larger framework in which the nation explored its sense of self. Turning inward, seeking an emblem of Englishness, many writers and artists focused on the image of the garden, which concomitantly acknowledged and assimilated desirable aspects of Empire while marking it as foreign, thus embodying the paradoxical pride and abhorrence then swirling about imperialism. Indeed, one could argue, as did Kipling, that the English capacity to master, display, and enhance the beauties of nature via the garden served as a metaphor for England's right to rule and for the service that England brought to so-called less developed lands.

In an age when nothing seemed secure – foreign competition drove down agricultural and manufactured production, labor struck against capital, the masses pressed for democracy, Ireland fought for home rule, and rival nations jostled for possession of overseas colonies – the garden – sufficiently elastic to repair the rent fabric of domestic life while shoring up England's preeminent position in the world – was something that everyone could agree on. The garden promoted solid down-to-earth sobriety, domesticity, and oneness with God and nature, as opposed to the crass production of multiple goods and the pursuit of technology and profit glorified in the ever-changing marketplace. It denied England's history as a modern industrial power and instead located true England in an idyllically remembered preindustrial age. The garden as England and England as garden rendered the nation into a stable homeland. This sense of home resonated most strongly for the most active participants in the garden discourse: the upper middle classes who laid claim to the countryside in unprecedented numbers.

These values created high stakes for garden designers, who disputed the form of the garden, and therefore notions of the nation. Should the garden be wild, with its connotations of rusticity, or formal, with its evocations of the courtly culture of the Elizabethan age? Should it take its cues from the homes of cottagers or grand country homes? Should it accommodate or reject the produce of Empire? Or did one have to make a choice; could one have it all in the reconciling displays of Lutyens and Jekyll?

Throughout these debates, one theme held constant: the garden, for Englanders at home and abroad, expressed the very nature of England. Whether on the ground or on the page, the garden circulated throughout the nation, binding it together in an imagined community. What remains to be investigated is what happened to the garden when it traveled out into Empire. Did it produce there a notion of homeland that both paradoxically denied and acknowledged the presence of Empire?

A seemingly innocuous cultural artifact, the garden participated in one of the most important projects at the turn of the century: the construction of national identity. It continued to play this role into the twentieth century. As Raphael Samuel noted, during the interwar period, gardens and gardening were touted as national virtues and conjured up an image of the English as "a domestic people rather than a master-race, home-lovers rather than conquerors," which fed into the position of splendid isolation and bolstered Britain's morale and image in World War II. With respect to the present day, Raphael Samuel found that the cottage style has become "little short of hegemonic, the quintessence of the Englishness presented to the tourist and an inspiration to gardeners of all kinds."[18] One might ask, what ramifications has this for England's national identity today?

Notes

INTRODUCTION

1 For more on the historical practice of reading the garden, see, for example, John Dixon Hunt, "Emblem and Expression in the Eighteenth-Century Landscape Garden," *Eighteenth-Century Studies* 4 (Spring 1971): 294–317, and Ronald Paulson, *Emblem and Expression: Meaning in English Art of the Eighteenth Century* (Cambridge: Harvard University Press, 1975). For examples of inquiries into gardens that employ notions of reading (as well as other methodological frameworks), see Simon Pugh, *Garden, Nature, Language* (Manchester and New York: Manchester University Press, 1988); Stephen Daniels and Denis Cosgrove, "Introduction: Iconography and Landscape," in *The Iconography of Landscape* (Cambridge: Cambridge University Press, 1988); and Stephen Daniels, *Fields of Vision: Landscape Imagery and National Identity in England and the United States* (Princeton: Princeton University Press, 1993).

2 J. C. Loudon, *An Encyclopedia of Gardening,* new ed. (London: Longman, Rees, Orme, Brown, Green, and Longman, 1835), 1187.

3 Ernest Newton, "Domestic Architecture of To-Day," in *The House and Its Equipment,* ed. Lawrence Weaver (London: Country Life, 1912), 4–5.

4 W. J. T. Mitchell, "Introduction," in *Landscape and Power,* ed. W. J. T. Mitchell (Chicago: University of Chicago Press, 1994), 1, 2.

5 Roland Barthes, "Myth Today," in *Mythologies,* selected and translated by Annette Lavers (New York: Noonday Press, 1972), 143 and 109–59 passim. For more on the politicization of the garden, see, for example, Chandra Mukerji, *Territorial Ambitions and the Gardens of Versailles* (Cambridge: Cambridge University Press, 1997).

6 Ernest Renan, "Qu'est-ce qu'une nation?," in *Nationalism,* ed. John Hutchinson and Anthony D. Smith (Oxford and New York: Oxford University Press, 1994), 17.

7 Max Weber, "The Nation," in *Nationalism,* ed. Hutchinson and Smith, 22, 25.

8 Walker Connor, "A Nation Is a Nation, Is a State, Is an Ethnic Group, is a . . . ," in *Nationalism,* ed. Hutchinson and Smith, 37.

9 "Introduction," in *Nationalism,* ed. Hutchinson and Smith, 5.

10 Ernest Gellner, *Nations and Nationalism* (Ithaca and London: Cornell University Press, 1983), 40.

11 Ernest Gellner, *Nationalism* (New York: New York University Press, 1997), 3–4.
12 Benedict Anderson, *Imagined Communities: Reflections on the Origin and Spread of Nationalism,* 2nd ed. (London and New York: Verso, 1991), 4, 6.
13 Ibid., 44, 133, 164.
14 Daniels, *Fields of Vision,* 5.
15 Eric Hobsbawm, "Introduction: Inventing Traditions," in *The Invention of Tradition,* ed. Eric Hobsbawm and Terence Ranger (New York: Cambridge University Press, 1983), 1, 9, 11, 13.
16 John Hutchinson, "Cultural Nationalism and Moral Regeneration," in *Nationalism,* ed. Hutchinson and Smith, 122–31.
17 Gerald Newman, *The Rise of English Nationalism: A Cultural History 1740–1830* (London: Weidenfeld and Nicolson, 1987), 58–9.
18 Linda Colley, *Britons: Forging the Nation, 1707–1837* (New Haven and London: Yale University Press, 1992), 5–7. For discussion of how recent events, such as the establishment of a separate Scottish Parliament, undermine Colley's thesis, see Christopher Harvie, "Uncool Britannia: Linda Colley's *Britons* reconsidered," *Times Literary Supplement* (January 8, 1999): 12; and Michael Gove, "The Flight From History: How Labour Has Unravelled the Union," *Times Literary Supplement* (January 8, 1999): 13.
19 Hugh Kearney, *The British Isles: A History of Four Nations* (Cambridge: Cambridge University Press, 1989), 174–96.

CHAPTER 1

1 John Beckett, *The Rise and Fall of the Grenvilles, Dukes of Buckingham and Chandos, 1710–1921* (Manchester and New York: Manchester University Press, 1994), 24.
2 George Bickham, *The Beauties of Stow,* with an introduction by George B. Clarke (London E. Owen, 1750; reprint, Los Angeles: William Andrews Clark Memorial Library, University of California, 1977), 39.
3 William Mason, *The English Garden,* new ed. (York: A. Ward, 1783), 3. Michael Leslie, "History and Historiography in the English Landscape Garden," in *Perspectives on Garden Histories,* ed. Michel Conan (Washington, D.C.: Dumbarton Oaks Research Library and Collections, 1999), 91–106.
4 Mukerji, *Territorial Ambitions and the Gardens of Versailles,* 298.
5 Hermann Muthesius, *The English House,* edited with an introduction by Dennis Sharp and a preface by Julius Posener, trans. Janet Seligman (New York: Rizzoli, 1979), 9.
6 "Country Homes and Gardens Old & New, Heatherbank and Oakwood, The Residence and Garden of Mr. G. F. Wilson, F. R. S.," *Country Life* 8 (September 8, 1900): 304; and John Cornforth, *The Search for a Style: Country Life and Architecture, 1897–1935* (London: André Deutsch Limited, 1988), 14.
7 Cornforth, *The Search for a Style,* 17.
8 The design of the conservatory was reportedly based on the plant it sheltered – the South African *Victoria Regia* water lily – and its use of weblike cantilevers to support its giant leaf. John Tallis, *Tallis's History and Description of the Crystal Palace* (London and New York: John Tallis and Co., 1852), 9; and John McKean, *Crystal Palace* (London: Phaidon Press, 1994), 15.
9 Tallis, *Tallis's History,* 9; McKean, *Crystal Palace,* 22.
10 Paxton facilitated this practice through his numerous publications, such as *Paxton's Flower Garden* (1850–3), a monthly series devoted to "the new and remarkable plants introduced into cultivation." John Lindley and Sir Joseph Paxton, *Paxton's Flower Garden,* revised by Thomas Baines, vol. I (London, Paris, and New York: Cassell, Petter, Galpin and Co., 1882), iii.

11 Mark Laird, *The Flowering of the Landscape Garden: English Pleasure Grounds, 1720–1800* (Philadelphia: University of Pennsylvania Press, 1999), xiv passim.

12 Laird, *The Flowering of the English Landscape Garden,* 384.

13 Kim D. Legate, "Replanting England's 'Pioneer Parks': A study of planting design, focusing on the disposition of trees and shrubs in the public parks of the 1840s and 1850s" (Master's thesis, The Institute of Advanced Architectural Studies, The King's Manor, University of York, 1997), 38.

14 Lucile H. Brockway, *Science and Colonial Expansion: The Role of the British Royal Botanic Gardens* (New York: Academic Press, 1979), 60.

15 J. C. Loudon, *The Landscape Gardening and Landscape Architecture of the Late Humphry Repton,* new ed. (London: Longman & Co., A. & C. Black, 1840), viii–ix. For more on Loudon's gardenesque, see Melanie Louise Simo, *Loudon and the Landscape: From Country Seat to Metropolis, 1783–1843* (New Haven and London: Yale University Press, 1988), 170–3.

16 Ibid., 28.

17 As quoted in Werner Plum, *World Exhibitions in the Nineteenth Century: Pageants of Social and Cultural Change* (Bonn-Bad Godesberg: Friedrich-Ebert-Stiftung, 1977), 21–2.

18 As quoted in Robert Brain, *Going to the Fair: Readings in the Culture of Nineteenth-Century Exhibitions* (Cambridge: Whipple Museum of the History of Science, 1993), 165.

19 John Ruskin, "Introduction, The Poetry of Architecture," in *The Works of John Ruskin,* ed. E. T. Cook and Alexander Wedderburn, vol. 1 (London: George Allen, 1903), 5.

20 Loudon, *Encyclopedia,* 3.

21 *The Crystal Palace Penny Guide* (London: Robert K. Burt, [1865]), 4.

22 Ibid., 26. See also Tallis, *Tallis's History,* 108–9. Fortunately, this contrast did not destroy the unity of the garden; according to the guidebook, the designer, Joseph Paxton, recognized that fully adhering to the Italian style was not permissible in the English climate and so modified it by introducing an "English character." *Crystal Palace Penny Guide,* 26.

23 For the architectural quandary, see J. Mordaunt Crook, *The Dilemma of Style: Architectural Ideas from the Picturesque to the Post-Modern* (Chicago: University of Chicago Press, 1987), 98–132. For more on Victorian associationism, see George L. Hersey, *High Victorian Gothic: A Study in Associationism* (Baltimore and London: Johns Hopkins University Press, 1972).

24 Charles M'Intosh, *The Flower Garden: Containing Directions for the Cultivation of all Garden Flowers,* new ed. (London: Wm. S. Orr and Co., 1839), 9, 12, 15, 17.

25 Christopher Ridgeway, "William Andrews Nesfield: Between Uvedale Price and Isambard Kingdom Brunel," *Journal of Garden History* 13 (Spring/Summer 1993): 73. Ridgeway reveals that many of Nesfield's designs were not historically authentic but instead reflected Nesfield's unique interpretation of the past (86).

26 Brent Elliott, "Nesfield in his Victorian Context," in *William Andrews Nesfield: Victorian Landscape Architect,* ed. Christopher Ridgeway (University of York: Institute of Advanced Architectural Studies, 1996), 13–14.

27 David Ottewill, *The Edwardian Garden* (New Haven and London: Yale University Press, 1989), 7.

28 Lynn L. Merrill, *The Romance of Victorian Natural History* (New York and Oxford: Oxford University Press, 1989), 39–41.

29 John Ruskin, "Lecture II. Lilies: Of Queen's Gardens," in *The Works of John Ruskin,* ed. E. T. Cook and Alexander Wedderburn, vol. 18 (London: George Allen, 1905), 109–144.

30 For a thoughtful exposition of the country/city theme in English culture, see Raymond Williams, *The Country and the City* (New York: Oxford University Press, 1973). Martin Wiener, in his much-debated text *English Culture and the Decline of the Industrial Spirit, 1850–1980* (New York: Cambridge University Press, 1981), also tackled the question of

English attitudes to rural culture. For an insightful review of Wiener's book, see John Bax-
endale, "Review of Martin J. Wiener: *English Culture and the Decline of the Industrial
Spirit 1850–1980*," *History Workshop Journal* 21 (Spring 1986): 174.

31 Ibid., 158.

32 Alun Howkins, "The Discovery of Rural England," in *Englishness, Politics and Culture,
    1880–1920,* ed. Robert Colls and Philip Dodd (London and Dover, N.H.: Croom Helm,
    1986), 62–88.

33 Wiener, *English Culture,* 41–63.

34 Henry James, "London," in *English Hours* (Boston: Houghton Mifflin, 1905), 36–7.

35 Williams, *The Country,* 186–8.

36 Henry James, "An English Easter," in *English Hours,* 127.

37 John Ruskin, "Lectures on Art, Lecture I, Inaugural," in *The Works of John Ruskin,* ed.
    Cook and Wedderburn, vol. 20, 36, 37, 42, 43.

38 J. A. Froude, *Short Stories on Great Subjects,* 2nd series (London: Longman, Green and
    Co., 1871), 151, 155, 157, 159, 160, 174–5.

39 This account of Britain's and London's historical condition at the end of the nineteenth
    century has been drawn largely from the following sources: Walter L. Arnstein, *Britain
    Yesterday and Today, 1830 to the Present* (Lexington, Mass.: D.C. Heath, 1983); Eric Hobs-
    bawm, *The Age of Empire, 1875–1914* (New York: Vintage, 1989); Gareth Stedman Jones,
    Outcast London: A Study in the Relationship between Classes in Victorian Society (Oxford:
    Clarendon Press, 1971); Donald J. Olsen, *The City as a Work of Art: London, Paris, Vienna*
    (New Haven: Yale University Press, 1986); Harold Perkin, "Introduction: An Age of Great
    Cities," in *Victorian Urban Settings: Essays on the Nineteenth-Century City and Its Con-
    texts,* ed. Debra N. Mancoff and D. J. Trela (New York: Garland, 1996); Harold Perkin,
    Origins of Modern English Society (London: Ark Paperbacks, 1986, 1985 edition); Harold
    Perkin, *The Rise of Professional Society, England since 1880* (New York: Routledge, 1989);
    and Peter Stansky, *England since 1867, Continuity and Change* (New York: Harcourt
    Brace Jovanovich, 1973).

40 John Kenyon, *The History Men: The Historical Profession in England since the Renais-
    sance* (London: Weidenfeld and Nicolson, 1983), 116.

41 Henry James to Miss Alice James, [London] March 10, [1869], in *The Portable Henry
    James,* ed. Morton Dauwen Sabel (New York: Penguin, 1979), 630.

42 Ibid., 300.

43 Perkin, *The Rise of Professional Society,* 94.

44 "They belong to a society, a large number of the members of which are much wealthier
    than they themselves are, and the general level of whose social usages and demands they
    must, in as far as they move in it, maintain." G. Colmore, "Family Budgets: Eight Hun-
    dred a Year," *The Cornhill Magazine* 10 (June 1901): 790.

45 Ibid., 791.

46 Gordon A. Craig, *Europe since 1815* (New York: Holt, Rinehart and Winston, 1961), 386.

47 Andrew Mearns, "The Bitter Cry of Outcast London," in *The Bitter Cry of Outcast Lon-
    don,* ed. Anthony S. Wohl (*Pall Mall Gazette,* 1883; New York: Humanities Press, 1970),
    58.

48 Ibid., 56.

49 *Report of the Inter-Departmental Committee on Physical Deterioration* (London: His
    Majesty's Stationery Office, 1904), 16. Over thirty years earlier, Froude had alerted readers
    of *Fraser's Magazine* that "the life of cities brings with it certain physical consequences,
    for which no antidote and no preventive has yet been discovered. When vast numbers of
    people are crowded together, the air they breathe becomes impure, the water polluted.
    The hours of work are unhealthy, [and] occupation passed largely within doors thins the

blood and wastes the muscles and creates a craving for drink, which reacts again as poison." Froude, *Short Stories on Great Subjects*, 167.

50 Perkin, *The Rise of Professional Society*, 53.

51 Ibid., 171–2.

52 For more on Imperial architecture, see M. H. Port, *Imperial London: Civil Government Building in London, 1850–1915* (New Haven and London: Yale University Press, 1995).

53 Arnstein, *Britain Yesterday*, 161.

54 Frans Coetzee, *For Party or Country: Nationalism and the Dilemmas of Popular Conservatism in Edwardian England* (New York and Oxford: Oxford University Press, 1990), 7.

55 Colley, *Britons: Forging the Nation*.

56 Newman, *The Rise of English Nationalism*, 53.

57 Martin Pugh, *State and Society: British Political and Social History, 1870–1922* (London, New York, Melbourne, and Auckland: Edward Arnold, 1994), 72–80.

58 J. A. Hobson, *Imperialism: A Study*, new introduction by Philip Siegelman (London: J. Nisbet, 1902; reprint, Ann Arbor: University of Michigan Press, 1971), 5, 6, 368.

59 For more on the Broadway circle, see Marc Simpson, "Windows on the Past: Edwin Austin Abbey and Francis Davis Millet in England," *American Art Journal* 22 (1990): 65–89.

60 Copy of the exhibition catalog annotated by Edmund Gosse held at the Huntington Library, San Marino, California (443645). *Catalogue of a Collection of Drawings by Alfred Parsons with a Prefatory Note by Henry James* (London: The Fine Art Society, 1891), 14.

61 *Catalogue of a Collection of Drawings by Alfred Parsons*, 3–11.

62 "Art: Four Exhibitions," *The Spectator* 66 (March 21, 1891): 411. "Art Exhibitions," *The Times* (March 10, 1891): 3.

63 "The Fine Art Society's Gallery." *Illustrated London News* (March 14, 1891): 350.

64 Anderson, *Imagined Communities*, 11.

65 Mandell Creighton, *The Romanes Lecture, 1896: The English National Character* (London: Henry Frowde; Oxford: Clarendon Press, 1896), 7.

66 Ibid., 7, 25.

67 "A History of Gardening in England," *The Spectator* 76 (May 2, 1896): 640.

68 Henry James, "Our Artists in Europe," *Harper's Magazine* 79 (June 1889): 58; and James, *English Hours*, 83.

69 K. Baedeker, *Great Britain: A Handbook for Travellers*, 2nd ed. (London: Dulau and Co., 1890), lvi, 13, 122, 363, 366, 402. For a history of this practice, see Adrian Tinniswood, *A History of Country House Visiting: Five Centuries of Tourism and Taste* (Oxford and New York: Basil Blackwell, 1989). See also Peter Mandler, *The Fall and Rise of the Stately Home* (New Haven and London: Yale University Press, 1997); and Ian Ousby, *The Englishman's England: Taste, Travel and the Rise of Tourism* (Cambridge: Cambridge University Press, 1990).

70 Arthur Cooke, *With the Tourist Tide* (New York: Neal, 1907), 180, 183, 200.

For more about notions of the past and their intersection with the practices of tourism and identity construction, see David Lowenthal, *The Past Is a Foreign Country* (Cambridge: Cambridge University Press, 1985), as well as Donald Horne, *The Great Museum: The Re-Presentation of History* (London: Pluto Press, 1984), and Patrick Wright, *On Living in an Old Country: The National Past in Contemporary Britain* (London: Verso, 1985).

71 Jonathan Culler, "Semiotics of Tourism," *American Journal of Semiotics* 1 (1981): 131–2.

See also James Buzard, *The Beaten Track: European Tourism, Literature, and the Ways to Culture, 1800–1918* (Oxford: Clarendon Press, 1993); and Dean MacCannell, *The Tourist: A New Theory of the Leisure Class* (New York: Schocken, 1976).

72 For more on guidebooks, landscape imagery, possession and circulation, see Elizabeth

K. Helsinger, *Rural Scenes and National Representation: Britain, 1815–1850* (Princeton: Princeton University Press, 1997), 162–74.

73 Rudyard Kipling, "The Glory of the Garden," in *A School History of England*, ed. C. R. L. Fletcher and Rudyard Kipling (Oxford: Clarendon Press, 1911), 249–50.

74 C. C. Eldridge, *The Imperial Experience from Carlyle to Forster* (New York: St. Martin's Press, 1996), 102.

75 Stephen Heathorn, "'Let us remember that we, too, are English': Constructions of Citizenship and National Identity in English Elementary School Reading Books, 1880–1914," *Victorian Studies* 38 (Spring 1995): 395–427. See also Robert H. MacDonald, *The Language of Empire: Myths and Metaphors of Popular Imperialism, 1880–1918* (Manchester and New York: Manchester University Press, 1984), 62–9; and John M. MacKenzie, *Propaganda and Empire: The Manipulation of British Public Opinion, 1880–1960* (Manchester: Manchester University Press, 1984), 173–97.

76 The house also signified Kipling's newly found admiration for the English countryside as well as his elevated social status: writing to a friend in November 1902, shortly after he had purchased the house, Kipling explained that he and his wife had "discovered England which we had never done before . . . and went to live in it. England is a wonderful land. It is the most marvellous of all foreign countries that I have ever been in. It is made up of trees and green fields and mud and the gentry, and at last I'm one of the gentry." Rudyard Kipling to C. E. Norton, November 30, 1902, quoted in Charles Carrington, *Rudyard Kipling: His Life and Work* (London: Macmillan, 1955), 369. The tenor of the place is lovingly evoked in Kipling's *Puck of Pook's Hill* (1906), a story set in the streams, meadows, and hills around his home in which three children awaken the fairies of ancient England. The text concludes with a tribute to England akin to "The Glory of the Garden" in the form of a poem, "The Children's Song," in which the speaker pledges "love and toil" to the "land of our birth" in order to ensure an unbroken, "undefiled heritage." Rudyard Kipling, *Puck of Pook's Hill* (New York: Doubleday, 1906), 276.

77 T., "Country Homes, Gardens Old and New: Bateman's, Sussex, The Residence of Mr. Rudyard Kipling," *Country Life* 24 (August 15, 1908): 230.

78 Ibid., 231.

79 A note in the Visitor's Book at Bateman's states "To Lunch Mr. Robinson. Suggests alterations in gardens." As William Robinson lived relatively close, was one of the most notable figures in gardening of the period, and by this point in his career traveled in some of the same social circles to which the Kiplings belonged, the identity of this Mr. Robinson is likely William Robinson. Adam Nicholson, *Bateman's, East Sussex* (London: The National Trust, 1996), 29. For Blomfield at Bateman's, see T. , "Country Homes, Gardens Old & New, Bateman's Sussex, The Residence of Mr. Rudyard Kipling," 231.

80 Nicholson, *Bateman's*, 29.

81 Reginald Blomfield, *The Formal Garden in England* (London: Macmillan and Co., 1892), 125–30, 135, 144–5, 208.

CHAPTER 2

1 For the use of early-nineteenth-century visual images in configuring the countryside in opposition to the city, see Ann Bermingham, *Landscape and Ideology: The English Rustic Tradition, 1740–1860* (Berkeley: University of California Press, 1986), 57–193. For literature, see Williams, *The Country and the City*, 191–214. As examples: George Eliot, *Middlemarch* (first published 1871–2), Thomas Hardy, *Far from the Madding Crowd* (1874), and Richard Jefferies, *Hodge and His Masters* (1880). For a discussion of the predilection for the pastoral in nineteenth-century literature and its role in the construction of English-

ness, see David Gervais, *Literary Englands: Versions of "Englishness" in Modern Writing* (Cambridge: Cambridge University Press, 1993), 1–27.

2 Geoffrey Taylor, *Some Nineteenth Century Gardeners* (Tiptree, Essex: Anchor Press, 1951), 68. Taylor states, "As for Ireland, he never forgot the country, though he concealed the fact that he was born there" (88). I am indebted to Mea Allan's study of William Robinson for these biographical details: Mea Allan, *William Robinson, 1838–1935: Father of the English Flower Garden* (London: Faber and Faber, 1982). For additional information on Robinson's life and career, see Betty Massingham, "William Robinson: A Portrait," *Garden History: The Journal of the Garden History Society* 6 (1978): 61–85; Ruth Duthie, "An Addendum to the Article 'William Robinson: a portrait' by Mrs. Betty Massingham in the last number of 'Garden History'," *Garden History: The Journal of the Garden History Society* 6 (1978): 20–1; and Ruth E. Duthie, "Some Notes on William Robinson," *Garden History: The Journal of the Garden History Society* 2 (1974): 12–21.

3 Robinson continued to design gardens after his writing career was established, although he often found it difficult to balance competing agendas of designing and writing: "I am doing several places now as it always interests me to study the thing on the ground but it only throws my books and business back to take up much work of the kind and it is also very ungrateful work as one rarely gets the thing done as it shd. [sic] be owing to wives husbands and gardeners and all the friends of the family having strong and opposing views, only a saint could step about them without losing his temper." Quoted in Nicole Milette, *Parsons-Partridge-Tudway: An Unsuspected Design Partnership 1884–1914* (York: Institute of Advanced Architectural Studies, University of York, 1995), 12.

4 For a history of the production and publishing of *The Wild Garden,* see Judith B. Tankard, "Introduction," in William Robinson, *The Wild Garden* (Portland: Sagapress/Timber Press, 1994), xi–xix.

5 For a history of the production and publishing of *The English Flower Garden,* see Judith B. Tankard, "A Perennial Favourite: 'The English Flower Garden'," *Hortus* 5 (1991): 74–85. See also Deborah Nevins, "Introduction," in William Robinson, *The English Flower Garden* (New York: Amaryllis Press, 1984), xiii–xxiv.

6 Horace Townsend, "An Artistic Treatment of Cottages," *The Studio* 6 (October 1895): 30.

7 "Rural England [A review of L. G. Seguin's *Rural England,* 1881]," *The Art Journal* 43 (December 1881): 376.

8 William Robinson, *The Wild Garden* (London: John Murray, 1870), 6–7.

9 William Robinson, *The Parks, Promenades & Gardens of Paris Described and Considered in Relation to the Wants of Our Own Cities* (London: John Murray, 1869), 21. Robinson was not the first to advocate a return to hardy plants. As both Richard Bisgrove and David Ottewill have pointed out, the garden writer and designer Shirley Hibberd wrote extensively on the use of hardy flowers at least ten years before Robinson began his work. Richard Bisgrove, *The National Trust Book of the English Garden* (New York: Viking, 1990), 197; and Ottewill, *The Edwardian Garden,* 53. On composing flower beds at mid-century, see Edward Kemp, *How to Lay out a Garden: Intended as a General Guide in choosing, forming, or improving an Estate,* 3rd ed. (London: Bradbury, Evans, and Co., 1864).

10 Brent Elliott, *Victorian Gardens* (London: B. T. Batsford, 1986), 89.

11 Robinson, *The Parks, Promenades, and Gardens of Paris,* 25.

12 Ibid., 22.

13 Ibid., 240.

14 Ibid., 29.

15 Robinson, *The Wild Garden* (1870), 33–4, and *The Wild Garden* (London: The Garden Office, 1881), vii.

16 Helsinger, *Rural Scenes and National Representation.*

17 Alfred Russel Wallace, *Bad Times* (London: Macmillan and Co., 1885), 60.

18 P. J. Perry, *British Agriculture* (London: Metheun and Co., 1973), Map I.

19 Alfred Russel Wallace, *Land Nationalisation: Its Necessity and Its Aims* (London: Trübner, 1882), 127.

20 "Save the commons and the grassy roadsides by all means, also every way really necessary for public convenience or even for seeing the charms of picturesque or beautiful districts; but to interfere with private rights, with stock, with delicate annuals in young, with game, is not just to those who have to bear the burdens of the land, and whose labours have created its charms." William Robinson, "Gravetye Manor, Tree and Garden Book and Building Record," 1888, 110. AMsS, Lindley Library, Royal Horticultural Society, London, England.

21 William Robinson, "Gravetye Manor," 1888, 114.

22 Robinson, *The Wild Garden* (1870), 13, 36.

23 Kim D. Legate, "Replanting England's 'Pioneer Parks'," 37.

24 Ibid., 93.

25 Ibid., 50.

26 For a history of the evolution of the shrubbery prior to the Victorian era, see Laird, *The Flowering of the Landscape Garden*, 264.

27 Robinson, *The Wild Garden* (1881), vii.

28 Alexander Pope, "Of False Taste. An Epistle to the Right Honourable Richard Earl of Burlington, occasion'd by his publishing Palladio's Designs of the Baths, Arches, Theaters, &c. of Ancient Rome" (London and Dublin: George Faulkner, 1732), 25.

29 Horace Walpole, "The History of the Modern Taste in Gardening," in *The Genius of the Place: The English Landscape Garden, 1620–1820* (London: Paul Elek, 1975), 314.

30 Robinson, *The Wild Garden* (1870), 39.

31 Francis Bacon, "Essay 46: Of Gardens," in Sally Weintz, *The Perpetual Spring of Francis Bacon* (Pittsburgh: Weintz, 1974), 3, 7.

32 Robinson, *The Wild Garden* (1870), 13.

33 Ibid., 12.

34 Ibid., 24.

35 Ibid., 5–7. Elliott, *Victorian Gardens*, 132, 159.

36 Robinson, *The Wild Garden* (1870), 4.

37 "English Ideals of Gardening," *The Times* (November 16, 1907): 3. See also Michael Waters, *The Garden in Victorian Literature* (Aldershot: Scolar Press, 1988), 48–71.

38 Wendy Kaplan, "Traditions Transformed: Romantic Nationalism in Design, 1890–1920," in *Designing Modernity: The Arts of Reform and Persuasion, 1885–1945*, ed. Wendy Kaplan (New York: Thames and Hudson; Miami Beach: The Wolfsonian, 1995), 19–21; and Barbara Miller Lane, *National Romanticism and Modern Architecture in Germany and the Scandinavian Countries* (Cambridge: Cambridge University Press, 2000), for a treatment of similar themes in Germany and Scandinavia.

39 William Morris, "Making the Best of It (A Paper read before the Trade's Guild of Learning and the Birmingham Society of Artists)," in *Hopes and Fears for Art* (London: Longmans, Green, and Co., 1903), 127. Robinson used Morris's discussion of his distaste for carpet bedding (akin to bedding out with an emphasis on ensuring that all the plants in the patterned bed grow to a low, uniform height) in gardens as an epigram for the 1898 edition of *The English Flower Garden*.

40 Ibid., 124–6.

41 Deborah Nevins, "Morris, Ruskin, and the English Flower Garden," *Antiques* 129 (June 1986): 1258.

42 Ruskin, "The British Villa," in *The Works of John Ruskin*, ed. Cook and Wedderburn, vol. 1, 156.

43 Ibid., 157.

44 Gary Taylor, *Reinventing Shakespeare: A Cultural History from the Restoration to the Present* (New York: Weidenfeld and Nicolson, 1989), 182–96.

45 Henry N. Ellacombe, *The Plant-Lore and Garden-Craft of Shakespeare,* new ed. (London and New York: Edward Arnold, 1896), xii–xiii. Around the turn of the century, the Countess of Warwick at Easton Lodge laid out a quite well-known Shakespeare garden, which the Arts and Crafts designer Walter Crane paid tribute to in his illustrated *Flowers from Shakespeare's Gardens, A Posy from the Plays* (1906) featuring anthropomorphized flowers.

46 Robinson, *The Wild Garden* (1870), 11.

47 Ibid., 43. The issue of collecting plant specimens for the wild garden was a bone of contention. For example, "A forester wrote to Robinson's magazine *The Garden* in 1876, telling how he had transplanted three cartloads each of daffodils and lilies of the valley to improve his woods; another correspondent in reply protested against such wholesale plundering: 'there is something selfish in wholesale cartloading away of the flowers of our meadows, banks, hedges, and copses, and . . . if encouraged it will certainly endanger not the wild gardens but the woodlands.'" Andrew Clayton-Payne and Brent Elliott, *Flower Gardens of Victorian England* (New York: Rizzoli, 1988), 104. Another article the same year cautioned, "collecting where Ferns are scarce is highly reprehensible, specimens should always be procured from where they are abundant, and in places where they are scarce they should be carefully preserved." J. O'B, "Our Native Plants and Ferns in the Wild Garden," *The Garden* 10 (1876): 177.

48 For a history of the back-to-the-land movement, see Jan Marsh, *Back to the Land: The Pastoral Impulse in England, from 1880 to 1914* (New York: Quartet Books, 1982).

49 *Sutton's Amateur's Guide for 1873* (Reading: Sutton and Sons, 1873), 69.

50 Robinson, *The Wild Garden* (1870), 157. The chapter on the "Garden of British Wild Flowers" was dropped from the 1881 edition, but a discussion of native species reappeared in the 1894 edition. For a contemporaneous appreciation of English native plants and trees, see Richard Jefferies, "Trees about Town (1881)," in *Landscape with Figures* (London: Penguin, 1983).

51 J. T. Burgess, *Old English Wild Flowers: To be found by the wayside, fields, hedgerows, rivers, moorlands, meadows, and seashore* (London: Fredericke Warne; New York: Scribner, Welford, 1868), 12.

52 Richard Jefferies, "Wild Flowers," in *The Open Air* (Philadelphia: J. B. Lippincott Co., 1908), 30.

53 Watson authored such studies as *Remarks on the Geographical Distribution of British Plants; Chiefly in Connection with Latitude, Elevation, and Climate* (1835), *The New Botanists' Guide to the Localities of the Rare Plants in Britain* (1835–7), and *Cybele Britannica; or, British Plants and Their Geographical Relations* (1842–52).

54 Robinson, *The Wild Garden* (1870), 162. Watson quoted in Alfred Russel Wallace, *Island Life or the Phenomena and Causes of Insular Faunas and Floras* (New York: Harper and Bros., 1881), 333.

55 For more on how native has become falsely confused with natural with regard to plant material, see Stephen Jay Gould, "An Evolutionary Perspective on Strengths, Fallacies, and Confusions in the Concept of Native Plants," in *Nature and Ideology: Natural Garden Design in the Twentieth Century,* ed. Joachim Wolschke-Bulmahn (Washington, D.C.: Dumbarton Oaks Research Library and Collection, 1997), 11–19.

56 John H. Harvey, "Botanical Incunabula," *Historic Gardens Review* (Summer 1998): 21, 25.

57 Robinson, *The Wild Garden* (1870), 164, 207.

58 Ibid., 13.

59 Ibid., 7.

60 Ibid., 24.

61 William Robinson, *The Subtropical Garden; or, Beauty of Form in the Flower Garden* (London: John Murray, 1871), 3–5, 13, 23, 25, 26.

62 Robinson, *The Wild Garden* (1870), 15–16, 10.

63 B. F. Brandon, "The Diffusion of Designed Landscapes in South-East England," in *Change in the Countryside: Essays on Rural England, 1500–1900,* ed. H. S. A. Fox and R. A. Butlin (London: Institute of British Geographers, 1979), 180, 183–4.

64 Richard Jefferies, *Wild Life in a Southern County* (Boston: Roberts Brothers, 1879), iii.

65 John Hedley Brooke, "Science and Theology in the Enlightenment," in *Religion & Science, History, Method, Dialogue,* ed. W. Mark Richardson and Wesley J. Wildman (New York and London: Routledge, 1996), 7–27; and Dov Ospovat, *The Development of Darwin's Theory, Natural History, Natural Theology, and Natural Selection, 1838–1859* (Cambridge: Cambridge University Press, 1981).

66 William Robinson, "Wild v. Highly Kept Gardens," *The Garden* 20 (1881): 209.

67 Robinson, *The Wild Garden* (1881), 61.

68 Ibid., 13–14.

69 Ibid., 14–15.

70 John Langdon Brooks, *Just before the Origin: Alfred Russel Wallace's Theory of Evolution* (New York: Columbia University Press, 1984), 73.

71 Wallace, *Island Life,* 12.

72 Alfred Russel Wallace, *Contributions to the Theory of Natural Selection* (London: Macmillan and Co., 1870), 279. David Ottewill has pointed out the nineteenth-century precedents to Robinson's proposals to naturalize foreign exotics. Ottewill, *The Edwardian Garden,* 53. See also Elliott, *Victorian Gardens,* 194–5.

73 Charles Darwin, *The Variation of Animals and Plants under Domestication* (London: John Murray, 1868), 3.

74 Ibid., 68–9.

75 Robinson, *The Wild Garden* (1870), 33.

76 Ibid., 11.

77 Robinson, *The Wild Garden* (1881), 102.

78 Ibid.

79 David Allen, *The Naturalist in Britain, A Social History* (London: Allen Lane, 1976), 201.

80 Vitalism is similar to the German monism movement, which Joachim Wolschke-Bulmahn has discussed in relation to the German wild garden. Joachim Wolschke-Bulmahn, "The 'Wild Garden' and the 'Nature Garden' – Aspects of the Garden Ideology of William Robinson and Willy Lange," *Journal of Garden History* 12 (July/September, 1992): 197–8.

81 Allen, *The Naturalist in Britain,* 240–1.

82 Charles Kingsley, *Glaucus; or The Wonders of the Shore* (London: Macmillan and Co., 1873), 14–15, 44–5.

83 John Ruskin, *Modern Painters,* vol. 2, in *The Complete Works of John Ruskin,* ed. Cook and Wedderburn, vol. 4, 146, 147, 148, 151, 154–5, 161.

84 John Ruskin, *Modern Painters,* vol. 1, in *The Complete Works of John Ruskin,* ed. Cook and Wedderburn, vol. 3, 33, 36.

85 Robinson, *The Wild Garden* (1870), 11. In his obituary for John Ruskin written for *The Garden,* Robinson admitted his debt to the art critic, writing that Ruskin "of all the artists of England . . . throughout the length of the century" had opened "eyes" and "hearts" to "the beauty of flower and leaf, of the sunny smile of peaceful pastoral land" and revealed and interpreted "the moods of Nature and her marvelous structure to minds dimmer and duller than his own." William Robinson, "John Ruskin, An Appreciation," *The Garden* 57 (1900): 73.

86 Robinson, *The Wild Garden* (1881), 4, 17.

87 James Aumonier (1832–1911) was best known as a landscape and animal painter.

88 Charles Holme, ed., *Masters of English Landscape Painting* (London: The Studio, 1903); and J. Comyns Carr, *Modern Landscape* (London: Remington and Co., 1883), 45.

89 For a discussion of Fantin-Latour's English patrons, see Douglas Druick and Michel Hoog, *Fantin-Latour* (Ottawa: National Gallery of Canada, 1983), 113–18. For a discussion of English interest in Barbizon painters, see Jacqueline Falkenhim, *Roger Fry and the Beginning of Formalist Art Criticism* (Ann Arbor: UMI Research Press, 1980), 3–4. For listings of William Robinson's art collection, see the manuscript "Gravetye Manor, Tree and Garden Book and Building Record," Lindley Library, Royal Horticulture Society, London. This record book contains Robinson's 1895 list of "Pictures in House," a list of paintings owned by Robinson sold at Christie's in 1898, an 1899 list of paintings sold at Christie's, and a brief mention of paintings sold at Christie's in 1900 and 1903 (vol. 2, pp. 100–6, 149, 183, 197, 219). See also the catalog of William Robinson's paintings sold upon his death, *Catalogue of Modern Pictures and Water Colour Drawings of the British and Continental Schools* (London: Christie, Manson, and Wood, 1935).

90 William Robinson, *The Wild Garden,* introduction by Richard Mabey (London: Century Hutchinson, 1983), 61. (This is a republication of the 1894 edition and is referred to henceforth as *The Wild Garden,* 1894.)

91 Quoted in Peter Herbert, "Henry George Moon, 1857–1905," TMs [photocopy], Gravetye Manor, October 1992, 1.

92 William Robinson, *The English Flower Garden* (London: John Murray, 1895), 5, 12.

93 For example, Parsons was contacted by author Edmund Gosse to provide illustrations for an article on Charles Darwin by Arabella Buckley. Letter from Edmund Gosse to Alfred Parsons, November 20, 1882. Letter from Richard Jefferies to Alfred Parsons, January 15, [no year given], Alfred Parsons Correspondence, BA 11, 302, Hereford and Worcester County Record Office, England. He also illustrated articles by Richard Jefferies and earned the praise of Thomas Hardy. Letter from Thomas Hardy to Alfred Parsons, July 24, 1910, Alfred Parsons Correspondence, BA 11, 302, Hereford and Worcester County Record Office, England.

94 Robinson, *The Wild Garden* (1881), vi.

95 Ibid., vii.

96 For example, "An interesting point in favor of the wild garden is the succession of effects which it may afford, and which are suggested by the illustrations on the next pages, both showing a succession of life on the same spot of ground." Robinson, *The Wild Garden* (1881), 71.

97 Robinson, *The Wild Garden* (1881), 4.

98 The *Art Journal,* for example, in its review of the 1894 edition of *The Wild Garden,* designated the scattering of spring bulbs as one of Robinson's major contributions to gardening. "Notes on Art Books," *Art Journal,* n.s. 33 (1894): 319.

99 Robinson, *The Wild Garden* (1881), 51, 53.

100 Parsons's image also repudiated J. C. Loudon's claim that trees and flowers should never be placed together to form one picture because landscapes by eminent artists and great masters never depicted detailed flowers in the foregrounds of their paintings. Loudon, "On Mixing Herbaceous Flowering Plants with Trees and Shrubs," *The Gardener's Magazine* 11 (1835): 413–14.

101 Readers also reportedly responded favorably to Parsons's illustrations, often relying on them for guidance more than Robinson's text. For example, although Robinson intended wild gardens to be created only at the edges of existing parks or gardens, readers often planted wild gardens throughout their grounds because Parsons's illustrations did not indicate that wild gardens were situated along the outer perimeters of pleasure grounds.

According to the garden historian Richard Bisgrove, readers took the illustrations "as a suggestion to scatter yuccas, pampas, reeds, and retinosporas freely over the whole lawn." Bisgrove, *The National Trust Book of the English Garden,* 194.

102 "Art in the Garden," *The Art Journal,* n.s. 21 (January 1882): 10–11.

103 Frances Jane Hope, *Notes and Thoughts on Gardens and Woodlands,* ed. Anne J. Hope Johnstone (London: Macmillan and Co., 1881), 207–18; and S. W. Fitzherbert, *The Book of the Wild Garden* (London and New York: John Lane/The Bodley Head, 1903).

104 Robinson, *The Wild Garden* (1881), 103.

105 C. W. Earle, *Pot-Pourri from a Surrey Garden* (London: Smith, Elder and Co., 1897), 170.

106 The H. A. Peto manuscript held at Dumbarton Oaks contains several pages of Peto's sketches for wild gardens. See H. A. Peto, *Garden designs 1900–1933*(?), 62–5, AMsS, Garden Library, Dumbarton Oaks, Washington, D.C. For more on H. A. Peto's design for Wayford Manor, which included a wild garden, see Ottewill, *The Edwardian Garden,* 150. For more on Ellen Willmott's garden at Warley Place, see Bisgrove, *The English Garden,* 235–6; and Audrey Le Lievre, *Miss Willmott of Warley Place, Her Life and Gardens* (Boston: Faber and Faber, 1980).

107 Ottewill, *The Edwardian Garden,* 53.

108 See, for example, Tewensis, "My Wild Garden," *The Garden* 13 (April 13, 1878): 327; and "My Wild Garden," *The Garden* 13 (May 25, 1878): 488.

109 Peter Brandon and Brian Short, *The South East from AD 1000* (London and New York: Longman, 1990), 353.

110 *High Beeches* (Handcross, West Sussex: High Beeches Gardens Conservation Trust, n.d.), 15.

111 The house and immediately surrounding gardens are now Gravetye Manor Hotel. The ornamental grounds around the house have been recently restored under the auspices of owner Peter Herbert.

112 William Robinson, *Home Landscapes* (London: John Murray, 1914), 19. For the chronological development of the garden, see William Robinson, *Gravetye Manor, or Twenty Years' Work round an Old Manor House* (London: John Murray, 1911).

113 Robinson, *Home Landscapes,* 1.

114 Michael Rosenthal, *Constable: The Painter and His Landscape* (New Haven and London: Yale University Press, 1983), 178.

115 Robinson, *Home Landscapes,* 3.

116 Rosenthal, *Constable,* 175–9.

117 Robinson, *Home Landscapes,* 5, 8.

118 Robinson, *Gravetye Manor,* 46.

119 Robinson, *Home Landscapes,* 4; and *Gravetye Manor,* 12, 72–6.

120 Robinson had once considered converting the fields into a park but decided it was inappropriate for his manor house because of the park's connotations of grand manner houses. Robinson, *Gravetye Manor,* 12.

CHAPTER 3

1 Gellner, *Nations and Nationalism,* 57.

2 "English Ideals of Gardening," *The Times* (November 16, 1907): 3.

3 For more on the first two types of cottages, see Eric Mercer, *English Vernacular Houses: A Study of Traditional Farmhouses and Cottages* (London: Her Majesty's Stationery Office, 1975); and Sutherland Lyall, *Dream Cottages: From Cottage Ornée to Stockbroker Tudor* (London: Robert Hale, 1988).

4 "Allotments and Cottage Gardens Compensation for Crops Act, 1887," in John Aubrey

Spencer, *The Agricultural Holdings (England) Acts, 1883–1900,* 2nd ed. (London: Stevens and Sons, 1901), 111.

5 Anne Scott-James, *The Cottage Garden* (London: Allen Lane, 1981), 9–10.

6 E. L. D.-A., "Cottage Gardens," *Country Life* 7 (April 14, 1900): 453.

7 Loudon, 1225.

8 To support this point, the author described a cottage garden full of flowers and fruit trees. Gesturing to the flowers, the male cottager exclaimed, "Do you see those flowers, sir? . . . its those flowers, Sir, which keep me out of the public house. You see, flowers take a deal of fiddling after." "Cottage Gardens," *Spectator* 73 (August 25, 1894): 236–7.

9 Ibid., 237.

10 Loudon, 1204.

11 Richard Jefferies, "The Labourer's Daily Life," first published in *Fraser's Magazine* (November 1874), in *Landscape with Figures,* 47–8.

12 Flora Thompson, *Lark Rise to Candleford,* introduction by H. J. Massingham (Harmondsworth: Penguin Books, 1939), 63.

13 Ibid., 78.

14 Ibid., 114–15.

15 Stephen Constantine, "Amateur Gardening and Popular Recreation in the 19th and 20th Centuries," *Journal of Social History* 14 (Spring 1981): 393.

16 Elliott, *Victorian Gardens,* 64.

17 L. G. Seguin, *Rural England: Loitering along the Lanes, the Common-sides and the Meadow-Paths with Peeps into the Halls, Farms, and Cottages* (London: Strahan and Co., 1881), 19.

18 Lucy Hardy, "The Cottage Garden," *Country Life* 2 (November 6, 1897): 483–4.

19 Robinson, *The Wild Garden,* 1870, 4.

20 John Dixon Hunt, "The Cult of the Cottage," in *The Lake District: A Sort of National Property* (Manchester: Countryside Commission and London: Victoria and Albert, 1986), 78.

21 George H. Ford, "Felicitous Space: The Cottage Controversy," in *Nature and the Victorian Imagination* (Berkeley: University of California Press, 1977), 34, 48.

22 Williams, *The Country and the City,* 72, 74.

23 Ibid., 77, 79. Oliver Goldsmith, *The Deserted Village* (London: W. Griffin, 1770; reprint, London: Noel Douglas, 1927), 8, 9.

24 Quoted in Merryn Williams, *Thomas Hardy and Rural England* (New York: Columbia University Press, 1972), 15. Thanks to Karen Steele for drawing this poem to my attention.

25 Tom Taylor, *Birket Foster's Pictures of English Landscape* (first published 1862; reprint, London: George Routledge and Sons, New Edition, 1881), XVII.

26 For example, see F. E. Green, *The Tyranny of the Countryside* (London: T. Fisher Unwin, 1913), 32.

27 E. J. Urwick, *Studies of Boy Life in Our Cities* (London: J. M. Dent and Company, 1904; reprint, New York: Garland Publishing, 1980), 267.

28 Pamela Horn, *The Changing Countryside in Victorian and Edwardian England and Wales* (London: The Athlone Press; Rutherford, Madison, and Teaneck: Fairleigh Dickinson University Press, 1984), 108.

29 Alun Howkins, "The Discovery of Rural England," in *Englishness: Politics and Culture,* ed. Colls and Dodd, 67–9.

30 For an example, see an 1887 investigation of two cottages in the village of Milton Keynes, property of Mr. George Henry Finch, M.P., for the county of Rutland in *Pall Mall Gazette* (May 5, 1887): 10. See also *Report of Agriculture and Fisheries, Report on the Decline of the Agricultural Population of Great Britain 1881–1906* (London: His Majesty's Stationery Office, 1906).

31 Seebohm Rowntree and May Kendall, *How the Labourer Lives: A Study of the Rural Labour Problem* (London and New York: T. Nelson, 1913; reprint, New York: Arno Press, 1975), 328–9.

32 Williams, *The Country and the City*, 102.

33 Lucy Hardy, "The Cottage Garden," 483.

34 Jefferies, "The Labourer's Daily Life," 48–9.

35 John Varley, *Treatise on the Principles of Landscape Design for Students & Amateurs in That Art* ([London]: J. Varley, [1816]), text accompanying plate 2.

36 "First of all, if he did not actually introduce, he was the artist to popularize the homes of the peasantry and life in the fields. . . . Half a century ago artists had never condescended to such things; and if they noted the one phase of it represented by tumble-down buildings they did so because they were an echo of the classic ruin which had for so long furnished a *raison d'etre* for a most unreal and uninteresting landscape. But as a body they had entirely overlooked the garden of nature, which cried out for notice, no man regarding it. He was almost the first to see beauty in the wayside cottage, with its tiled roof ridged with moss and house leek, its timbered sides half hidden in vines, its apple-trees pushing their blossoms almost in at the leaden lattices; the first to put on paper the hedgerows decked with honeysuckles and wild rose, and the woods gay with hyacinth and primroses." "Birket Foster," *The Art Journal*, n.s., 29 (December 1890): 20.

37 "Always works directly from nature, painting exactly what she sees but leaving out things which are in the way and which do not help the subject – any gaps which result are filled in with other material painted from nature." Annotation in the hand of A. J. Baldry on a letter from Helen Allingham to A. J. Baldry, February 14, 1911, 86.PP.25, National Art Library, Victoria and Albert Museum, London.

38 John Ruskin, "The Art of England, Lecture IV Fairy Land," in *The Works of John Ruskin*, ed. Cook and Wedderburn, vol. 33, 341.

39 "Art Exhibitions," *The Times* (March 28, 1898): 5.

40 "Spring Exhibitions," *The Illustrated London News* (April 10, 1886): 369. "Spring Exhibitions," *The Illustrated London News* (May 18, 1889): 626.

41 David Watkin, *The Rise of Architectural History* (London: The Architectural Press; Westfield, N.J.: Eastview Editions, 1980), 104.

42 P. H. Ditchfield, *Picturesque English Cottages and Their Doorways* (Philadelphia: John C. Winston, 1905), 15.

43 M. J. Sallis Schwabe, "Shere and Its Neighborhood," *Art Journal* (May 1882): 129.

44 [W. Allingham], *Catalogue of a Collection of Drawings by Mrs. Allingham, R.W.S. Illustrating Surrey Cottages* (London: Fine Art Society, 1886), 3, 4, 6.

45 David Lowenthal and Marcus Binney, eds., *Our Past before Us: Why Do We Save It?* (London: Temple Smith, 1981), 18.

46 Gillian Naylor, ed., *William Morris, by Himself* (London: Macdonald & Co., 1988), 118–19; and Chris Miele, "The First Conservation Militants: William Morris and the Society for the Protection of Ancient Buildings," in *Preserving the Past: The Rise of Heritage in Modern Britain*, ed. Michael Hunter (Stroud, Gloucestershire: Alan Sutton, 1996), 20.

47 Morris, "The Beauty of Life (Delivered Before the Birmingham Society of Arts and School of Design, Feb. 19, 1880)," in *Hopes and Fears for Art*, 99.

48 G. E. Mingay, *A Social History of the Countryside* (London and New York: Routledge, 1990), 184. See also William Savage, *Rural Housing* (London: T. Fisher Unwin, 1914).

49 A. F. Topham, "Building By-Laws in Rural Districts," *Architectural Review* 19 (March 1906): 110. "Minor Exhibitions," *The Athenaeum* no. 3109 (May 28, 1887): 710.

50 Townsend, "An Artistic Treatment of Cottages," 29–30.

51 C. J. Cornish, "Village Houses for Holiday Homes," *Country Life* 3 (May 7, 1898): 552.

52 M. H. Baillie Scott, "A Country Cottage," *The Studio* 25 (March 15, 1902): 93.

53 Anon., "The Sabine Farm.-New Style," *Country Life* 4 (November 29, 1898): 661–3. See also Anon., "New Homes in Old Houses," *Country Life* 2 (October 9, 1897): 378–82; and C. J. Cornish, "Village Houses for Holiday Homes," *Country Life* 3 (May 7, 1898): 552–4.

54 Gertrude Jekyll, *Old West Surrey* (London: Longmans, Green, and Co., 1904), 5, 287.

55 Anon., "The Lay Figure: On Cottage Architecture," *The Studio* 60 (December 15, 1913): 250.

56 "Spring Exhibitions," *Illustrated London News* (April 10, 1886): 369.

57 Marsh, *Back to the Land,* 56. For more information on Alfriston, which was reportedly restored by William Morris's Anti-Scape group after its purchase, see Kenneth Gravett, "The Clergy House, Alfriston: A Reappraisal," in *National Trust Studies 1981,* ed. Gervase Jackson-Stops (London: Sotheby Parke Bernet Publications), 103–8.

58 "Home Counties, On Going to Live in the Country and Trying to Make Ends Meet," *World's Work* 11 (March 1908): 391.

59 F. E. Green, "The Architect in the Garden," *World's Work* 17 (April 1911): 507.

60 Peter C. Gould, *Early Green Politics: Back to Nature, Back to the Land, and Socialism in Britain, 1880–1900* (New York: St. Martin's Press, 1988), 231.

61 Horn, *The Changing Countryside,* 108; and E. Lawrence Mitchell, *The Law of Allotments and Allotment Gardens (England and Wales)* (London: P. S. King and Son, 1922), 38. See also David Crouch and Colin Ward, *The Allotment, Its Landscape and Culture* (London: Faber and Faber, 1988).

62 *Spring Catalogue: Sutton's Amateur Guide for 1873* (Reading: Sutton and Sons, 1873), 47, 69.

63 Anon., "An Estate in the Making-II.," *Country Life* 8 (September 22, 1900): 361–2.

64 Sir William Lever, *Art and Beauty and the City, Three Addresses* (Port Sunlight: Lever Bros. Limited, 1915), 5–6.

65 For more on the garden city movement, see, for example, Stanley Buder, *Visionaries and Planners: The Garden City Movement and the Modern Community* (New York: Oxford University Press, 1990); Gillian Darley, *Villages of Vision* (London: The Architectural Press, 1977); and Robert Fishman, *Urban Utopias in the Twentieth Century: Ebenezer Howard, Frank Lloyd Wright, Le Corbusier* (New York: Basic, 1977).

66 Edward Hubbard and Michael Shippobottom, *A Guide to Port Sunlight Village* (Liverpool: Liverpool University Press, 1988), 20.

67 J. H. Whitehouse, "Bournville," *The Studio* 24 (December 16, 1901): 168.

68 W. Alexander Harvey, *The Model Village and Its Cottages: Bournville* (London: B.T. Batsford, 1906), 10. See also Standish Meacham, *Regaining Paradise, Englishness and the Early Garden City Movement* (New Haven and London: Yale University Press, 1999), 15–19.

69 Wilhelm Miller, *What England Can Teach Us about Gardening* (Garden City, N.Y.: Doubleday, Page, and Co., 1911), 137.

70 Marsh, *Back to the Land,* 229, 230.

71 See, for example, Ewart G. Culpin, *The Garden City Movement Up-to-Date* (London: The Garden Cities and Town Planning Association, 1913); T. Raffles Davison, *Port Sunlight: A Record of Its Artistic and Pictorial Aspect* (London: B. T. Batsford, 1917); Ralph Neville, *Garden Cities* (Manchester: Manchester University Press, 1904); and A. R. Sennett, *Garden Cities in Theory and Practice* (London: Bemrose and Sons, 1905).

72 Stewart Dick, *The Cottage Homes of England* (New York: Longmans, Green and Co., 1909; London: Edward Arnold, 1909), 2, 4, 227.

73 Sydney Jones, *The Village Homes of England* (London: The Studio, 1912), 3.

74 Helsinger, *Rural Scenes and National Representation,* 61–4.

75 Hunt, "The Cult of the Cottage," 81.

76 John Ruskin, "The Poetry of Architecture: The Lowland Cottage – England and France (1837)," in *The Complete Works of John Ruskin,* ed. Cook and Wedderburn, vol. 1, 12–13.

77 Tricia Cusack, "The Irish Cottage Landscape and "Banal Nationalism," paper delivered in the session "The Structure and Narratives of National Identity Formation," at the annual Association of Art Historians conference, Exeter, England, April 3–5, 1998. See also Tricia Cusack, "A 'Countryside Bright with Cosy Homesteads': Irish Nationalism and the Cottage Landscape," *National Identities 3* (2001): 228.

78 William Robinson, *The English Flower Garden,* 2nd ed. (London: John Murray, 1889), 8.

79 E. T. Cook, *The Gardens of England* (London: A. & C. Black, 1911), 3.

80 Seguin, *Rural England,* 1–4, 120.

81 Dick, *The Cottage,* 4, 8.

82 The copy of *Old English Country Cottages* (1906) inscribed "Betty Xmas 1906 Calcutta" is now in the collections of the Huntington Library, San Marino, California.

83 Anon., "Cottage Gardens in England," *Country Life 5* (January 21, 1899): 84–6. For more on the role of character in the construction of national identity, see Newman, *The Rise of English Nationalism,* 123–56.

84 Thompson, *Lark Rise to Candleford,* 27. See also Horn, *The Changing Countryside,* 109.

85 Leonore Davidoff, Jean L'Esperance, and Howard Newby, "Landscape with Figures: Home and Community in English Society," in *The Rights and Wrongs of Women,* ed. Juliet Mitchell and Anne Oakley (New York: Penguin Books, 1976).

86 MacDonald, *The Language of Empire.* See also John M. MacKenzie, *Propaganda and Empire: The Manipulation of British Public Opinion, 1880–1960* (Manchester: Manchester University Press, 1984).

87 Although not describing a cottage garden, a related example is found in Frances Hodgson Burnett's children's story *The Secret Garden* (1911). The story focuses on Mary Lennox, who was born in India to English parents and is returned to England after her parents and nurse die of cholera. Peevish, sallow, and selfish, Mary grows into mental and physical maturity through tending a "secret" garden on her uncle's Yorkshire estate. Burnett uses the motif of gardens to track the development of her heroine: in the gardens that Mary attempts in India, the plants wither and die, whereas in England, in the face of a brisk climate, the seeds she plants, like the child herself, flourish. An implicit contrast between hot, languid, and degenerate India and cool, energizing, and moral England is set in place through the garden motif, but the two are also necessarily coupled together. Lennox needs England to survive, just as the Empire needs the homeland as a supportive foundation and a recuperative influence. For more, see Mandy Morris, "'Tha'lt be like a blush-rose when tha' grows up, my little lass', English Cultural and Gendered Identity in *The Secret Garden*," *Environment and Planning D: Society and Space* 14 (1996): 59–78.

CHAPTER 4

1 For more on the founding of this journal, see Reginald Blomfield, *Memoirs of an Architect* (London: Macmillan and Co., 1932), 103.

2 "Modern Garden Design," *The Architectural Review* 28 (August 1910): 68, 70.

3 Reginald Blomfield, *The Formal Garden in England,* with illustrations by F. Inigo Thomas, 3rd ed. (London: Macmillan and Co., 1901), 2. The first edition was published in January 1892 and the second edition in October 1892.

4 Blomfield, *The Formal Garden in England,* 1901, 4, 19–20.

5 Ibid., 10, 235.

6 Quoted in Helen Walker, "Lawn Tennis," in *Sport in Britain, A Social History,* ed. Tony Mason (Cambridge: Cambridge University Press, 1989), 247.

7 Ibid., 126.

8 Richard Holt, *Sport and the British, A Oxford Modern History* (Oxford: Clarendon Press, 1989), 125.

9 "Garden Parties," *The Spectator* 99 (September 14, 1907): 354–5.

10 "Let us remember that formal quaintness, sometimes tending to exaggeration, was the delight of our more cultured ancestors and of the famous men of England and the Continent. It was found at Penshurst and Moor Park, at Hampton Court and Levens, just as at Versailles and St. Cloud and at the Ludovisi, Medici, Doria Pamphili, and other state gardens of Rome." *Gardens Old & New, The Country House & It's [sic] Environment,* 4th ed., Vol. 1 (London: Country Life, c. 1900), xii.

11 See Keith N. Morgan, *Shaping an American Landscape: The Art and Architecture of Charles A. Platt* (Hanover, N.H.: Hampshire: Hood Museum of Art, Dartmouth College and University Press of New England, 1995).

12 Reginald Blomfield, *A History of Renaissance Architecture in England, 1500–1800,* vol. 1 (London: George Bell and Sons, 1897), vi, 1, 121–2.

13 According to the preface of the first edition, Blomfield was the author of the text, written from materials collected by both himself and Thomas. Thomas supplied the illustrations (some of which are based on drawings by Blomfield). Hence, throughout this study, Blomfield is referred to as the author of *The Formal Garden* and Thomas as the illustrator. Blomfield, 1901, x.

14 I am indebted to Richard Fellows's biography for this account of Blomfield's early career. Richard A. Fellows, *Sir Reginald Blomfield, An Edwardian Architect* (London: A. Zwemmer, 1985).

15 For more on Shaw, see Andrew Saint, *Richard Norman Shaw* (New Haven: Yale University Press for the Paul Mellon Centre for Studies in British Art, 1976).

16 Lethaby, Horsely, Macartney, Newton, and Prior had all worked for Shaw, and Blomfield wrote a biography of the architect. Reginald T. Blomfield, *Richard Norman Shaw, R.A., Architect 1831–1912* (London: Batsford, 1940).

17 Report No. 6, Committee Meeting, The Minutes of the St. George's Art Society, 1883, Archives of the Art Workers Guild. For histories of the guild, see H. J. L. J. Massé, *The Art-Workers' Guild, 1884–1934* (Oxford: Shakespeare Head Press for the Art-Workers' Guild, 1935), and *Beauty's Awakening: The Centenary Exhibition of the Art Workers Guild* (Brighton: Royal Pavilion, Art Gallery and Museums, 1984).

18 Peter Stansky, *Redesigning the World: William Morris, the 1880s, and the Arts and Crafts* (Princeton: Princeton University Press, 1985), 122.

19 William Morris, "Making the Best of It (A Paper Read before the Trade's Guild of Learning and the Birmingham Society of Artists)," in *Hopes and Fears for Art,* 123–8.

20 Quoted in Derek Baker, *The Flowers of William Morris* (London: Barn Elms, 1996), 42. Amyer Vallance, *William Morris: His Art, His Writings and His Public Life* (London: George Bell and Sons, 1909), 49.

21 Sir Reginald Blomfield, *Memoirs of an Architect* (London: Macmillan and Co., 1932), 81–2.

22 "It is curious that in an age of minute historical research, and professed enthusiasm for the subject, the history of English Art should be still unwritten. Though our architecture has a distinct individuality, we know little of its makers. . . . Every instance, therefore, becomes precious, and not least among them any examples of that minor domestic architecture which is still the most suggestive record of English life from the sixteenth to the seventeenth century." Reginald Blomfield, "Half-Timber Houses in the Weald of Kent and Neighbourhood [No. I]," *The Portfolio* 18 (1887): 1.

23 Reginald Blomfield, "Half-Timber Houses in the Weald of Kent and Neighbourhood, No. III," *The Portfolio* 18 (1887): 50.

24 "I became the more confirmed as to the general rightness of the old ways of applying Art, and interpreting Nature the more I studied old gardens and the point of view of their makers; until I now appear as advocate of old types of design, which, I am persuaded, are more consonant with the traditions of English life, and more suitable to an English homestead than some now in vogue." John D. Sedding, *Garden-Craft Old and New,* with memorial notice by the Rev. E. F. Russell (London: Kegan Paul, Trench, Trübner and Co., 1891), v.

25 F. Inigo Thomas, "Of Garden Making," *Country Life* 7 (April 21, 1900): 489.

26 This point is expertly explained by Robert Williams in "Edwardian Gardens, Old and New," *Journal of Garden History* 13 (Spring/Summer 1993): 90–103.

27 Malcolm Rogers, *Montacute House* (London: National Trust, 1991), 87–8.

28 H. Inigo Triggs, *Formal Gardens in England and Scotland* (London: B. T. Batsford, 1902; reprint, Woodbridge: Antique Collectors' Club, 1988), 11.

29 Blomfield, *The Formal Garden,* 1901, 21, 30.

30 Ibid., 34.

31 Ibid., 34–5.

32 Ibid., 53.

33 Ibid., 58–9.

34 Ibid., 65.

35 Ibid., 70.

36 Ibid., 92.

37 Ibid., 84.

38 Ibid., 85.

39 Ibid., 85.

40 Ibid., 88.

41 Quoted in Richard Etlin, *Frank Lloyd Wright and Le Corbusier: The Romantic Legacy* (Manchester and New York: Manchester University Press, 1994), 166.

42 Reginald Blomfield, *Catalogue of a Collection of Water-Colour Drawings of Gardens in Many Lands by George S. Elgood* (London: Fine Art Society's, 1895), 3.

43 Reginald Blomfield, *A History of Renaissance Architecture in England,* 1500–1800, vol. II (London: George Bell and Sons, 1897), 398.

44 Ibid., 399.

45 Ibid.

46 Ibid., 399, 403.

47 Ibid., 404.

48 For example, musicologist Cecil Sharp, like others of his generation, believed the last century or more had witnessed an abandonment of English values. In his history of English folksong, Sharp argued that since the "death of Purcell [1695] . . . the educated classes have patronised the music of the foreigner, to the exclusion of that of the Englishman."Alun Howkins, "The Discovery of Rural England," in *Englishness Politics and Culture,* ed. Colls and Dodd, 69.

49 J. A. Froude, *History of England, from the Fall of Wolsey to the Defeat of the Spanish Armada,* Vol. 1, *Henry the Eighth* (London: Longman, Green, and Co., 1872), 475.

50 Blomfield, *The Formal Garden,* 1901, 236.

51 F. Inigo Thomas, "The Garden in Relation to the House," *The Gardener's Magazine* (February 22, 1896): 118.

52 Sir George Sitwell, *On the Making of Gardens* (first published 1909 under the title "An Essay on the Making of Gardens"; reprint, London: Dropmore Press, 1949), xv, 10.

53 Sedding, *Garden-Craft,* 49, 50.

54 Ibid., 68–9.
55 Sedding, *Garden-Craft,* 56, 57.
56 Ibid., 64–5.
57 Ibid., 93.
58 Ibid., 95.
59 Ibid., 21.
60 Ibid., 17.
61 Ibid., 148.
62 Ibid., 10.
63 Stephen Daniels, *Humphry Repton, Landscape Gardening and the Geography of Georgian England* (New Haven and London: Published for the Paul Mellon Centre for Studies in British Art by Yale University Press, 1999), 62–5.
64 For a discussion of the values of domesticity and their impact on American architecture at the end of the nineteenth century, see Gwendolyn Wright, *Moralism and the Model Home, Domestic Architecture and Cultural Conflict in Chicago, 1873–1913* (Chicago and London: University of Chicago Press, 1980), particularly pp. 97–102.
65 William Morris, *News from Nowhere or an Epoch of Rest,* ed. James Redmond (London: The Commonweal, 1890; reprint, London and Boston: Routledge & Kegan Paul, 1970),1, 2, 6.
66 Walter Crane, *A Floral Fantasy in an Old English Garden* (New York and London: Harper and Bros., 1899), 6.
67 Aymer Vallance, "Good Furnishing and Decoration of the House: Wall-Papers," *Magazine of Art* 2 (March 1904): 226–8.
68 "The Garden in Relation to the House," *Architectural Review* 1 (November–May 1897): 222.
69 Thomas Mawson, *The Art and Craft of Garden Making,* 2nd ed. (London: B. T. Batsford, 1901), xi.
70 John Belcher, "The Architectural Treatment of Gardens," *The British Architect* 31 (June 28, 1889): 460.
71 Ibid., 459.
72 Sedding, *Garden-Craft,* 156.
73 Belcher, "The Architectural Treatment of Gardens," 460.
74 Edward S. Prior, "Garden-Making," *The Studio* 21 (October 1900): 31.
75 Sedding, *Garden-Craft,* 162.
76 Prior, "Garden-Making," 31.
77 "Country Homes and Gardens Old and New, Shipton Court, Oxfordshire, The Seat of Sir Compton Read," *Country Life Illustrated* 7 (February 3, 1900): 148.
78 E. S. Prior, "Garden Making II– The Conditions of Practice," *The Studio* 21 (November 1900): 86–95.
79 Ibid., 90–1.
80 Blomfield, *The Formal Garden,* 1901, 135.
81 F. Inigo Thomas, "Gardens," *Journal of the Royal Institute of British Architects* 33 (1926): 432.
82 For example, in a letter of May 11, 1999, Captain Partridge, in a landscape design partnership with Alfred Parsons, requested a copy of *Country Life* to assist with his designs. Nicole Milette, "Landscape-Painter as Landscape-Gardener, The Case of Alfred Parsons, R.A.," Ph.D. dissertation, University of York, 1997, 211. F. Inigo Thomas stated that *Country Life*'s articles inspired practioners to "return to the old English ways of laying out grounds." Thomas, "Gardens," 433.
83 Thomas, "The Garden in Relation to the House," 135. See also E. S. Prior, "Garden Making," 28–36, and E. S. Prior, "Gardening Making II– The Conditions of Practice," 86–95.

84 "Country Homes, Gardens Old & New, Athelhampton Hall-III. Dorsetshire, The Seat of Mr. Alfred de Lafontaine," *Country Life* 19 (June 23, 1906): 906. "Country Homes, Gardens Old & New, Athelhampton Hall, Dorchester, The Seat of Mr. A. C. Lafontaine," *Country Life* 6 (September 2, 1899): 274–5.

85 Jill Franklin, *The Gentleman's Country House and Its Plan, 1835–1914* (London, Boston, and Henley: Routledge & Kegan Paul, 1981), 25.

86 Perkin, *The Rise of Professional Society,* 64.

87 Ibid., 78. See also David Cannandine, *The Decline and Fall of the British Aristocracy* (New Haven: Yale University Press, 1990), 88–139.

88 Ibid., 149, 358.

89 Thomas, "The Garden in Relation to the House," 135.

90 F. E. Green, "The Architect in the Garden," *The World's Work* 17 (April 1911): 506–8.

91 Thomas, "The Garden in Relation to the House," 135.

92 Robert Williams, "Edwin Lutyens and the Formal Garden in England," *Die Gartenkunst* 2 (1995): 204.

93 "The Gardener's Reckoning," *The Times* (January 30, 1909): 19.

94 Williams, "Edwardian Gardens," 96.

95 Thomas Mawson, *The Life and Work of an English Landscape Architect* (London: Richards Press, 1927), 123.

96 "Country Homes, Gardens Old & New, Barrow Court, Somerset, The Seat of Mr. H.M. Gibbs," *Country Life* 11 (January 18, 1902): 80–7. For plans of Barrow Court and Chantmarle, see Ottewill, *The Edwardian Garden,* 16 and 19, respectively.

97 T. [H. Avray Tipping], "Country Homes, Gardens Old & New, Rotherfield Hall, Sussex, The Seat of Sir Lindsay Lindsay-Hogg, Bt.," *Country Life* (August 14, 1909): 235–6.

98 Fellows, *Architects in Perspective, Reginald Blomfield,* 63.

99 "Country Homes, Gardens Old & New, Godinton, Kent, the Seat of Mr. George Ashley Dodd," *Country Life* 21 (May 11, 1907): 671.

100 Ibid., 673.

101 For more on this design, see Jane Brown, *The Art and Architecture of English Gardens* (New York: Rizzoli, 1989), 170–1.

102 Ottewill, *The Edwardian Garden,* 146–57.

CHAPTER 5

1 Crook, *The Dilemma of Style,* 19.

2 Thomas, "Gardens," 433.

3 Milner, *The Art and Practice of Landscape Gardening,* 2, 23.

4 William Robinson, *Garden Design and Architects' Gardens* (London: John Murray, 1892), 25.

5 Blomfield, *The Formal Garden in England,* 1901, 11, 81.

6 William Robinson, *The English Flower Garden* (London: John Murray, 1883), vi.

7 Belcher, "The Architectural Treatment of Gardens," 459.

8 See, for example, F. Inigo Thomas, "The Garden in Relation to the House," *The Gardener's Magazine* 39 (February 15, 1896): 104.

9 Sedding, *Garden-Craft Old and New,* 169, 135, 153–4, 213–4.

10 Blomfield, *The Formal Garden,* 1901, 4–11.

11 Robinson, *Garden Design,* vii–viii.

12 Robinson, *Garden Design,* ix.

13 Ibid., x–xi, 2, 20–2.

14 Ibid., x, 38.

15 Ibid., 23, 24.

16 Ibid., 26, 27.

17 Ibid., facing p. 6, facing pp. 46, 69.

18 Ibid., facing p. 26, facing p. 16.

19 Ibid., 1.

20 Ibid., 5.

21 Much of the exterior of the house was by Sir Charles Barry, who also laid the lower garden in "architectural formed beds." Reverend Alfred Barry, *The Life and Works of Sir Charles Barry, R. A., F. R. S.* (London: John Murray, 1867; reprint, New York: Benjamin Blom, 1972), 118–19.

22 Daniels, *Humphry Repton.*

23 William Robinson, *The Garden Beautiful: Home Woods, Home Landscape* (London: John Murray, 1906), 49.

24 Perkin, *The Rise of Professional Society,* xiii, 117.

25 Robinson, *Garden Design,* 17.

26 Robinson, *The Garden Beautiful,* 14–15.

27 Reginald Blomfield, *The Formal Garden in England,* with illustrations by F. Inigo Thomas, 2nd ed. (London: Macmillan and Co., 1892), viii, xiii.

28 Robinson, *Garden Design,* 2.

29 Ibid., 41, 42.

30 "On Gardens," *British Architect* 38 (September 2, 1892): 166.

31 Blomfield, *Garden Design,* vi, xiii.

32 Belcher, "The Architectural Treatment," 460.

33 Blomfield, *The Formal Garden,* 1892, xx.

34 Ibid., xix.

35 Blomfield, *The Formal Garden,* 1901, 225–6.

36 "Formal Gardens," *Magazine of Art* 16 (March 1893): 170–1.

37 Mandler, *The Fall and Rise of the Stately Home,* 7–69.

38 C. R. Ashbee, *American Sheaves & English Seed Corn* (Bow: Essex House Press, c. 1901), 9, 29, 34, 113.

39 Julia Cartwright, "Gardens," *The Portfolio* 23 (1892): 211–18.

40 Wiener, *English Culture and the Decline of the Industrial Spirit,* 46.

41 Comprehensive histories had been attempted before. J. C. Loudon included an extensive discussion in his *Encyclopedia of Gardening* (first published 1822), and George Johnson offered *A History of English Gardens* in 1829, which, despite the breadth implied in the title, focused largely on "the reigns of Edward the II, Elizabeth and George the I," as the most significant eras, but a new generation was needed to bring the history up to date. George W. Johnson, *A History of English Gardening* (London: Baldwin & Cradock and Long & Co.; W. H. Wright; J. Ridgeway; and H. Wicks, 1829), ii; and Brent Elliott, *Victorian Gardens* (London: B. T. Batsford, 1986), 55.

42 Amherst's father was the first Baron of Amherst, created in 1892, and served as an M.P. for Norfolk. Her husband, whom she married in 1898, became the first Baron of Rockley after an influential political career (serving, for example, as private secretary for the prime minister in 1891–2 and 1895–1902). Alicia Amherst, *A History of Gardening in England* (London: Bernard Quaritch, 1895), ix, x.

43 Ibid., 279, 105.

44 Ibid., 305–6.

45 Leyland was a general writer who also contributed to a number of London papers, and Tipping was an Oxford-trained historian from the landed gentry who also designed gardens.

46 *Gardens Old and New, The Country House & It's [sic] Environment,* xxii.

47 H. Avray Tipping, ed., *Gardens Old and New, The Country House & Its Garden Environment,* Vol. 3 (London: Country Life, [c. 1908]), xi.

48 Tipping, *Gardens Old and New,* 327.

49 Clive Ashwin, "The Founding of *The Studio,*" *High Art and Low Life: The Studio and the Fin de Siècle Special Centenary Number,* 201 (1993): 5, 7.

50 A. L. Baldry, "The History of Garden Making," *The Gardens of England in the Southern & Western Counties,* ed. Charles Holme (London: The Studio, 1907), v, xviii, xx, xxi, xxxiv.

51 [A. L. Baldry], "Types of Gardens," *The Gardens of England, in the Northern Counties,* ed. Charles Holme (London: The Studio, 1911), iii, iv.

52 [A. L. Baldry], "The Use of Gardens," *The Gardens of England, in the Midland & Eastern Counties,* ed. Charles Holme (London: The Studio, 1908), xvi.

53 [G. Jekyll], "Gardens and Garden Craft," *The Edinburgh Review* 184 (July 1896): 178–9.

54 "Country Homes, Gardens Old & New, Athelhampton Hall, Dorchester, The Seat of Mr. A. C. Lafontaine," 272, 274.

55 Lawrence Weaver, ed., *Small Country Houses of To-day* (London: Country Life, 1910), 99.

56 Thomas Mawson, *The Art and Craft of Garden Making,* 2nd ed. (London: B. T. Batsford, 1901), vii.

57 Ibid., viii.

58 [C. E. Mallows], "Architectural Gardening – II with Illustrations after Designs by C. E. Mallows, F. R. I. B.A.," *The Studio* 45 (October 15, 1908): 34.

59 Lucy Dynevor, *A Dissertation on the Work of C. E. Mallows, Architectural Gardener & Illustrator,* Post-Graduate Diploma Course on the Conservation of Historic Landscapes and Gardens, The Architectural Association, London, June 1993, 42.

CHAPTER 6

1 "Gardens, Old and New," *The Spectator* 90 (January 31, 1903): 155.

2 Jekyll, *Old West Surrey,* 249.

3 Jekyll, *Old West Surrey,* ix, vii, vi.

4 Jekyll, *Old West Surrey,* viii.

5 Charles Hastings, "Recent Photography," *Art Journal* (February 1891): 52.

6 John Taylor, *A Dream of England: Landscape, Photography, and the Tourist's Imagination* (Manchester and New York: Manchester University Press, 1994), 57.

7 Ibid., 62.

8 Ibid., 25.

9 Jekyll, *Old West Surrey,* viii.

10 Ibid., 262, 264.

11 For a brief discussion of the "nationalization" of rural culture, see Alun Howkins, *Reshaping Rural England: A Social History, 1850–1925* (London: HarperCollins Academic, 1991), 238–9.

12 P. H. Emerson, *Naturalistic Photography* (New York: E. and F. Spon, 1890), 23.

13 Jekyll's photograph of Angela MacKail from 1901, for example, is extremely contrived: the sitter is posed with her head turned downward, swathed in draperies and holding a staff. It echoes Robinson's images of single figures, such as his depiction of a young girl holding a vase on her shoulder illustrated in his *Pictorial Effect in Photography* (1869), which took its cue, as did Margaret Cameron's similar images, from the conventions of academic painting. Jekyll's photographs of monks were even more forthrightly artificial: they depicted her gardener P. Brown dressed in a habit she borrowed from a Sussex monastery. For an analysis of the published monk photograph, see Michael Charlesworth,

"Rhetoric of the Image: Charles Collins' 'Convent Thoughts' and a Photograph by Gertrude Jekyll the Garden Designer," *Word & Image* 7 (January–March 1991): 49–57.

14 H. P. Robinson, *Pictorial Effect in Photography* (London: Piper & Carter and Marion & Co., 1869), 11, 18.

15 Taylor, *A Dream of England,* 42.

16 Jekyll, *Old West Surrey,* 286–7.

17 For an overview of Munstead House, see Judith B. Tankard, "The Garden before Munstead Wood," *Hortus* 20 (Winter 1991): 17–26; and also Judith Tankard and Martin Wood, *Gertrude Jekyll at Munstead Wood: Writing, Horticulture, Photography, Homebuilding,* with a foreword by Graham Stuart Thomas (Thrupp, Stroud, Gloucestershire: Sutton Publishing; Sagaponack: Sagapress, 1996), 28–39.

18 William Goldring in *The Garden* (1881), quoted in Tankard and Wood, *Gertrude Jekyll at Munstead Wood,* 31.   **255**

19 Brandon and Short, *The South East from AD 1000,* 50.

20 Ibid., 102.

21 P. F. Brandon, "The Diffusion of Designed Landscapes in South-East England," in *Change in the Countryside,* ed. Fox and Butlin, 169.

22 William Cobbett, *Rural Rides* (London: William Cobbett, 1830), 54.

23 Ibid., 169–70.

24 Quoted in Paul Everson, "The Munstead Wood Survey, 1991, The Methodology of Recording Historic Gardens by the Royal Commission on the Historical Monuments of England," in *Gertrude Jekyll, Essays on the Life of a Working Amateur,* ed. Michael Tooley and Primrose Arnander (Witton-le-Wear, Durham, England: Michaelmas, 1995), 75.

25 In *Wood and Garden,* Jekyll described placing bands of paper on those trees she considered cutting and subjecting them to a period of aesthetic contemplation prior to the actual execution of her pruning plan. Gertrude Jekyll, *Wood and Garden, Notes and Thoughts, Practical and Critical, of a Working Amateur* (London, New York, and Bombay: Longmans, Green, and Co., 1899), 151.

26 Ibid., 34, 48, 61.

27 Ibid., 107.

28 "Country Homes, Gardens Old & New: Munstead House and Its Mistress," *Country Life* 8 (December 8, 1900): 735.

29 Elliott, *Victorian Gardens,* 166.

30 Ibid., 168.

31 S. Reynolds Hole, *Our Gardens* (London: J. M. Dent, 1899), 73–4.

32 Ibid., 78.

33 For more on this topic, see Douglas Chambers, *The Planters of the English Landscape Garden: Botany, Trees, and the Georgics* (New Haven and London: Published for The Paul Mellon Centre for Studies in British Art by Yale University Press, 1995).

34 Laird, *The Flowering of the Landscape Garden,* 98.

35 The meanings of shrubbery and wilderness, it must be acknowledged, were not firmly fixed, and the forms and materials of these features were debated intensely in gardening literature. Ibid., 8.

36 Jekyll, *Wood and Garden,* 100.

37 Laird, *The Flowering of the Landscape Garden,* 92.

38 Ibid., 94.

39 Jekyll, *Wood and Garden,* 147.

40 Gertrude Jekyll, *Colour in the Flower Garden* (London: Country Life, 1908), 13.

41 Gertrude Jekyll, *Home and Garden, Notes and Thoughts, Practical and Critical, of a Worker in Both* (London: Longmans, Green and Co., 1900), 97–8.

42 Jekyll, *Wood and Garden*, 9.

43 Ibid., 64.

44 Jekyll, *Home and Garden*, 190.

45 For the species used in Jekyll's azalea plantation, see Tankard and Wood, *Gertrude Jekyll at Munstead Wood*, 8.

46 Jekyll, *Wood and Garden*, 69–70.

47 Ibid., 1.

48 Ibid.

49 Anon., "Wood and Garden," *Country Life* 5 (March 18, 1899): 332, 333.

50 Walter Wright, *The Perfect Garden: How to Keep It Beautiful and Fruitful* (London: Grant Richards, 1908), 12.

51 "Ladies in Agriculture," *Country Life* 6 (November 11, 1899): 578.

52 Dianne Harris, "Cultivating Power: The Language of Feminism in Women's Garden Literature, 1870–1920," *Landscape Journal* 13 (Fall 1994): 115.

53 Ann Shtier, *Cultivating Women, Cultivating Science* (Baltimore and London: Johns Hopkins University Press, 1996), 197, 205, 207.

54 Harris, "Cultivating Power," 113, 121.

55 Jane Brown, *Lutyens and the Edwardians, An English Architect and His Clients* (London: Viking, 1996), 37.

56 Gertrude Jekyll, "Women as Gardeners," *Country Life* 39 (April 29, 1916): 541.

57 Jekyll, *Wood and Garden*, 156.

58 Jekyll, *Home and Garden*, 274–5.

59 Robinson, *Pictorial Effect*, 12.

60 Ibid., 13.

61 Jekyll, *Home and Garden*, 26.

62 Ibid., 45. The appreciation of hedgerows predates Jekyll's treatise by at least one hundred years. At Philip Southcote's Woburn Farm, a *ferme ornée,* a flower border "backed by a plantation of shrubs and trees . . . all set against 'The Old Hedgerow' was planted and created a contrast between the 'rusticity of the farm' and the neatness and artificiality of the flower border." Laird, *The Flowering of the English Landscape Garden,* 102.

63 As Judith Tankard and Martin Wood have observed, Jekyll's house clearly looked to the tile-hung cottages Jekyll and Lutyens had studied on their travels and "the dormers and deeply-hipped roof closely follow the lines of the half-timbered cottage in Eashing she had photographed years before." Judith Tankard and Martin Wood, *Gertrude Jekyll at Munstead Wood,* 77.

64 For example, a sepia ink drawing of the west elevation includes pencil annotations that appear to be in Jekyll's hand. This drawing (1996.22) is in the collections of the Royal Institute of British Architecture.

65 Jekyll, *Home and Garden*, 2.

66 Ibid., 3.

67 Ibid., 14.

68 "From the way it is built it does not stare with newness; it is not new in any way that is disquieting to the eye; it is neither raw nor callow. On the contrary, it almost gives the impression of a comfortable maturity of something like a couple of hundred years. And yet there is nothing sham-old about it; it is not trumped-up with any specious or fashionable devices of spurious antiquity; there is no pretending to be anything that it is not – no affectation whatever. . . . The house is not in any way a copy of any old building, though it embodies the general characteristics of the older structures of its own district." Ibid., 2.

69 Stephen King, *Munstead Wood* (Published at Munstead Wood; Printed by Cradocks of Godalming, 1996), 3.

70 Ibid., 4.

71 My thanks to Mark Laird for pointing out this contrast to me.

72 Jekyll, *Wood and Garden*, 49.

73 Ibid., 35.

74 Ibid., 101.

75 Ibid.

76 Jekyll, *Wood and Garden*, 219.

77 Jekyll, *Colour in the Flower Garden*, 51–2.

78 Ibid., 24.

79 J. C. Loudon, *An Encyclopedia of Gardening*, 4th ed. (London: Longman, Rees, Orme, Brown and Green, 1826), 798.

80 J. C. Loudon, *An Encyclopedia of Gardening*, 2nd ed. (London: Longman, Hurst, Rees, Orme, Brown, and Green, and Longman, 1824), 799.

81 For more on the *plate-bande*, see Laird, *The Flowering of the Landscape Garden*, 181–4.

82 Jane Loudon, *The Ladies' Companion to the Flower Garden*, 5th ed. (London: Bradbury & Evans, 1849), 34.

83 J. C. Loudon, *An Encyclopedia of Gardening*, ed. Jane Loudon (London: Longmans, Green, and Co., 1869), 1017.

84 Hope, *Notes and Thoughts on Gardens and Woodlands*, 99.

85 Elliott, *Victorian Gardens*, 206.

86 "I have learnt much from the little cottage gardens that help to make our English waysides the prettiest in the temperate world. One can hardly go into the smallest cottage gardens without learning or observing something new. It may be some two plants growing beautifully together by some happy chance, or a pretty mixed tangle of creepers, or something that one always thought must have a south wall doing better on an east one." Jekyll, *Wood and Garden*, 4.

87 "Rising gradually from the smallest flower to holli-oaks, paeonies, sun-flowers, carnations, poppies, and others of the boldest growth; and varying their tints, by easy gradations from white, straw colour, purple and incarnate, to the deepest blues, and the most brilliant crimsons and scarlets." Laird, *The Flowering of the Landscape Garden*, 340.

88 John Gage, *Color and Culture: Practice and Meaning from Antiquity to Abstraction* (Boston: Little, Brown, 1993), 168, 171.

89 Ibid., 173.

90 Elliott, *Victorian Gardens*, 125.

91 M. E. Chevreul, *The Principles of Harmony and Contrast of Colours, and Their Application to the Arts*, translated from the French by Charles Martel, 3rd ed. (London: Bell and Daldy, 1872). For more on Chevreul and Jekyll, see Jane Brown, *Gardens of a Golden Afternoon: The Story of a Partnership: Edwin Lutyens and Gertrude Jekyll* (New York: Van Nostrand Reinhold; London: Allen Lane, 1982; reprint, London: Penguin Books, 1994), 42–3. For a more in-depth discussion of nineteenth-century color principles and guidelines for flower border arrangements, see Elliott, *Victorian Gardens*, and, in particular, 123–34, 205–9.

92 Jekyll, *Wood and Garden*, 197.

93 Ibid., 65.

94 Elliott, *Victorian Gardens*, 207.

95 Huish, *Happy England*, 164. For more on the plants used in Jekyll's border, see Jane Brown, *Gardens of a Golden Afternoon*, 44–50.

96 Jekyll, *Wood and Garden*, 270.

97 Ibid., Photographic Illustration, "Cottage Porch Wreathed with the Double White Rose," facing p. 39; Photographic Illustration "Free Cluster-Rose as Standard in a Cot-

tage Garden," facing p. 77; Photographic Illustration "A Roadside Cottage Garden," facing p. 185.

98 Ibid., 185.
99 Ibid., 249–55.
100 Ibid., 61.
101 Jekyll, *Colour in the Flower Garden*, 50, 115–16. Jekyll, *Wood and Garden*, 267, and photographic illustration opposite "Geraniums in Neopolitan Pots."
102 Tankard and Wood, *Gertrude Jekyll at Munstead Wood*, 24.
103 Jekyll, *Colour in the Flower Garden*, 115. See also Jekyll, *Wood and Garden*, 264–5.
104 For a brief discussion of the relationship between gardens and consumerism in the eighteenth century, see Mark Laird, *The Flowering of the Landscape Garden*, 17. For a more extensive discussion, see his forthcoming essay "The Culture of Horticulture: Class, Consumption, and Gender in the English Landscape Garden," to be published by Dumbarton Oaks, Washington, D.C.
105 Thorstein Veblen, *The Theory of the Leisure Class, an Economic Study of Institutions* (New York: Macmillan, 1899; reprint, New York: Mentor Books, 1953), 100–101.
106 Asa Briggs, *Victorian Things* (Chicago: University of Chicago Press, 1988), 15.
107 Jekyll, *Wood and Garden*, 95–7.
108 Ibid., 2.

CHAPTER 7

1 Brown, *Gardens of a Golden Afternoon*, 159–76. For those works executed independently of Lutyens, see Appendix A, "A List of Miss Jekyll's Commissions 1880–1932," 188–91. The dates of Jekyll's and Lutyens's sites used in this chapter were taken from Brown's study. See also Michael Tooley, "Gertrude Jekyll's Garden Plans," in *Gertrude Jekyll: Essays on the Life of a Working Amateur*, ed. Tooley and Arnander, 198–202.
2 Brown, *Lutyens and the Edwardians*.
3 Ibid., 43.
4 Lutyens knew Robinson and designed a garden seat for him in 1898. Christopher Hussey, *The Life of Sir Edwin Lutyens* (London: Country Life, 1950; reprint Woodbridge, Suffolk: Antique Collectors' Club, 1984), 175.
5 E. L. Lutyens, Sketchbook for Munstead Corner Surrey, 1891, 7. E1 (1-70)-1991, Victoria and Albert Museum, London. Brown, *Lutyens and the Edwardians*, 114.
6 Hussey, *The Life of Sir Edwin Lutyens*, 175.
7 Brown, *Gardens of a Golden Afternoon*, 106–7. Peter Inskip, *Architectural Monographs 6, Edwin Lutyens* (London: Academy Editions, New York: St. Martin's Press, 1986), 20.
8 For a reproduction of this garden design, see Hussey, *The Life of Sir Edwin Lutyens*, 52.
9 Edwin Lutyens, "What I Think of Modern Architecture," *Country Life* 69 (June 20, 1931): 775. I am indebted to Robert Williams and his excellent analysis of Lutyens's sites for these remarks on rhythm and proportion. See Robert Williams, "Edwin Lutyens and the Formal Garden in England," *Die Gartenkunst* 2 (1995): 201–9.
10 *Fulbrook: The Sketchbook, Letters, Specification of Works & Accounts for a House by Edwin Lutyens, 1896–1899*, ed. Jane Brown and foreword by Mary Lutyens (Marlborough, Wiltshire: Libanus Press, 1989), 62–3.
11 Jane Brown, *Gardens of a Golden Afternoon*, 96.
12 Daniel O'Neill, *Sir Edwin Lutyens: Country Houses*, with a preface by Sir Hugh Casson (New York: Whitney Library of Design, 1981), 5–6.
13 Jane Brown, *Lutyens and the Edwardians*, 32.

14 Gertrude Jekyll, "Country Homes, Gardens Old and New, Orchards, Surrey, The Residence of Mr. William Chance," *Country Life* 10 (August 31, 1901): 275–6.

15 Brown, *Gardens of a Golden Afternoon,* 58; and Jekyll, "Orchards," 272.

16 Jekyll, "Orchards," 272, 275.

17 T.[Avray Tipping] "Country Homes, Gardens Old and New, Orchards, Surrey, The Residence of Sir William Chance, Bart.," *Country Life* 23 (April 11, 1908): 520. In the eighteenth century, the term *Dutch,* in the English imagination, was associated with small enclosed gardens governed by a strong sense of order as well as an "incremental" quality. John Dixon Hunt, "'But Who Does Not Know What a Dutch Garden Is?' The Dutch Garden in the English Imagination," *The Dutch Garden in the Seventeenth Century,* ed. John Dixon Hunt (Washington, D.C.: Dumbarton Oaks Research Library and Collection, 1990), 175–206. In the nineteenth century, a Dutch garden was characterized by "rectangular formality, and what may sometimes be termed clumsy artifice, such as yew trees cut in the form of statues," according to nineteenth-century garden writer Charles M'Intosh. Elliott, *Victorian Gardens,* 56.

18 Williams, "Edwin Lutyens and the Formal Garden in England," 202–3.

19 Jekyll, "Country Homes, Gardens Old & New, Orchards, Surrey, The Residence of Mr. William Chance," 272–9.

20 Jekyll, *Old West Surrey,* 1–6.

21 Brown, *Lutyens and the Edwardians,* 38.

22 Materials identified in Brian Edwards, *Goddards: Sir Edwin Lutyens* (London: Phaidon Press, 1996), 11, 16.

23 Ibid., 16.

24 "Country Homes: Goddards, Abinger Common, Surrey, A Home of Rest," *Country Life* 15 (January 30, 1904): 162.

25 Jekyll, *Old West Surrey,* 15.

26 Brown, *Gardens of a Golden Afternoon,* 66.

27 Blomfield, *The Formal Garden in England,* 1901, 189.

28 John Leyland, "Country Homes: Loseley Park," *Country Life* 2 (December 25, 1897): 720–2; and "Country Homes: Gardens Old & New, Loseley Park, Surrey, The Seat of Mr. W. More-Molyneux," *Country Life* 5 (March 4, 1899): 272–4.

29 John Cornforth, "Lutyens and 'Country Life': 81 Not Out," in *Lutyens: The Work of the English Architect Sir Edwin Lutyens (1869–1944)* (London: Hayward Gallery, 1982), 25–31.

30 O'Neill, *Sir Edwin Lutyens: Country Houses,* 42.

31 The garden has been restored by Rosamund Wallinger, who provides a history of the project in Rosamund Wallinger, *Gertrude Jekyll's Lost Garden: The Restoration of an Edwardian Masterpiece* (Suffolk: Garden Art Press, 2000).

32 Ibid., 28, 35, 50.

33 Blomfield, *The Formal Garden in England,* 1901, 208–10.

34 Brown, *Gardens of a Golden Afternoon,* 75.

35 "In architecture Palladio is the Game!! It is so big – few appreciate it now, and it requires training to value and to realise it. The way Wren handled it was marvellous. Shaw has the gift. To the average man it is dry bones, but under the hand of a Wren it glows and the stiff materials become as plastic clay. . . . It is a game that never deceives, dodges never disguise. It means hard thought all through – if it is laboured it fails. There is no fluke that helps it – the very what one might call the machinery of it makes it impossible except in the hands of a Jones or a Wren." Hussey, *The Life of Sir Edwin Lutyens,* 122.

36 Brown, *Gardens of a Golden Afternoon,* 75.

37 O'Neill, *Sir Edwin Lutyens,* 62.

38 Jane Brown, "Sir Edwin Lutyens and Miss Jekyll at Folly Farm," unpublished pamphlet, 1984.

39 O'Neill, *Sir Edwin Lutyens,* 88.

40 Blomfield, *The Formal Garden,* 1901, 149.

41 Sir Lawrence Weaver, *Lutyens Houses and Gardens* (London: Country Life, 1921), 282.

42 Brown, *Lutyens and the Edwardians,* 73.

43 Weaver, *Lutyens Houses and Gardens,* 70.

44 Ibid.

45 Blomfield, *The Formal Garden,* 1901, 191.

46 Weaver, *Lutyens Houses and Gardens,* 71.

47 Edwin Lutyens to Emily Lutyens, Buckhurst, April 23, 1904, in *The Letters of Edwin Lutyens to His Wife Lady Emily,* ed. Clayre Percy and Jane Ridley (London: Collins, 1985), 110.

48 Robert Williams, "Edwin Lutyens," 207. For a discussion of the mathematical proportional structure undergirding Hestercombe, see 208–9.

49 Blomfield, *The Formal Garden,* 1901, 108.

50 Ibid., 104.

51 Weaver, *Lutyens Houses and Gardens,* 149.

52 Hussey, *The Life of Sir Edwin Lutyens,* 570.

53 Watkin, *The Rise of Architectural History,* 104.

54 Newton, "Domestic Architecture of To-Day," in *The House and Its Equipment,* ed. Weaver, 3–4.

CONCLUSION

1 "Country Homes and Gardens Old & New, Heatherbank and Oakwood, The Residence and Garden of Mr. G. F. Wilson, F. R. S.," *Country Life* 8 (September 8, 1900): 304.

2 Kerry Downes, *Hawksmoor* (London: A. Zwemer, 1959), 82.

3 Mark Bennitt, ed., *History of the Louisiana Purchase Exposition* (St. Louis: Universal Exposition Publishing Company, 1905; reprint, New York: Arno Press, 1976), 264.

4 Sir Isidore Spielmann on Behalf of the Royal Commission International Exhibition St. Louis 1904, Sir Isidore Spielmann, *The British Section* (London: The Royal Commission, 1906), 25.

5 Blomfield, *The Formal Garden in England,* 1901, 72, 80.

6 Murat Halstead, *Pictorial History of the Louisiana Purchase and the World's Fair at St. Louis* (n. p., 1904), 306–7.

7 M. J. Lowenstein, comp., *Official Guide to the Louisiana Purchase Exposition* (St. Louis: The Official Guide Co., 1904), 47.

8 Quoted in Halstead, *Pictorial History,* 305.

9 Royal Commission, International Exhibition, Saint Louis, 1904, *Official Catalogue of the British Section* (London: William Cloves and Sons, 1904), xxxi.

10 Because all the guides to the exhibition consulted for this study utilized generally black and white photographs taken shortly after the garden was planted, it is difficult to determine the planting arrangement from photographic evidence.

11 *The Greatest of Expositions, Completely Illustrated* (St. Louis: Official Photographic Company of the Louisiana Purchase Exposition, 1904), 19.

12 Royal Commission, International Exhibition, Saint Louis 1904, *Official Catalogue,* xxviii.

13 *Ireland's Exhibit at the Fair with addresses by President Francis, Mayor Wells of St. Louis, His Grace Archbishop Glennon of St. Louis, and Hon. P. Gill of Dublin* [n.p., 1904].

14 Ibid.
15 Bennitt, *History,* 268.
16 Thomas Pakenham, *The Boer War* (New York: Random House, 1979), xix.
17 Paul Greenhalgh, *Ephemeral Vistas: the Exposition Universelles, Great Exhibitions and World's Fairs, 1851–1939* (Manchester and New York: Manchester University Press, 1988), 57.
18 Raphael Samuel, "Introduction: Exciting to Be English," *Patriotism: The Making and Unmaking of British National Identity,* ed. Raphael Samuel, vol. 1 (London and New York: Routledge, 1990), xxv, cxxxvii.

Select Bibliography

PRIMARY SOURCES

[Allingham, William]. Prefatory Note to *Catalogue of a Collection of Drawings by Mrs. Alling-ham, R.W. S. Illustrating Surrey Cottages.* London: Fine Art Society, 1886.

Amherst, Alicia. *A History of Gardening in England.* London: Bernard Quaritch, 1895.

Ashbee, C. R. *American Sheaves & English Seed Corn, Being a Series of Addresses Mainly Deliv-ered in the United States, 1900–1901.* Bow: Essex House Press, c. 1901.

Blomfield, Reginald. *The Formal Garden in England.* 3rd ed. London: Macmillan and Co., 1901.

    A History of Renaissance Architecture in England, 1500–1800, vols. 1 and 2. London: George Bell and Sons, 1897.

    Memoirs of an Architect. London: Macmillan and Co., 1932.

    Prefatory Note to *Catalogue of a Collection of Water-colour Drawings Illustrating Gardens, Grave and Gay by George S. Elgood.* London: The Fine Art Society, 1893.

Burgess, J. T. *Old English Wild Flowers: To be found by the wayside, fields, hedgerows, rivers, moorlands, meadows, mountains, and seashore.* London: Frederick Warne; New York: Scribner, Welford, 1868.

Chevreul, M. E. *The Principles of Harmony and Contrast of Colours, and Their Application to the Arts,* 3rd ed. Translated by Charles Martel. London: Bell and Daldry, 1872.

Cook, Edward Tyas, and Alexander Wedderburn, eds. *The Complete Works of John Ruskin.* Vols. 1, 3, 4, 8, 16, 18, 20, and 33. London: George Allen, 1903–5.

Cook, Ernest Thomas. *The Gardens of England.* London: A. & C. Black, 1911.

Crane, Walter. *A Floral Fantasy in an Old English Garden.* New York and London: Harper and Bros., 1899.

Creighton, Mandell. *The Romanes Lecture, 1896: The English National Character.* London: Henry Frowde; Oxford: Clarendon Press, 1896.

Culpin, Ewart G. *The Garden City Movement Up-to-Date.* London: The Garden Cities and Town Planning Association, 1913.

Darwin, Charles. *The Variation of Animals and Plants under Domestication.* London: John Murray, 1868.

Davison, T. Raffles. *Port Sunlight: A Record of Its Artistic and Pictorial Aspect.* London: B.T. Batsford, 1917.

Dawber, E. Guy, and W. Galsworthy Davie. *Old Cottages and Farmhouses in Kent and Sussex.* London: B.T. Batsford, 1900.

Dawber, E. Guy. *Old Cottages, Farm Houses and Other Stone Buildings in the Cotswold District.* London: B.T. Batsford, 1905.

Dick, Stewart. *The Cottage Homes of England.* London: Edward Arnold; New York: Longmans, Green, and Co., 1909.

Earle, Alice. *Sun Dials and Roses of Yesterday.* London: Macmillan and Co., 1902.

Earle, S. W. *Pot-Pourri from a Surrey Garden.* London: Smith, Elder and Co., 1897.

Ellacombe, Henry N. *The Plant-Lore and Garden-Craft of Shakespeare,* new ed. London and New York: Edward Arnold, 1896.

Fitzherbert, S.W. *The Book of the Wild Garden.* London and New York: John Lane/The Bodley Head, 1903.

Foster, Mrs. J. Francis. *On the Art of Gardening, A Plea for English Gardens of the Future, with Practical Hints for Planting Them.* London: W. Satchell & Co., 1881.

Gardens Old & New, The Country House & It's [sic] Environment, 4th ed. Vol. 1. London: Country Life, [c. 1900].

Green, W. Curtis, and W. Galsworthy Davie. *Old Cottages and Farmhouses in Surrey.* London: B.T. Batsford, 1908.

Harvey, W. Alexander. *The Model Village and Its Cottages: Bournville.* London: B. T. Batsford, 1906.

Hibberd, Shirley. *The Amateur's Flower Garden.* London: Groombridge and Sons, 1871.

Hole, S. Reynolds. *Our Gardens.* London: J. M. Dent, 1899.

Holme, Charles, ed. *Old English Country Cottages.* London: The Studio, 1906.

   The Gardens of England in the Midland & Eastern Counties. London: The Studio, 1908.

   ed. *The Gardens of England in the Northern Counties.* London: The Studio, 1911.

   ed. *The Gardens of England in the Southern & Western Counties.* London: The Studio, 1907.

Hope, Frances Jane. *Notes and Thoughts on Gardens and Woodlands,* ed. Anne J. Hope Johnstone. London: Macmillan and Co., 1881.

Housing in Town and Country. London: Garden City Association, 1906.

Howard, Ebenezer. *Garden Cities of Tomorrow,* ed. F. J. Osborn. London: Faber and Faber, 1951.

Huish, Marcus. *Happy England.* London: Adam and Charles Black, 1903.

James, Henry. *English Hours.* Boston: Houghton Mifflin Co., 1905.

   Prefatory Note to *Catalogue of a Collection of Drawings by Alfred Parsons.* London: The Fine Art Society, 1891.

Jekyll, Gertrude. *Children and Gardens.* London: Country Life, 1908.

   Colour in the Flower Garden. London: Country Life, 1908.

   Colour Schemes for the Flower Garden. London: Country Life, 1914.

   Home and Garden, Notes and Thoughts, Practical and Critical, of a Worker in Both. London: Longmans, Green, and Co., 1900.

   Old West Surrey. London: Longmans, Green, and Co., 1904.

   Some English Gardens. London: Longmans, Green, and Co., 1904.

   Wood and Garden, Notes and Thoughts, Practical and Critical, of a Working Amateur. London, New York, and Bombay: Longmans, Green, and Co., 1899.

   and Lawrence Weaver. *Gardens for Small Country Houses.* London: Country Life, 1912.

Johnson, George W. *The Gardener's Dictionary,* 2nd ed. London: George Bell and Sons, 1877.

Jones, Sydney. *The Village Homes of England.* London: The Studio, 1912.

Kemp, Edward. *How to Lay Out a Garden: intended as a general guide in choosing, forming, or improving an estate,* 3rd ed. London: Bradbury, Evans, and Co., 1864.

Kipling, Rudyard, and C. R. L. Fletcher. *A School History of England.* Oxford: Clarendon Press, 1911.

Lever, Sir William. *Art and Beauty and the City, Three Addresses.* Port Sunlight: Lever Bros. Limited, 1915.

Leyland, John, ed. *Gardens Old and New, The Country House & Its Environment.* Vol. 2. London: Country Life, c. 1902.

Loudon, Jane. *The Ladies' Companion to the Flower Garden,* 5th ed. London: Bradbury & Evans, 1849.

Loudon, John Claudius. *An Encyclopedia of Gardening,* 2nd ed. London: Longman, Hurst, Rees, Orme, Brown, and Green, 1824.

   An Encyclopedia of Gardening, 4th ed. London: Longman, Rees, Orme, Brown, and Green, 1826.

   An Encyclopedia of Gardening, new ed. London: Longman, Rees, Orme, Brown, and Green, 1835.

   The Landscape Gardening and Landscape Architecture of the Late Humphry Repton, new ed. London: Longman & Co., A. & C. Black, 1840.

Macartney, Mervyn. *English Houses and Gardens.* London: B. T. Batsford, 1908.

Mawson, Thomas. *The Art and Craft of Garden Making,* 2nd ed. London: B.T. Batsford, 1901.

   The Life and Work of an English Landscape Architect. London: Richards Press, 1927.

M'Intosh, Charles. *The Flower Garden: Containing Directions for the Cultivation of All Garden Flowers,* new ed. London: Wm. S. Orr and Co., 1839.

Miller, Wilhelm. *What England Can Teach Us about Gardening.* Garden City, N.Y.: Doubleday, Page, and Co., 1911.

Milner, Henry Ernest. *The Art and Practice of Landscape Gardening.* London: Simpkin, Marshall, Hamilton, Kent and Co., 1890.

Minutes of the Art Workers Guild, AMs, Art Workers Guild, London, England.

Minutes of the St. George's Art Society, AMs, Art Workers Guild, London, England.

Morris, William. *Hopes and Fears for Art.* London: Longmans, Green, and Co, 1903.

   News from Nowhere or an Epoch of Rest, ed. James Redmond. London: The Common Weal, 1890; reprint, London, Boston, and Henley: Routledge & Kegan Paul, 1970.

Neville, Ralph. *Garden Cities.* Manchester: Manchester University Press, 1904.

   Old Cottage and Domestic Architecture in South-West Surrey. Guildford: Billing and Sons, 1889.

Newton, William Godfrey. *The Work of Ernest Newton, R.A.* With an Introduction by Sir Reginald Blomfield. London: The Architectural Press, 1925.

Nicholson, George. *Illustrated Dictionary of Gardening.* London: Upcott Gill, 1887.

Oliver, Basil. *Old Houses and Village Buildings in East Anglia, Norfolk, Suffolk & Essex.* London: B. T. Batsford, 1912.

Ould, E. A., and James Parkinson. *Old Cottages, Farm Houses and Other Half-Timber Buildings, in Shropshire, Herefordshire, and Cheshire.* London: B. T. Batsford, 1904.

Peto, H. A. *Garden designs, 1900–1933*(?), AMsS, Garden Library, Dumbarton Oaks, Washington, D.C.

Purdom, C. B. *The Garden City, A Study in the Development of a Modern Town.* London: Garden City at the Time Press and J. M. Dent, 1908.

Report of Agriculture and Fisheries. *Report on the Decline in the Agricultural Population of Great Britain, 1881–1906.* London: His Majesty's Stationery Office, 1906.

Report of the Inter-Departmental Committee on Physical Deterioriation. London: His Majesty's Stationery Office, 1904.

Robinson, William. *The English Flower Garden.* London: John Murray, 1883.

   The Garden Beautiful, Home Woods, Home Landscape. London: John Murray, 1906.

   Garden Design and Architects' Gardens. London: John Murray, 1892.

   Gravetye Manor, or Twenty Years' Work round an Old Manor House. London: John Murray, 1911.

   Gravetye Manor, Tree and Garden Book and Building Record, 1885–1911. AMsS, Lindley Library, Royal Horticulture Society, Vincent Square, London.

   Hardy Flowers, 4th ed. London: John Murray, 1883.

   Home Landscapes. London: John Murray, 1914.

The Parks, Promenades & Gardens of Paris Described and Considered in Relation to the Wants of Our Own Cities. London: John Murray, 1869.

The Subtropical Garden; or, Beauty of Form in the Flower Garden. London: John Murray, 1871.

The Wild Garden or, Our Groves & Shrubberies Made Beautiful. London: John Murray, 1870.

Rowntree, B. Seebohm, and May Kendall. *How the Labourer Lives: A Study of the Rural Labour Problem.* London and New York: T. Nelson, 1913; New York: Arno Press, 1975.

Savage, William G. *Rural Housing.* London: T. Fisher Unwin, 1914.

Scott, M. H. Baillie. *Houses and Gardens.* London: George Newness, 1906.

Sedding, John. *Garden-Craft Old and New.* With Memorial Notice by the Rev. E. F. Russell. London: Kegan Paul, Trench, Tübner, and Co., 1891.

Seguin, L. G. *Rural England: Loitering along the Lanes, the Common-sides and the Meadow – Paths with Peeps into the Halls, Farms, and Cottages.* London: Strahan and Co., 1881.

Sennett, A. R. *Garden Cities in Theory and Practice.* Vols. 1 and 2. London: Bemrose and Sons, 1905.

Sitwell, Sir George. *On the Making of Gardens,* 2nd ed. London: Dropmore Press, 1949.

Spencer, Aubrey John. *The Agricultural Holdings (England) Acts, 1883–1900,* 2nd ed. London: Stevens and Sons, 1901.

Tankard, Judith. *Annotated Catalog of Gertrude Jekyll's Six Photo-Albums at College of Environmental Design Documents Collection.* TMs, University of California, Berkeley, 1990.

[Catalogue of] *Gertrude Jekyll Collection.* TMs, Documents Collection, College of Environmental Design, University of California, Berkeley.

Taylor, Tom. *Birket Foster's Pictures of English Landscapes,* new ed. London: George Routledge and Sons, 1881.

Tipping, Avray, ed. *Gardens Old and New, The Country House & Its Garden Environment.* Vol. 3. London: Country Life, c. 1908.

Triggs, Inigo H. *Formal Gardens in England and Scotland, Their Planning and Arrangement,* 2nd ed. London: B.T. Batsford, 1902; Suffolk: Antique Collector's Club, 1988.

Wallace, Alfred Russel. *Bad Times, An Essay on the Present Depression of Trade.* London: Macmillan and Co., 1885.

Contributions to the Theory of Natural Selection. London: Macmillan and Co., 1870.

Island Life or, the Phenomena and Causes of Insular Faunas and Floras. New York: Harper and Bros., 1881.

Watson, Forbes. *Flowers and Gardens, Notes on Plant Beauty.* London: Strahan and Co., 1872.

Weaver, Lawrence, ed. *The House and Its Equipment.* London: Country Life, 1912.

Houses and Gardens by E. L. Lutyens, described and criticised by Lawrence Weaver. London: Country Life, 1913.

Lutyens Houses and Gardens. London: Country Life, 1921.

ed. *Small Country Houses of To-Day.* London: Country Life, 1910.

Small Country Houses, Their Repair and Enlargement. London: Country Life, 1914.

JOURNALS AND NEWSPAPERS

The Academy

The Architectural Review

The Art Journal

The Athenaeum

British Architect

The Builder

The Burlington

Cornhill Magazine

Country Life

Edinburgh Review

The Fortnightly Review

The Garden

Gardener's Magazine

Harper's Magazine

Journal of the Royal Institute of British Architects

London Illustrated News

The Magazine of Art

Select Bibliography

The Nation	*The Spectator*
Pall Mall Gazette	*The Standard*
The Portfolio	*The Studio*
Punch	*The Times*
The Quarterly Review	*The World's Work*
The Saturday Review	*The World*

SECONDARY SOURCES

An English Arcadia, 1600–1990, Designs for Gardens and Garden Buildings in the Care of the National Trust. Compiled and with an Introduction by Gervase Jackson-Stops. Washington, D.C.: The American Institute of Architects Press in association with The National Trust, 1993.

Allan, Mea. *William Robinson, 1838–1935: Father of the English Flower Garden.* London: Faber and Faber, 1982.

Allen, David. *The Naturalist in Britain: A Social History.* London: Allen Lane, 1976.

Anderson, Benedict. *Imagined Communities: Reflections on the Origin and Spread of Nationalism,* 2nd ed. London: Verso, 1991.

An English Arcadia, Landscape and Architecture in England and America, Papers Delivered at a Huntington Symposium. San Marino, Calif.: Henry E. Huntington Library and Art Gallery, 1992.

Arts Council of Great Britain. *Lutyens, the Work of the English Architect Sir Edwin Lutyens (1869–1944).* London: Hayward Gallery, 1982.

Barber, Lynn. *The Heyday of Natural History, 1820–1870.* New York: Doubleday, 1980.

Barnes, Susan J., and Walter S. Melion, eds. *Cultural Differentiation and Cultural Identity in the Visual Arts.* Washington, D.C.: National Gallery of Art, 1989.

Barthes, Roland. *Mythologies.* Selected and translated by Annette Lavers. New York: Noonday Press, 1972.

Bermingham, Ann. *Landscape and Ideology: The English Rustic Tradition, 1740–1860.* Berkeley: University of California Press, 1986.

Billig, Michael. *Banal Nationalism.* London, Thousand Oaks, and New Delhi: Sage, 1995.

Bisgrove, Richard. *The National Trust Book of the English Garden.* London: Viking, 1990.

Brooks, John Langdon. *Just before the Origin: Alfred Russel Wallace's Theory of Evolution.* New York: Columbia University Press, 1984.

Brown, Jane. *The Art and Architecture of English Gardens: designs for the garden from the collection of the Royal Institute of British Architect, 1609 to the present.* New York: Rizzoli, 1989.

———. *The English Garden in Our Time: From Gertrude Jekyll to Geoffrey Jellicoe.* Woodbridge, Suffolk: Antique Collectors' Club, 1986.

———. *Gardens of a Golden Afternoon: The Story of a Partnership, Edwin Lutyens and Gertrude Jekyll.* New York: Van Nostrand Reinhold; London: Allen Lane, 1982; reprint, London: Penguin Books, 1994.

———. *Lutyens and the Ewardians: An English Architect and His Clients.* London: Viking, 1996.

Buder, Stanley. *Visionaries and Planners: The Garden City Movement and the Modern Community.* New York: Oxford University Press, 1990.

Butler, A.S.G., with the collaboration of George Stewart and Christopher Hussey. *The Architecture of Sir Edwin Lutyens.* Vols. 1 and 2. London: Country Life, 1950; reprint, Woodbridge, Suffolk: Antique Collectors' Club, 1984.

Chambers, Douglas. *The Planters of the English Landscape Garden: Botany, Trees, and the Georgics.* New Haven and London: Published for The Paul Mellon Centre for Studies in British Art by Yale University Press, 1995.

Clayton-Payne, Andrew, and Brent Elliott. *Flower Gardens of Victorian England.* New York: Rizzoli, 1988.

Colley, Linda. *Britons: Forging the Nation, 1707–1837.* New Haven and London: Yale University Press, 1992.

Colls, Robert, and Philip Dodd, eds. *Englishness, Politics and Culture, 1880–1920.* London and Dover, N.H.: Croom Helm, 1986.

Constantine, Stephen. "Amateur Gardening and Popular Recreation in the 19th and 20th Centuries." *Journal of Social History* 14 (Spring 1981): 387–406.

Corner, John, and Sylvia Harvey, eds. *Enterprise and Heritage: Crosscurrents of National Culture.* London: Routledge, 1991.

Cornforth, John. *The Search for a Style: Country Life and Architecture, 1897–1935.* London: André Deutsch in association with Country Life, 1988.

Cosgrove, Denis, and Stephen Daniels, eds. *The Iconography of Landscape: Essays in the Symbolic Representation, Design, and Use of Past Environments.* Cambridge: Cambridge University Press, 1988.

Cosgrove, Denis E. *Social Formations and Symbolic Landscape.* Totowa: Barnes and Noble, 1984.

Crook, J. Mordaunt. *The Dilemma of Style: Architectural Ideas from the Picturesque to the Post-Modern.* Chicago: University of Chicago Press, 1987.

Crouch, David, and Colin Ward. *The Allotment, Its Landscape and Culture.* London: Faber and Faber, 1988.

Daniels, Stephen. *Fields of Vision: Landscape Imagery and National Identity in England and the United States.* Princeton: Princeton University Press, 1993.

———. *Humphry Repton, Landscape Gardening and the Geography of Georgian England.* New Haven and London: Published for the Paul Mellon Centre for Studies in British Art by Yale University Press, 1999.

Davey, Peter. "Arts and Crafts Gardens." *The Architectural Review* 178 (1985): 32–7.

Elliott, Brent. *The Country House Garden: From the Archives of Country Life, 1897–1939.* London: Mitchell Beazley, 1995.

———. *Victorian Gardens.* London: B.T. Batsford, 1986.

Fedden, Robin. *The Continuing Purpose: A History of the National Trust, Its Aims and Work.* London: Longmans, Green, 1968.

Fellows, Richard. *Sir Reginald Blomfield: An Edwardian architect.* London: A. Zwemmer, 1985.

Festing, Sally. *Gertrude Jekyll.* London and New York: Viking, 1991.

Fishman, Robert. *Bourgeois Utopias: The rise and fall of suburbia.* New York: Basic, 1987.

———. *Urban Utopias in the Twentieth Century: Ebenezer Howard, Frank Lloyd Wright, Le Corbusier.* New York: Basic, 1977.

Fox, H. S. A., and R. A. Butlin, eds. *Change in the Countryside: Essays on Rural England, 1500–1900.* London: Institute of British Geographers, 1979.

Francis, Mark, and Randolph T. Hester, eds. *The Meaning of Gardens, Idea, Place, and Action.* Cambridge, Mass.: MIT Press, 1990.

Franklin, Jill. *The Gentleman's Country House and Its Plan, 1835–1914.* London, Boston, and Henley: Routledge & Kegan Paul, 1981.

Gage, John. *Color and Culture, Practice and Meaning from Antiquity to Abstraction.* Boston: Little, Brown, 1993.

Gaze, John. *Figures in a Landscape, A History of the National Trust.* London: Barrie and Jenkins in association with the National Trust, 1988.

Gellner, Ernest. *Nationalism.* New York: New York University Press, 1997.

———. *Nations and Nationalism.* Ithaca and London: Cornell University Press, 1983.

Gertrude Jekyll, 1843–1932, Gardener. London: Architectural Association, 1981.

Girouard, Mark. *Life in the English Country House: A Social and Architectural History.* New Haven: Yale University Press, 1978.

Sweetness and Light, The 'Queen Anne' Movement, 1860–1900. Oxford: Clarendon Press, 1977.

The Victorian Country House. Oxford: Clarendon Press, 1971.

Goode, Patrick, and Michael Lancaster, eds. *The Oxford Companion to Gardens.* Oxford: Oxford University Press, 1986.

Gradidge, Roderick. *Dream Houses, The Edwardian Ideal.* London: Constable, 1980.

Green, Nicholas. *The Spectacle of Nature, Landscape and Bourgeois Culture in Nineteenth-Century France.* Manchester and New York: Manchester University Press, 1990.

Greenhalgh, Paul. *Ephemeral Vistas: the Expositions Universelles, Great Exhibitions and World's Fairs, 1851–1939.* Manchester and New York: Manchester University Press, 1988.

Harris, Dianne. "Cultivating Power: The Language of Feminism in Women's Garden Literature, 1870–1920." *Landscape Journal* 13 (Fall 1994): 113–23.

Harris, John. *The Artist and the Country House, A History of Country House and Garden View Painting in Britain, 1540–1870.* London: Sotheby Parke Bernet, 1979.

Helmreich, Anne. "Contested Grounds: Garden Painting and the Invention of National Identity in England, 1880–1914." Ph.D. dissertation, Northwestern University, 1994.

Helsinger, Elizabeth. *Rural Scenes and National Representation: Britain, 1815–1850.* Princeton: Princeton University Press, 1997.

Hinge, David. "Gertrude Jekyll: 1843–1932, A Bibliography of Her Writings." *Journal of Garden History* 2 (July/September 1982): 285–92.

Hobhouse, Penelope, and Christopher Wood. *Painted Gardens, English Watercolours, 1850–1914.* New York: Athenaeum, 1988.

Hobsbawm, Eric. *Nations and Nationalism since 1780: Programme, Myth, Reality.* Cambridge: Cambridge University Press, 1990.

and Terence Ranger, eds. *The Invention of Tradition.* New York: Cambridge University Press, 1983.

Horne, Donald. *The Great Museum: The Re-Presentation of History.* London: Pluto Press, 1984.

Hunt, John Dixon, ed. *Garden History, Issues, Approaches, Methods.* Washington, D.C.: Dumbarton Oaks Research Library and Collections, 1992.

"The Cult of the Cottage." In *The Lake District: A Sort of National Property.* Manchester: Countryside Commission and London: Victoria and Albert, 1986.

Gardens and the Picturesque, Studies in the History of Landscape Architecture. Cambridge, Mass.: MIT Press, 1992.

Hunter, Michael, ed. *Preserving the Past: The Rise of Heritage in Modern Britain.* Stroud: Alan Sutton, 1996.

Hussey, Christopher. *The Life of Sir Edwin Lutyens.* London: Country Life, 1950.

Hutchinson, John, and Anthony D. Smith, eds. *Nationalism.* Oxford and New York: Oxford University Press, 1994.

Inskip, Peter. *Architectural Monographs 6, Edwin Lutyens.* London: Academy Editions; New York: St. Martin's Press, 1986.

Kaplan, Wendy, ed. *Designing Modernity: The Arts of Reform and Persuasion, 1885–1914.* New York: Thames and Hudson; Miami Beach: The Wolfsonian, 1995.

Knoepflmacher, U. K., and G. B. Tennyson, eds. *Nature and the Victorian Imagination.* Berkeley: University of California Press, 1977.

Laird, Mark. *The Flowering of the Landscape Garden: English Pleasure Grounds, 1720–1800.* Philadelphia: University of Pennsylvania Press, 1999.

The Formal Garden, Traditions of Art and Nature. London: Thames and Hudson, 1992.

Lambourne, Lionel. *Utopian Craftsmen: The Arts and Crafts Movement, from the Cotswolds to Chicago.* London: Astragal, 1980.

Landow, George P. *The Aesthetic and Critical Theories of John Ruskin.* Princeton: Princeton University Press, 1971.

Lazzaro, Claudia. *The Italian Renaissance Garden: From the Conventions of Planting, Design, and Ornament to the Grand Gardens of Sixteenth-century Central Italy.* New Haven and London: Yale University Press, 1990.

Legate, Kim D. "Replanting England's 'Pioneer Parks': A Study of Planting Design, Focusing on the Disposition of Trees and Shrubs in the Public Parks of the 1840s and 1850s." Master's thesis, The Institute of Advanced Architectural Studies, The King's Manor, University of York, 1997.

Lowenthal, David. "British National Identity and the English Landscape." *Rural History* 2 (1991): 205–30.

The Past Is a Foreign Country. Cambridge: Cambridge University Press, 1985.

Lowenthal, David, and Marcus Binney, eds. *Our Past before Us, Why do We Save It?* London: Temple Smith, 1981.

Lutyens: The Work of the English Architect Sir Edwin Lutyens (1869–1944). London: Hayward Gallery, 1982.

Lyall, Sutherland. *Dream Cottages: From Cottage Ornée to Stockbroker Tudor.* London: Robert Hale, 1988.

MacDougall, Elisabeth B., ed. *John Claudius Loudon and the Early Nineteenth Century in Great Britain.* Washington, D.C.: Dumbarton Oaks, 1980.

Mader, Günter, and Laila Neubert-Mader. *Der Architecktonische Garten in England.* Stuttgart: Deutsche Verlags-Anstalt, 1992.

Mandler, Peter. *The Fall and Rise of the Stately Home.* New Haven and London: Yale University Press, 1997.

Marsh, Jan. *Back to the Land: The Pastoral Impulse in England, from 1880 to 1914.* New York: Quartet, 1982.

Massé, H. J. L. J. *The Art Workers Guild, 1884–1934.* Oxford: Shakespeare Head Press for the Art-Workers Guild, 1935.

Massingham, Betty. *Miss Jekyll, Portrait of a Great Gardener.* London: Country Life, 1966.

"William Robinson: A Portrait." *Garden History: The Journal of the Garden History Society* 6 (1978): 61–85.

Meacham, Standish. *Regaining Paradise, Englishness and the Early Garden City Movement.* New Haven and London: Yale University Press, 1999.

Mercer, Eric. *English Vernacular Houses: A Study of Traditional Farmhouses and Cottages.* London: Her Majesty's Stationery Office, 1975.

Merrill, Lynn L. *The Romance of Victorian Natural History.* New York and Oxford: Oxford University Press, 1989.

Mitchell, W. J. T., ed. *Landscape and Power.* Chicago: University of Chicago Press, 1994.

Mosser, Monique, and Georges Teyssot, eds. *The Architecture of Western Gardens: a design history from the Renaissance to the present day.* Cambridge, Mass.: MIT Press, 1991.

Mukerji, Chandra. *Territorial Ambitions and the Gardens of Versailles.* Cambridge: Cambridge University Press, 1997.

Newman, Gerald. *The Rise of English Nationalism: A Cultural History, 1740–1830.* London: Weidenfeld and Nicolson, 1987.

O'Neill, Daniel. *Sir Edwin Lutyens: Country Houses.* With a Preface by Sir Hugh Casson. New York: Whitney Library of Design, 1981.

Ottewill, David. *The Edwardian Garden.* New Haven and London: Yale University Press, 1989.

Pugh, Simon, ed. *Reading Landscape: Country, City, Capital.* Manchester and New York: Manchester University Press, 1990.

Garden, Nature, Language. Manchester and New York: Manchester University Press, 1988.

Richardson, Margaret. *Architects of the Arts and Crafts Movement.* London: Trefoil, 1983.

Ridgeway, Christopher. "William Andrews Nesfield: Between Uvedale Price and Isambard Kingdom Brunel." *Journal of Garden History* 13 (Spring/Summer 1993): 69–89.

   ed. *William Andrews Nesfield: Victorian Landscape Architect, Papers from the Bicentenary Conference, The King's Manor, York.* York: University of York, Institute of Advanced Architectural Studies, 1996.

Ritvo, Harriet. *The Platypus and the Mermaid and other Figments of the Classifying Imagination.* Cambridge, Mass.: Harvard University Press, 1997.

Saint, Andrew. *Richard Norman Shaw.* New Haven: Yale University Press for the Paul Mellon Centre for Studies in British Art, 1976.

Samuel, Raphael, ed. *Patriotism, the Making and UnMaking of British National Identity.* Vol. 1. London and New York: Routledge, 1989.

Schulz, Max F. *Paradise Preserved, Recreation of Eden in Eighteenth- and Nineteenth-Century England.* Cambridge: Cambridge University Press, 1985.

Scott-James, Anne. *The Cottage Garden.* London: Allen Lane, 1981.

Scourse, Nicolette. *The Victorians and Their Flowers.* London: Croom Helm; Portland, Ore.: Timber Press, 1983.

Simo, Melanie Louise. *Loudon and the Landscape: From Country Seat to Metropolis, 1783–1843.* New Haven and London: Yale University Press, 1988.

Stamp, Gavin, and Andre Goulancourt. *The English House, 1860–1914: The Flowering of English Domestic Architecture.* Chicago: University of Chicago Press, 1986.

Stansky, Peter. *Redesigning the World: William Morris, the 1880s, and the Arts and Crafts.* Princeton: Princeton University Press, 1985.

Strong, Roy. *The Renaissance Garden in England.* London: Thames and Hudson, 1979.

Strong, Roy, Marcus Binney, and John Harris. *The Destruction of the Country House, 1875–1975.* London: Thames and Hudson, 1974.

Tankard, Judith B., and Michael R. Van Valkenburgh. *Gertrude Jekyll: A Vision of Garden and Wood.* New York: Harry N. Abrams, 1988.

   and Martin A. Wood. *Gertrude Jekyll at Munstead Wood: Writing, Horticulture, Photography, Homebuilding.* With a Foreword by Graham Stuart Thomas. Thrupp, Stroud, Gloucestershire: Sutton; Sagaponack: Sagapress, 1996.

Taylor, Geoffrey. *Some Nineteenth Century Gardeners.* Tiptree, Essex: Anchor Press, 1951.

Taylor, John. *A Dream of England: Landscape, Photography, and the Tourist's Imagination.* Manchester and New York: Manchester University Press, 1994.

Tinniswood, Adrian. *A History of Country House Visiting: Five Centuries of Tourism and Taste.* Oxford and New York: Basil Blackwell, 1989.

Tooley, Michael, ed. *Gertrude Jekyll, Artist, Gardener, Craftswoman.* Witton-le-Wear: Michaelmas, 1984.

   and Primrose Arnander, eds. *Gertrude Jekyll: Essays on the life of a Working Amateur.* Witton-le-Wear: Michaelmas, 1995.

Treib, Marc. "Frame, Moment and Sequence, the Photographic Book and the Designed Landscape." *Journal of Garden History* 15 (Summer 1995): 126–34.

Waters, Michael. *The Garden in Victorian Literature.* Aldershot: Scolar Press, 1988.

Watkin, David. *The English Vision, The Picturesque in Architecture, Landscape, and Garden Design.* New York: Harper & Row, 1982.

   The Rise of Architectural History. London: The Architectural Press; Westfield, N.J.: Eastview Editions, 1980.

Wiener, Martin. *English Culture and the Decline of the Industrial Spirit, 1850–1980.* New York: Cambridge University Press, 1981.

Williams, Raymond. *The Country and the City.* New York: Oxford University Press, 1973.

271

Williams, Robert. "Edwardian Gardens, Old and New." *Journal of Garden History* 13 (Spring/Summer 1993): 90–103.

"Edwin Lutyens and the Formal Garden in England." *Die Gartenkunst* 2 (1995): 201–9.

Williamson, Tom. *Polite Landscapes: Gardens and Society in Eighteenth-Century England.* Baltimore: Johns Hopkins University Press, 1995.

Wolschke-Bulmahn, Joachim. "The 'Wild Garden' and the 'Nature Garden' – Aspects of the Garden Ideology of William Robinson and Willy Lange." *Journal of Garden History* 12 (July/September 1992): 183–206.

ed. *Nature and Ideology: Natural Garden Design in the Twentieth Century.* Washington, D.C.: Dumbarton Oaks Research Library and Collection, 1997.

Index

Index